The FamilyPC

GREGG KEIZER
&
SERIES EDITOR
ROBIN RASKIN

Guide
to
Homework

 HYPERION

 BOOKS

NEW YORK

371.3
K28
cop.1

CO-PUBLISHED BY
Hyperion & FamilyPC
114 Fifth Avenue
New York, New York 10011

ISBN 0-7868-8206-9

First Edition
10 9 8 7 6 5 4 3 2 1

Vice President and Publisher: Bob Miller
Executive Editor: Rick Kot
Manuscript Editor: John Pont
Cover Design: Jim Phillips
Interior Design/Layout: Andrea DeBevoise
Proofreader: Jeannie Smith
Indexer: Liz Cunningham
Book Packager: Trudy Neuhaus

Photo credits: Pages 203, 214 - Christopher Baldwin; page 81 - Gary Benson; pages 1, 149, 243 - Michael Carroll; page 289 - Ken Davies; page 57 - Jim Gipe; page 103 - Danny Gonzalez; page 221 - Ed Judice; pages 15, 23, 24, 25, 31, 257 - Lightworks Photographic; page 179 - William Mercer McLeod; page 129 - William Whitehurst.

24.95
8/14/97

Contents

Foreword

In my 16-plus years of parenting, I've come to appreciate homework for many reasons. First of all, it helps parents keep in touch with what their children are doing in school. By the time I get home from work, my kids have what I've come to call school amnesia — when I ask, they have absolutely no recollection of what they did that day. Homework often helps rekindle their memories.

Second, homework helps you spot problems your children might be having in a particular subject. Schools can't possibly provide for all your children's educational needs, and homework gives you a good heads-up on potential problems that might require some extra effort on your part.

Third, homework gives you a chance to supplement teachers' efforts. Teachers can introduce good research and writing skills, but kids simply don't get enough time to practice and refine those skills during school hours. Homework allows your children to hone those skills by putting them to active use.

On the other hand, homework creates its share of burdens, too. For busy parents, taking on the role of homework helper for your children adds yet another chore to your seemingly endless list of responsibilities.

Intuitively, most parents know that the computer can play a vital role in the homework scene. However, most parents aren't sure how to go about making the computer play its part. When teachers assign home-work, they don't usually offer suggestions for using the computer to complete the assignment. As parents trying to figure out how the family computer can serve as a homework helper, we've been left to our own devices, picking up bits and pieces of knowledge from disparate sources.

The FamilyPC Guide to Homework solves that problem by providing a one-stop information source that covers everything you need to know about using the family computer as a homework helper for kids in grades K–12. This book mixes practical, step-by-step advice with dozens of project ideas that will help you inspire your kids to create reports and presentations that put them at the head of their class. And for kids who need some help getting started, *The FamilyPC Guide to Homework* offers lots of great project ideas, ranging from at-home science experiments to a family tree project that will be the envy of the history class.

Perhaps most important, *The FamilyPC Guide to Homework* helps you recognize the various ways in which your family's computer can lend a hand with homework skills.

The most common type of homework-help software is the traditional drill-and-practice program. These programs fill in for you by helping your kids master those subjects that require rote memorization — for example, multiplication tables, a foreign language, even the ABCs. Drill-and-practice programs ease the tedium of rote memorization by providing some entertainment along with their practice sessions. Although such programs sometimes fall a bit short in terms of fostering creativity and building critical thinking skills, parents have come to rely on these mundane homework helpers as patient, even-keeled tutors who work well with children.

The computer also helps kids develop cognitive, or thinking, skills. CD-ROMs such as Passage to Vietnam and The Material World give children a deeper understanding of a particular era or subject. Simulation programs make science come alive, allowing children to investigate anything from ecology to physics, in an entertaining way. These programs don't give children the answers; they invite kids to explore, make connections, and draw conclusions on their own.

The computer also serves as an electronic pencil or printing press. When your children need to create reports, the computer simplifies the process of organizing, editing, revising, and refining. With the proper writing and research tools, children learn to present their thoughts in a clear, compelling manner. Thanks to homework-helping software, your kids learn how to create bibliographies, choose the right fonts and layouts, insert charts in their reports, and even create multimedia presentations. In other words, the family computer helps your children express themselves in new ways.

Finally, and perhaps most important, the computer can help your children by functioning as a research tool. Whether your kids want to connect to the Internet or use a CD-ROM encyclopedia, the computer opens up a whole new world of research material and a brand new way to do research — at any hour from anywhere. The computer can let your kids speak to experts all over the world and connect to online libraries offering amazing collections of source materials. In the online world and on CD-ROMs where one topic is linked to another, a child learns to ferret out the best of the information.

The Family PC Guide to Homework systematically explores these different roles of the computer. Author Gregg Keizer, one of the best-known and most versatile authors on the use of computers, has the uncanny ability to serve up important information for every type of homework — whether it's a kindergartner's collage or a high-school student's essay on Shakespeare. Gregg's approach is entertaining and still practical, comprehensive but not overwhelming.

Homework will probably always remain a mixed blessing for parents. At its best, it draws parents and children closer together and reinforces important skills learned in school. At its worse, it results in rewards lost, punishments gained, and family tensions for homework assignments that go undone.

At *FamilyPC*, we're convinced that the computer makes homework more rewarding, more engaging, and more personal. We believe that students who learn how to use computers for help with schoolwork have an advantage over those who don't. And most important, we know that the ideas on the pages of this book can help you make the homework in your life more of a joy than a burden.

ROBIN RASKIN
Editor-in-Chief, *FamilyPC*

Chapter 1

The Family Computer

Your Private Tutor

TEACHER, TEACHER! ME, ME! I KNOW, I know!

With hands raised high in the air, kids with the right stuff have the answers. Maybe not always the *right* answers, but hey, that's learning, too, isn't it?

As parents, our job is to make sure that our kids have the best possible shot at knowing the right answers to educational questions, and so give them the best chance of succeeding in school. Of course, that's one of the reasons why we buy a home computer in the first place, and why we keep buying software.

In fact, the home computer is a primo private tutor for at-home and in-school children of all ages. When your family circle includes a computer, your kids don't have to wait until the school bell rings to ask questions and get answers; hone their math, writing, and research skills; or explore the mysteries of science, history, geography, and language. The teacher is *always* IN.

That's especially crucial at homework time. Although our kids keep most of us in the dark about day-to-day details of school time (You: "What did you do in school today?" Your child: "Nothin' much."), we can keep track of the schoolwork they bring home. We have a say — or we should — in how much time our kids spend doing homework. We can point them in the right direction. We can demand and urge and cajole and nag them into practicing skills that come with repetition. And most important, we can provide a pipeline to information.

Our parents may have purchased an encyclopedia and occasionally pitched in with an attempt to figure out the new math, but we can give our kids more. We can give them the computer.

Here at *FamilyPC*, we're excited about computers. We think they make terrific at-home tools for teaching. But they're neither replacements for school nor — if you home-school your children — substitutes for the lessons you provide. Why? Because they're only as smart as the software they run. Because they're far less flexible than a living, breathing teacher, who can shift from explaining how wind drives weather one moment to demonstrating how to shape clay into pottery the next.

However, the home computer is an excellent supplement to what goes on during official school hours. That's what this book is all about. *The FamilyPC Guide to Homework* shows you how to extend learning beyond the all-too-brief school day.

Using *The FamilyPC Guide to Homework*

We've organized *The FamilyPC Guide to Homework* in a way that helps you and your children tap the power of your home computer for after-hours schoolwork. Each major subject of study has its own chapter, letting you turn straight to the area of learning you want to emphasize. Each chapter includes several self-contained sections. Each section highlights one or more learning projects, describes the best software for the job, provides some pithy tips, and often points you to other resources with which you and your kids can dig even deeper.

But *The FamilyPC Guide to Homework* is different from other books aimed at computer-owning parents. We don't recommend just any software. (And when you think about it, it's the software, not the computer by itself, that becomes the private tutor for your kids.) Almost all of the learning, creativity, and kid-appropriate productivity software we endorse in this book has gone through exhaustive, real-world testing by real families. The hallmark of *FamilyPC* magazine, this testing puts programs in the hands of dozens of families and asks them to objectively evaluate the software's learning performance and overall value. Only the very best programs garner the coveted *FamilyPC* Recommended seal (which indicates a score of 85 or more out of a possible 100).

"Teacher, teacher!" If you want your kids to shout out those words — and do better in school — *The FamilyPC Guide to Homework* should be the first book you crack.

Know Your Teacher

You can sit down with your children's teachers at parents' night to get a feeling for their teaching techniques and possible personality quirks. You can't carry on the same kind of conversation with the at-home computer teacher, but you'd better spend time getting to know this teacher, too.

This is really the first step — and it's an important one — toward using the power of your PC or Mac to help your children do schoolwork. Although your kids may know as much as you do about the home computer (and if they're particularly nasty about it, they'll let you know they know more), you should at least be comfortable around the machine. To guide your kids through many of the activities in *The FamilyPC Guide to Homework*, you need to be familiar with some computer basics. That's especially true when you're working with young children — preschoolers and kindergarteners — who haven't spent much time at the keyboard.

You don't need to know anything fancy — just enough to get started. For more specialized help, you can probably count on your older kids to lend a hand. If you're looking for other sources of hands-on advice, don't forget *FamilyPC* magazine; each issue provides a wealth of tips, hints, and how-to information.

How to Install Software

Most computers now come with a wealth of preinstalled software. The computer manufacturer places these packages on the computer's hard disk — where all programs and files are stored — and sets them up so they're ready to run. Some of the programs commonly configured on a new computer — for example, Microsoft Works, ClarisWorks, and Encarta — are useful schoolwork tools that we tout in *The FamilyPC Guide to Homework*. But to really turn your PC or Mac into a private tutor, you must eventually install some software yourself.

This is a true test of your parenting skills. There's nothing more frustrating to a child than sitting and waiting — and waiting and sitting — while Mom or Dad struggles with a balky installation procedure for a can't-wait-till-it's-working program. (A couple

years ago, some software made national news when many parents weren't able to get the programs running after the children had unwrapped these Christmas gifts.) Advertisements for Macintosh computers even go so far as to stress how easy it is to put programs on those machines — and how difficult it is to put them on the competitions'.

GET SMART: *Although installing software is often a snap, a parent should be present during the process, to troubleshoot problems and ensure that the files get deposited in the right place.*

Frankly, installing software on the Macintosh is easy. Stick the disc into the Mac's CD-ROM drive (or, if you have a machine that uses a CD-ROM caddie — a thin plastic cartridge — place the disc in the caddie and then insert the caddie in the drive slot), and up pops a window. This window usually contains one or more icons — those tiny, on-screen objects that represent programs and files — with titles such as Install and Read Me (or Read Me First). Take a look at the Read Me file before you install the software, because this file may contain helpful installation and operation hints or further installation instructions. To open the Read Me file, double-click on the icon titled Read Me (*double-clicking* means positioning the mouse pointer on the icon and then clicking the mouse button twice). When you're ready to start the installation program, double-click on the Install icon, and virtually everything else is done for you.

PC software installation is a bit trickier.

Fortunately, almost all of today's learning programs for the PC run in Windows or Windows 95, where installation is a tad slicker than in the older DOS environment. Typically, you install a Windows program by running an installation procedure. You do that by selecting Run from the Program Manager's File menu and then typing something like D:\INSTALL.EXE or D:\SETUP.EXE (the exact wording is often specified right on the CD; if not, look for directions in the first few pages of the program's documentation).

Windows 95, Microsoft's newest operating system for the PC, promises even speedier, easier installation than in previous versions of Windows. Some programs use Windows 95's Autoplay feature, which automatically starts the program, moments after you put the CD-ROM in the drive. (You may have to click on an Install button the first time you insert the disc, but after that, Autoplay CDs fire up without any intervention on your part.) To install other programs in Windows 95, select Settings from the Start menu, pick Control Panel, and double-click on the Add/Remove Programs icon. Put the disk or the CD-ROM in the drive and click the Next button, to begin installation.

How to Organize What You See

The home computer's hard disk — where files and programs are stored — is a big place. You need a way to organize things so you and the kids can easily run programs, locate your previous work, and open documents.

Today's PCs and Macs all use a similar interface — think of it as the face the computer puts on when you turn it on — based on a familiar concept: a file cabinet and the folders it contains.

Windows, Windows 95, and the Macintosh all organize programs and

Unlike Windows 3.1 (bottom), Windows 95's software installer (top) doesn't demand that you enter cryptic text.

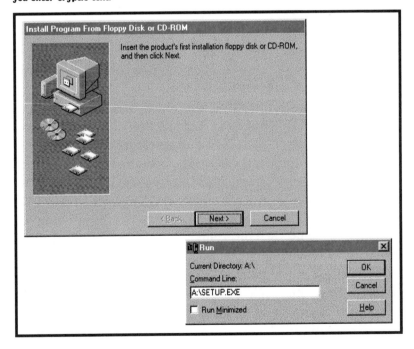

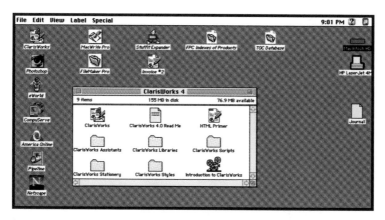

On the Macintosh, you can put icons on the desktop for convenient launching, and within folders for better organization.

files in these virtual folders. To open a folder and see what's inside, you simply double-click on it with the mouse pointer. The icons within each folder represent programs you can run or files or documents you've created with those programs. To run a program or open a document, double-click on its icon.

GET SMART: *Double-click to open a folder. Double-click to run a program. Remember those two rules, and you're set.*

When you install new software, the installation procedure almost always creates a new folder for you and places the program icons inside that folder. Leave those icons where they are.

But many programs also deposit the documents you

create in that same folder. What if you want to organize those files and documents in a system that makes sense to you? Simple. In just a few minutes, you can create new folders with names you choose, to store your work and your children's homework and for-fun files:

● **Macintosh.** To create a new folder on the Mac, select the New Folder command from the File menu. Give the folder a name by typing over the default name (that is, *untitled folder*) that appears in the text box below the folder icon.

Windows 95?

Windows 95 puts a more Macintosh-like face on the family computer. A bar with clickable buttons at the bottom of the screen makes it easy to switch between programs; icons and folders are much easier to manage than in the earlier Windows 3.1; and a Start menu simplifies launching programs and documents. But is Windows 95 right for you and your family PC?

Based on *FamilyPC*'s long-term testing after Windows 95's release, we recommend that you upgrade to Windows 95 only if your home PC is equipped with a Pentium processor and at least 8MB of memory (preferably, 16MB). Ideally, wait to move to Windows 95 until you buy your next computer. The new machine will come with Windows 95 ready to run, so you won't have to fight through upgrade and installation problems.

Folders in Windows 95 look — and act — much like those on the Mac. This is one of the reasons why Windows 95 is touted as being "more like a Mac."

• **Windows 3.1.** Pull down the Program Manager's File menu and select New. Click on the Program Group button (that's what Windows 3.1 calls its folder-like icons) and then click on the OK button. Finally, enter a name in the Description box that appears, such as Emily's Stories.

• **Windows 95.** In My Computer or the Explorer, pick New from the File menu and click on the Folder choice in the submenu. A new folder appears, with the default name — New Folder — already highlighted. Just enter the desired name.

Of course, you can move icons from one folder to another whenever you want. Moving an icon doesn't actually move the file on the hard disk (not usually, anyway, though if you put an icon in the Mac's Trash can,

you're getting ready to delete the real file). To move an icon, open both folders, click on the icon, and drag it to the new location.

Spend time organizing folders and the icons within them so that you and the kids can easily find programs and files. You can try different ways to group programs. We use a combination of organizing files and programs by type (for example, all art programs in one folder) and by user (say, Scott's Stuff). If you don't like the organization of icons and folders, don't sweat it; you can easily change things later.

On the Mac and in Windows 95, you can put icons for any program or file in more than one folder, or in a folder and on the desktop. Here's how you create a duplicate of an existing icon. On the Mac, select the icon and choose Make Alias from the File menu. In Windows 95, *right-click* on the icon (that is, position the mouse pointer on the icon and press the right mouse button) and pick Create Shortcut from the menu that's displayed. You can rename these duplicates, and you can deposit them within a folder or on the desktop.

GET SMART: *Use the Make Alias feature on the Mac or the Create Shortcuts command in Windows 95 to put icons of your children's most-frequently-used programs right on the desktop. Then, the kids won't have to go digging through folders to find the programs they want.*

Why go to all this trouble? This lets you run a program from more than one place, giving you and the kids even more flexibility. Say you have Kid Pix Studio on your PC; by using Windows 95's Shortcuts, you can create several icons representing that program and put one icon in a folder called Art Supplies, a second in a folder marked Tim's Art Projects, and a third in a folder named Janet's Things. Each icon points to the same program, so no matter who runs it or from where, Kid Pix Studio pops up.

How to Run Programs

Running programs and opening documents is, as we've already said, just a matter of some clicking. But a few basics will help you brush up on the process and give you an idea of what you need to pass along to the homework-ready kids in the house.

Running Macintosh Programs

To run a program or open a document on your Macintosh, just open the folder containing the program icon or the document, point at the icon, and click twice. You can also put icons right on the desktop (not within a folder) and double-click to run a program from there.

Most Macs also include a program called Launcher (it's one of the items on the Con-

trol Panel, which you open from the Apple menu). You can place programs and other files on the Launcher — which appears when you start up the Mac — by dragging icons from the desktop and dropping them onto its display. (The process is a bit more complicated in older versions of the Launcher. You have to create a duplicate of the program's icon by using the Make Alias command and then place the duplicate icon in the Launcher Items folder, which you find inside your System folder.)

Running Windows 3.1 Programs

To start a program in Windows 3.1, open the appropriate Program Group and double-click on the icon for the program you want. Unlike the Mac or Windows 95, Windows 3.1 doesn't let you place an icon on the desktop; all icons must be within a Group.

You can also run a program by choosing Run from the Program Manager's File menu and then entering the program's name in the dialog box that's displayed. But with the cryptic, eight-character filenames of most programs and documents in Windows, you're better off sticking with icons and the Program Manager.

You can customize the Mac's Launcher to meet your kids' needs. Single-click a large button to run that program.

Register!

Open up any software package, and out flutters a registration card. It's a good idea to fill out this card and send it back to the software publisher. You'll usually get better response from technical support personnel if you've registered the program. In addition, most companies notify registered users of program problems (and provide fixes), and you'll often receive infor-

mation about new versions as well as discounts for upgrading to these new editions.

As long as you're registering the program with the publisher, why not turn the tables and register the publisher with you? Keep a record of all the programs you buy, noting the name of the program, the date you purchased it, and most importantly, the technical support phone num-

ber to call if problems arise. A word processor document works fine for this, but if you're adventurous, you can create a database using your integrated package. Putting all this information in one place makes sense; after a program is installed, it's all too easy to lose pieces of the package, including the card or manual that lists the tech support phone number.

Running Windows 95 Programs
Although Windows 95 offers even more ways to run a program than either Win-

With Windows 95, you may have to dig down through several levels to find the program you want to run.

dows 3.1 or the Mac, you should use the Start menu for most of your launching. Installed programs automatically create a folder under the Start menu's Programs item. Click on the Start button — it's on the Toolbar, which, unless you've moved it, appears at the bottom of your screen — and then select Programs. Another menu slides out, showing all the folders there. Choose the one containing the program you want to run and click on the name/icon combination.

How to Manage Files and More Files
Although shuffling icons into and out of folders may make it easier to launch programs and open documents, that doesn't really reorganize the way files are stored on the hard disk. (At least on PCs. The Mac is another matter; when you move a program or document icon, you are actually moving

the file.) To organize your computer's hard disk, you — not the kids, because this kind of digital remodeling is best left to parents — need to know how to manage files and directories.

Moving Files in Windows 3.1

To move a file in Windows 3.1, click on the Program Group named Main and double-click on the File Manager icon. Windows displays a tree-style representation of the hard disk's contents. To move a file — maybe you want to group all your daughter's school report documents in one subdirectory — just click on the file, drag it to the destination folder, and drop it. Windows moves the file to that subdirectory. (In File Manager, what looks like a folder is really a subdirectory.) To create a new subdirectory, pick Create Directory from the File Manager's File menu.

Moving Files in Windows 95

The procedure for moving files in Windows 95 is much the same as in Windows 3.1, though you use Windows 95's Explorer instead of the File Manager. To run the Explorer, click on the Start button, choose Programs, and then click on Windows Explorer. As in Windows 3.1, you move files around by clicking, dragging, and dropping. To build a new subdirectory, however, pick New

from the File menu and then choose Folder from the submenu that appears.

Of course, you can also perform other file management chores in the File Manager or the Explorer. For example, you can delete files, copy files to a floppy disk, and even run programs and open documents from these displays.

GET SMART: *On the Mac, leave program icons in the folders created when you installed the programs. If you want to group applications by type — for example, all the paint programs in one folder — use the Make Alias command in the Mac's File menu.*

How to Protect the Computer

Sharing the family computer? Probably. If so, you should make sure the machine is childproof, to prevent children — especially young children — from accidentally erasing all the family's financial records or your take-home work.

For handling files in Windows 95, you usually use the Explorer.

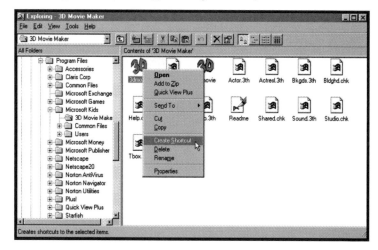

KidDesk Family Edition lets kids keep their stuff private but keeps them from getting to everything else on the computer's hard disk.

To gain even greater peace of mind, you may want to invest in a child-proofing program such as KidDesk Family Edition (available in versions for Windows, Windows 95, and the Mac). Kid-Desk is an attractive interface that gives children access to the files and programs you set up on their desktop, but prevents them from reaching any other files and programs on the hard disk. The result? They can work with their software, but they can't reach yours.

Here are some elementary precautions you can take:

• Use the Read-Only save option of most word processors and spreadsheets; this protects your work from being overwritten.

• Write-protect important floppy disks. To do this, slide open the write-protect tab found on the disk's underside.

• Use the password-protection option found on many screen savers to keep kids out of areas where they don't belong.

• Supervise younger children when they use the computer, and teach older kids which buttons and options they should avoid. Remember, the best prevention is education.

How to Keep the Computer in Tip-Top Shape

The best defense is a good offense. To keep your computer from developing problems, you need to know how to maintain it. This isn't an exhaustive list by any means, but by following our suggestions, you can ensure that the home learning center keeps teaching and doesn't give you trouble.

Build an Emergency Boot Disk

When a serious problem emerges with a DOS or Windows PC, your system often displays an error message (for example, Configuration Error, Invalid Setup, or Boot Disk Failure) and then locks up. In such cases, you can't diagnose and repair the problem until you get your system up and running. The only way to override these messages is to restart your computer from the floppy disk drive, rather than from the hard disk drive. To do this, you need an emergency boot disk, which you can create using any blank floppy disk.

If you're running Windows 3.1, begin by quitting Windows. Then, insert the blank floppy disk into drive A. At the C:\> prompt, type **FORMAT /S A:** and press the Enter key. This formats the floppy disk and copies crucial system files onto the disk.

Now, you need to add some other important start-up files. Type each of the following lines, pressing the Enter key at the end of each line and waiting for the C:\> prompt before typing the next line:

COPY C:\AUTOEXEC.BAT A:
COPY C:\CONFIG.SYS A:
COPY C:\WINDOWS\SYSTEM.INI A:
COPY C:\WINDOWS\WIN.INI A:

Make sure your children know how to exit Windows 95 properly — by picking Shut Down from Windows 95's Start menu.

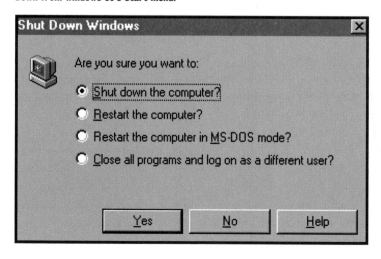

Windows 95 simplifies the process by giving you an option to create an emergency start-up disk during installation (you can also do it at any other time). Insert a blank floppy disk in the disk drive and open the Add/Remove Programs application in the Control Panel. Click on the Startup Disk tab and then click on the Create Disk button. Windows 95 walks you through the steps necessary for creating an emergency boot disk.

When your boot disk is complete, keep it in a cool, dry place.

Unlike DOS and Windows systems, Macs come with either a bootable floppy disk or a bootable CD-ROM you can use if your hard disk gives out. Make sure your emergency floppy disk contains copies of any SCSI drivers that came with your hard disk.

Rebuild Your Mac's Desktop Regularly
By rebuilding your desktop, you allow your Mac to keep better track of data on your start-up disks. To rebuild your desktop, hold down the option and command (clover) keys while starting your computer. Keep pressing these keys until you see a message asking whether you want to rebuild your desktop. Click on OK, and your Mac handles the rest. Repeat this process about once a month — more often if you work with many files.

Exit Programs and Shut Down Properly
Before turning off your computer, save all open files and then exit all applications, including Windows (press Alt-F-X or Alt-F4). Under Windows 95, click on the Start button, choose Shut Down, and wait for the message telling you it's safe to turn off the PC. The Mac is even easier: Choose the Shut Down command from the Special menu, and on most models, the machine turns itself off. (Some Macs simply tell you it's safe to switch off the machine, which you need to do manually.)

Have the Necessary Information Ready When You Call Tech Support
When preventive medicine doesn't work and you need to call the technical support

Online Support

VENDOR	AOL	COMPUSERVE	PRODIGY	WEB
Acer	Acer	PCVENF	Acer	http://www.acer.com
Apple	None	PCS-81	None	http://www.apple.com/
AST	None	ASTFOR	AST	http://www.ast.com
Canon	None	CAN-1	None	http://www.canon.com/
Compaq	Compaq	Compaq	Compaq	http://www.compaq.com
Digital	Digital	DEC-1	None	http://www.digital.com/
Gateway	Gateway	Gateway	Gateway	http://www.gw2k.com/
HP	hp	HYSYST	None	http://www.hp.com/
IBM	ibm	BOC-1	ibm	http://www.ibm.com/
Micron	None	PCVEND	None	http://www.micron.com
Microsoft	Microsoft (Web)	MIE-1	None	http://www.microsoft.com/support/
MidWest Micro	None	None	None	http://www.mwmicro.com/
NEC	NEC	None	None	http://www.nec.com/
Packard Bell	None	PACKAR	None	http://www.packardbell.com
Quantex	None	None	None	http://www.quantex.com

line to a computer manufacturer or a software publisher, make sure you're ready with the following information:

• The amount of memory installed in your system

• The amount of free disk space

• The version number of the operating system you are running

• For DOS and Windows PCs, printouts of the AUTOEXEC.BAT and CONFIG.SYS files from your system's root directory

• For Windows PCs, printouts of your WIN.INI and SYSTEM.INI files from the Windows directory

• The version number of the program (when calling about a specific program)

When things go wrong, who ya gonna call? See the sidebar "Online Support" for information about where to go on the major online services and the World Wide Web to get fix-it-now help from computer manufacturers and operating system suppliers. Be sure you have the necessary information *before* you call.

Chapter 2

The Bare Necessities

THIS HOMEWORK GUIDE IS CHOCK-FULL OF projects, schoolwork advice, tips for parents, and recommendations for a slew of software. So full, in fact, that you may wonder where to start, where to quit, and what you need to fill the middle.

The place to start, of course, is at the beginning, with the necessities. You need a multimedia-ready computer — that is, one with a CD-ROM drive — because that's the format used for almost all of today's learning software. A PC also needs speakers and an audio board (however, Macs have these built in). You need some software. And, you need at least one more piece of hardware: a printer. Finally, you need a way for your children to dip into the vast reservoir of information that's out there for the taking.

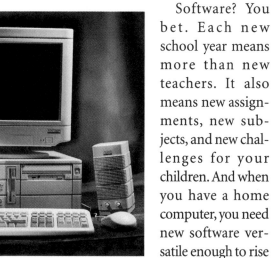

Sound like a lot? It's not. Not really. In fact, you probably already have most of what you need. As for the rest, you can get by with a bare minimum that won't set you back too much.

The Software Bare Necessities

You're looking at the school-supply shopping list. "Binder, three-ring." Check. "Spiral notebooks, four." Check. "Colored pencils." Check. "Software." Check.

Software? You bet. Each new school year means more than new teachers. It also means new assignments, new subjects, and new challenges for your children. And when you have a home computer, you need new software versatile enough to rise to those challenges.

But with so many computer programs packing the shelves, how do you know which are tough enough to make it through the school year? Your wallet isn't bottomless (though at this time of the year, with forays for clothing, supplies, and shoes, you probably wish it was), so you're probably looking for help in selecting the one or two packages that your kids will find invaluable during the next nine months. We think we've found them.

We've reviewed the *FamilyPC* Family-Tested evaluations — in which real families install and use software and then report their findings — and selected the seven most effective programs for kids in four age ranges. These titles have proved themselves where it counts: in the home. And they're age-appropriate not only in their content and ease of use, but for the kinds of projects kids are expected to handle during the school year. As you begin to collect your home-work-helping library, you should put these learning programs on your shopping list.

Software? Check.

Bailey's Book House, Millie's Math House, Sammy's Science House

Ages 3-6

Preschoolers and kindergarteners may not come home from school with stacks of homework, but they can still learn a lot on the family computer. If you're looking for a software series that can help boost your children's reading, math, and elementary science skills, *FamilyPC* and its FamilyTested families recommend the House line from Edmark. All three titles — Bailey's Book House, Millie's Math House, and Sammy's Science House — won accolades and high scores from families in the field.

Not only do these three programs provide some top-notch teaching games, they all offer two routes to learning. In the Explore and Discover mode, kids can wander through these packages' activities and learn at their own pace. With the Question and Answer mode, cartoon characters direct the child toward a specific task or ask a specific question. This flexibility — your little ones can choose which mode they use, or you can decide for them, if you're trying to emphasize something — is one of the main reasons why these three programs are such good picks for back-to-school software.

Each title comes with a Parent's Notebook that offers lots of parent-child activities you can use for exploring the software together. You can also print out parts of the Parent's Notebook and use them as the basis for some worthwhile away-from-the-computer learning.

Bailey's Book House uses several cartoon characters — Bailey the cat is just one of them — and five wacky activities to improve early reading skills. In Make-A-Story, kids assemble a four-sentence story by picking a subject, a mode of transportation, a destination, and an activity. (No bother-some noun-verb-adverb terminology for this age group.) Bailey animates the result, reads — and rereads — the story, and even prints it out so that you or your kids can fold the paper into a handy little storybook.

Read-A-Rhyme asks children to finish a

familiar nursery rhyme by picking a new, but still rhyming, ending. Kid Cards lets children design greeting cards, plaster them with stamps, and pick from a lineup of messages. For little ones, it's a good replacement for — and a good introduction to — programs such as Print Shop or Kid Pix.

Two other activities are more structured: Learning the Alphabet uses an on-screen keyboard to introduce letters and letter sounds, and Edmo & Houdini uses animation to illustrate prepositions such as *over*, *under*, *in*, and *out*.

Using much the same approach as Bailey's Book House, Millie's Math House introduces basic math concepts such as counting, sizes, and shapes. With cute cartoon characters, animation, and children's voices for narration, the six games in this package are perfect for preschoolers, though our

FamilyTested results indicate that they may not hold the interest of kids at the upper end of the target age range.

Number Machine shows the relationship between Arabic numerals and numbers of objects. Mouse House is a shape-matching game in which kids build a house for a family of mice by using geometric shapes. Bing and Boing highlights patterns and pattern matching. Little, Middle, and Big gives kids a chance to match sizes properly, and Cookie Factory combines number recognition and sequencing. Build-A-Bug helps develop counting skills as kids create weird creatures with spots, legs, eyes, and antennae.

Sammy's Science House introduces young children to a more difficult subject. Although this program includes elements of natural science — weather and a bit of biology — it's also strong in teaching some basic concepts such as sorting and sequencing.

In the Weather Machine, kids create different climate conditions by picking from lists of temperatures, wind, and precipitation. The Weather Machine shows the results in a colorful window, with a cartoon character dressed appropriately for the weather.

In Acorn Pond — essentially an elementary reference work about

Bailey's Book House's Make-A-Story activity lets children create and then listen to really short stories.

• One day, Dorothy traveled to an island.

wildlife — children can discover facts about familiar animals such as raccoons and fish, and print pages that they can then color. Sorting Station asks kids to classify plants, animals, birds, and rocks into bins by looking for common characteristics. In Make-A-Movie, kids string together frames of some simple films to learn about the order of events, and they get a feel for beginnings, middles, and ends.

Sammy's most unstructured activity is Workshop, in which kids assemble weird machines and toys from a bunch of parts. In Q & A mode, they must follow a blueprint to build something specific; in the Explore and Discover mode, they can make anything they want and then put the creation on paper for sharing with friends.

For about $120, you can equip your home PC or Mac with this excellent series of school starter software.

Kid Pix Studio
Ages 7-9
Kid Pix Studio doesn't make crayons, markers, paints, and paper obsolete, but it does turn the family computer into a superb creativity center. That's why Kid Pix Studio is

The notes within Acorn Pond turn Sammy's Science House into a simple biology reference work that's perfect for preschoolers.

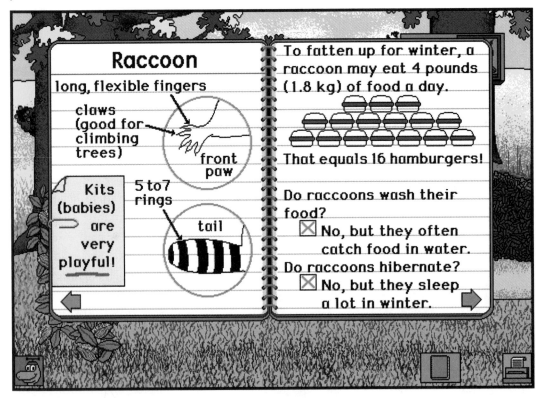

our pick for this age group; even though it's not really a homework helper, almost every kid likes to draw and paint and create. Kid Pix Studio received a perfect 10 for replay value, and an overall score of 91 — one of the highest scores — in our FamilyTested exams.

Like its ancestor, the popular children's painting program Kid Pix, this version includes paintbrushes

The opening screen of Kid Pix Studio sends pint-sized painters to all its tools.

that draw silly shapes and make strange sounds and animations that turn even dull tasks such as erasing the screen into something fun. But Kid Pix Studio is an even better buy than its predecessor; three new tools — Moopies, Digital Puppets, and Stampimator — add more fun and creative flexibility to the program.

Moopies animate the Wacky Brushes to make lines dance and colors flash. Digital Puppets let children control on-screen moppets without worrying about tangling strings. And the Stampimator animates any of the software package's 800 stamps (one of the most popular parts of the original Kid Pix program) with a variety of flip and move tricks. Kid Pix Studio also offers other features first seen in Kid Pix 2. With Wacky TV, for example, children can blend scenes from the more than 100 video clips on the CD-

ROM with their own artwork.

Kids like to share their artwork, and with Kid Pix Studio's SlideShow, they can assemble drawings, sounds, and photos (Kid Pix Studio accepts images from Photo CD discs) and give these presentations — as well as Moopies, Digital Puppets, and Stampimations — to their friends, who can run them without Kid Pix Studio.

Kid Pix Studio is one whale of a back-to-school program for kids in the 7–9 age range.

Microsoft Encarta 96
Ages 10-11

Reports and projects come fast and furious for fourth and fifth graders, and that means lots of research. Although you can't beat a traditional encyclopedia for providing in-depth information, a multimedia version serves almost as well for this age group.

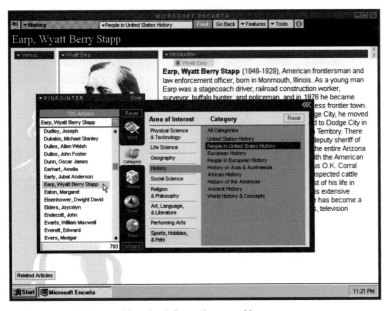

The Pinpointer in Encarta 96 makes information searching easy.

And because a CD-ROM reference makes looking up facts seem easy, kids are much more likely to dive into the fact pool.

Based on Funk & Wagnalls New Encyclopedia, Encarta offers an impressive collection of audio, illustrations, and video to go along with its traditional text-based articles. Earlier versions of Encarta received top honors from *FamilyPC* families, but this edition is even better. The Pinpointer, an extraordinarily easy-to-use search tool, helps kids find exactly what they want. They can search by entering specific words, by choosing a subject topic, and by time or place. A Wizard, which is Microsoft's term for a hand-holding helper, guides children through the research process.

Other elements of Encarta also encourage research, as well as the use of the information your kids find. Kids can mark articles with notemarks — think of them as electronic versions of Post-it notes — which can contain the kids' own notes. And it takes just a click of a button to print anything — including pictures — or copy material to another Windows program, such as a word processor. This digital encyclopedia includes a dictionary/thesaurus combination, so young researchers can uncover the meanings of tough words or terms.

Even better, Encarta now includes something called Yearbook Builder, which lets you update the encyclopedia throughout the year by downloading monthly revisions. These additions — which are similar to the annual yearbooks that paper-based encyclopedias try to sell you — are free during the first half of 1996 (as of this writing, Microsoft hasn't decided whether it will charge for updates after August 1996). And if you have an account on The Microsoft Network (MSN), you can use the online version of Encarta, which is based on the 1995 edition. It looks and works just like the CD-ROM version (although screens and searches are slower).

If your family includes kids doing research reports and projects, you need Microsoft Encarta 96.

Microsoft Works or ClarisWorks

Ages 12 and Up

For older children, the single most useful piece of software for schoolwork is an integrated package such as Microsoft Works or ClarisWorks. Both of these all-in-one software suites give kids the important tools they need — a word processor, a spreadsheet, a database, and a drawing program — for writing reports, manipulating numbers, keeping track of information, and producing charts.

For example, your child might use the spreadsheet to perform complex mathematical operations on data collected from science experiments. The database is useful for assembling address books or lists of the references your child consulted for a project. And these programs' word processors, though not as feature-packed as stand-alone programs, are certainly sufficient for middle-school students.

Both packages are available in versions for the PC and the Mac, and both scored equally well when used by *FamilyPC*'s Family-Tested real-world panels. And, both have recently been updated. ClarisWorks 4.0 and Works for Windows 95 (which operates only under Microsoft's new operating system, Windows 95) provide the same sets of tools as their predecessors but are easier to use, thanks to more electronic assistants, which guide kids through complicated procedures, and sample *templates* — ready-to-use document examples that kids can modify to suit their own needs.

What's important to middle schoolers wrestling with a report, though, is that these two packages make it relatively easy to create documents using material from a variety of sources. Your kids can easily design newsletter-like reports, complete with charts created with the spreadsheet tool and graphics imported from the drawing module. ClarisWorks has an edge in this area, because its word processor does a better job of creating snappy-looking, multicolumn documents.

However, either integrated package will help your kids do their work with a bit more flair.

The Hardware Bare Necessities

You have a home PC or Mac. It's set up, ready to run great learning software, and ready to launch

Just paste your own text in this Microsoft Works document, and you've got a sharp-looking book report.

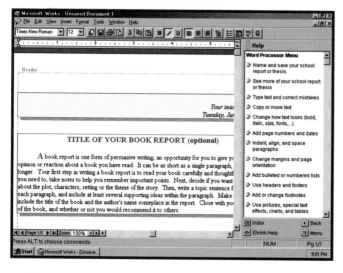

your children into projects galore. Everything is ready, right? Not quite. Before you begin, you need a few other pieces of computer-related hardware.

What else do you need to make the computer a suitable substitute teacher? Actually, not much. You might already have almost everything you need. If not, we'll outline the best you can buy.

Color the Rainbow with a Color Printer

After your computer, the most important piece of equipment — and the most costly — is a printer. It may be the digital age, but paper — and the pictures, words, and numbers on that paper — is still a necessary part of life, including life in school. Older kids will use the printer to publish short stories and churn out reports. Younger children will want to print artwork to hang on the refrigerator or hand to their teachers. (And you'll want a printer for family chores such as finances and correspondence.) No home computer setup is complete until it includes a printer.

But what kind of printer, and which one?

Two basic types of printers are popular with families: laser printers and color ink-jet printers. (Another once-common type — dot-matrix printers — is virtually obsolete; dot-matrix printers are now relegated to such tasks as printing multipage business forms.) Laser printers produce better-quality black-and-white pages, and they are faster than ink-jet printers. In addition, laser printers are designed to turn out more pages per month — and to do so at a lower cost per

page — than ink-jet printers.

But ink-jet printers have a big advantage in the home: color. Almost all of today's ink-jet printers produce color pages that range from good to showstopping. The biggest problem with ink-jets is that, although they usually (but not always) cost less than lasers, they are more expensive to operate. Depending on whether you use plain or more expensive coated paper, you can spend as much as 30 cents for a page of color output. A page from a black-and-white laser costs about one-tenth as much.

We believe that color ink-jets have a lot more appeal for most families than do laser printers, so that's what we recommend for homework help. But which of the dozens of ink-jet printers is best?

For $300, you can get Hewlett-Packard's 600C color ink-jet printer, which garnered a *FamilyPC* Best Buy award shortly after its release. The 600C turns out admirable color, is easy to work with, and makes short work of documents. This printer features flexible paper handling, first-rate black-and-white output, and a top-notch resolution — essentially a measure of the clarity of the images and text it produces — of 600- by 600-dots per inch (dpi). In addition to the printer driver (the software that you install on your computer and that controls printing), the 600C comes with ColorSmart technology, which automates the complexities of color printing by matching the colors you see on the screen with the ones your printer produces.

However, the 600C isn't perfect. Unlike other ink-jet printers, it has space for just a single ink cartridge. So if you want color, you must snap out the black cartridge and insert the three-color cartridge. (With the color cartridge in place, the 600C prints black by mixing the other three colors.) The result is pretty good color, but without the extra sharpness and detail that black plus three-color printing provides.

The 600C comes with a three-year limited warranty, the longest among the *FamilyPC*-tested products. Even more important, HP offers extended technical support hours during the week and on Saturday, so you can get help when it's convenient for you.

The Kidboard keyboard can take the rough handling kids dish out.

Type Me, Point Me

Computer keyboards and mice are made for adults, not kids. To a child — really, to anyone not schooled in touch-typing — the pattern of keys on a standard keyboard doesn't make much sense. Likewise, a typical mouse is made to fit an adult hand, not the smaller, less nimble fingers of a kid. What's a homework-savvy parent to do? One solution is to buy an alternative input device that's designed specifically for kids. Available for both PCs and Macs, these devices help make the computer easier to use for younger members of your family.

Most kid keyboards and pointing devices are intended to replace your existing controllers, offering enhanced durability and ease of use over traditional types. Although some secondary keys may have been relocated, several kid-appropriate keyboards use the standard QWERTY layout, making them a relatively painless replacement option for adults. They use color or symbols to help kids recognize letters, and provide software games so that children can get acquainted with the keys. Mice and trackballs built for kids vary in shape and size, usually offering scaled-down dimensions more comfortable for little hands.

Before you buy, decide whether your family's learning center needs these options. The ages of your children and the level of their computer skills are paramount here. The younger the child, the more important these devices become. Consider price, too. Kid keyboards and mice are usually slightly more expensive than standard models. And take the time to visit a computer store or two for a chance to put fingers on these gizmos.

Of the many kid-style keyboards on those store shelves, *FamilyPC* gives the nod to the $60–$100 Kidboard (from, wouldn't you know it, a company called KidBoard).

Although this 101-key keyboard is well-suited to adults, its color-coded blue and red keys show kids where to put their hands as they learn to type. Each key also features a picture of an animal or an object (for example, *L* shows a lion's face) to teach younger children through letter association. Test families loved the durable construction of the Kidboard but were less impressed with the simple activity software included with the device.

If you're looking for a pint-sized pointing device, check out Mouse 'N House, which got a pat on the back from *FamilyPC*'s parents and kids. Somewhat smaller than other mice, the brightly colored Mouse 'N House has indentations in its sides and buttons to help guide small hands into proper position. Other pluses include its smooth rolling action and quick button response. The Cursor Power software included with the Mouse 'N House lets you change the look of the pointer and increase the size of the blinking cursor, making it easier for kids (and adults) to see.

Art Is in the Pen

Kids may not be born with a crayon, a marker, or a colored pencil in their hands, but it sometimes seems so. Give them these tools, and they can whip up a masterpiece in nothing flat. But skills learned with these tools don't automatically translate to computer artistry, because a mouse is an awkward

When kids press hard on the Wacom ArtPad II's stylus, colors come out richer and lines thicker.

substitute for traditional drawing and painting supplies.

To ease the transition from traditional media to the PC or the Mac, consider buying a digitizing tablet for your artistic child. These precision drawing tools consist of a hard plastic electromagnetic tablet and a pen-like stylus. Professional artists have long relied on graphics tablets, and in the past couple of years several manufacturers have introduced scaled-down versions aimed at the family market.

The most versatile tablets and pens have software that lets you map a small portion of the tablet (say, 1 square inch) so that you can move back and forth across your entire screen with only tiny movements of your wrist. They also do a good job of duplicating the feel of a pencil or a paintbrush by using pressure sensitivity. With this capability, lines are drawn and color is applied according to how hard you press the stylus on the tablet.

We recommend the $190 Wacom Art-Pad II — available for both PCs and Macs — above all other digitizing tablets. Its Ul-traPen stylus works without batteries and is as comfortable and natural as using a tra-ditional pencil or pen. Because the UltraPen is pressure-sensitive, kids can draw thick lines and dense color by pressing hard or produce thin lines and lighter color by press-ing gently. Flip the UltraPen over, and it erases just like a real pencil. Installation is also easy, because the ArtPad II is Plug-and-Play compliant — in other words, Windows 95 automatically detects the device and prompts you for a driver disk. The 4- by 5-inch ArtPad II has a solid, well-construct-ed feel and a pen holder, both important when kids are involved. A copy of Dabbler, an excellent paint program, is included with the ArtPad II.

Now Scanning

It's true. Pictures are often worth a thousand — or more — words, especially when it comes to school-assigned reports and projects or for the around-the-house learning that kids and parents do on their own.

You can find zillions of im-ages on the Internet, on online services, and in CD-ROM art collections, but for the really personal touch, you'll want some way to put your own pictures on the family's PC or Macin-tosh. (Some of the activities and projects in *The FamilyPC Guide*

to Homework can be completed only if you have a way to move physical images onto the computer.)

We think a scanner is the right way to go. Other techniques — for example, using a digital camera or sending pictures to a ser-vice bureau, which scans them into elec-tronic form for you — are too expensive for most families.

And when it comes to scanners, we think Storm's $250 EasyPhoto Reader is the one best suited to home-learning chores. It may cost a bit more — $50 to $100 more — than comparable hand-held scanners, but its ex-cellent software and attention to simplici-ty convinced us that it's the most family-friendly scanner around.

The motorized EasyPhoto plugs into your PC's parallel port or the back of the Mac for quick setup and scans your photographs automatically at the press of a button. The

The EasyPhoto Reader is simple to set up, has great software, and is per-fect for digitizing photos as large as 4-by-6 inches.

scanner then draws the photo through its image-capture mechanism, while the control software makes all the decisions about brightness and other scanning options. With a resolution of 600 dpi, the EasyPhoto's scan quality is as good as any family printer can duplicate.

Without a doubt, the EasyPhoto software is the best we've seen for helping families quickly scan photos and edit them once they're stored on disk. It doesn't matter if your original photographs aren't perfect — the EasyPhoto software helps you improve their appearance with tools for removing red-eye and eliminating scratches. The straightforward interface includes the basic tools for adjusting, resizing, and rotating photos. And Photo Gallery displays filmstrip-like thumbnails of your photos, helping you organize the photos scanned into your computer.

EasyPhoto has two limitations. It can scan only what fits into its 4-inch input slot (it handles 3-by-5 and 4-by-6 prints with no problems), and it doesn't support optical character recognition (OCR), so you won't be able to scan text.

The Information Bare Necessities

You're two-thirds of the way toward building a top-notch home learning center. You have assembled a small library of software and extra hardware. What's left? Now you need a connection to the outside world.

That connection — to information, news, prospective pen pals, and much, much more — is so important to homework and learning potential that you simply can't do without it. If linking your PC or your Mac to the phone line means you have to skimp on

How the Online Services Rate

FamilyPC recently rated three of the most popular online services and graded each in nine critical information areas.

SERVICE	NEWS	HOMEWORK HELP	BUSINESS & PROFESSIONAL	COMPUTER STUFF	SPORTS & GAMES	HOBBIES	KIDS	TRAVEL	INTERNET
America Online	A	A	B-	A	B	A-	A	B+	A-
Compu-Serve	B	B-	A	A	B+	B+	C	B	B-
Prodigy	B-	C	C	C+	B	C	B	B+	B

America Online's picture-based interface is not only easy on the eyes but easy to navigate, too.

other items — for example, hardware such as a scanner or even some software — we think it's a worthwhile trade-off.

As with many other bare necessities in this chapter, you may already have some of the pieces of the information connection. Others, you may have only heard about.

Let's get going — going online, that is.

Modem to Modem and the Two-Line Family

If you've recently bought a computer — say, in the last year or so — the machine probably came with a modem. This device connects your computer to the phone line, allowing you to transmit and receive data via an online service or the Internet.

When choosing a modem, the most important feature is its speed. Listed in kilobits per second (this is often abbreviated to *kbps*), this speed represents the top-end rate at which the modem will send and receive information. For example, a 14.4-kbps modem is slower than a 28.8-kbps model.

A faster modem saves you online and Internet connect-time charges in the long run, and it minimizes frustration — always important to keep in mind with kids. Although you can go online using a 14.4-kbps modem, we recommend a 28.8-kbps modem. Most

How Much Does It Cost?

FamilyPC subscribers who belong to an online service report average use of roughly 24 hours per month. Not counting surcharges, here is what it would cost if your family spent 5, 10, 20, or 30 hours a month using each online service.

	AMERICA ONLINE	COMPUSERVE	MICROSOFT NETWORK*	PRODIGY
Telephone	800-827-6364	800-848-8199	800-386-5550	800-776-3449
5 hours	$9.95	$9.95	$9.95	$9.95
10 hours	$24.70	$24.70	$22.45	$24.70
20 hours	$54.20	$24.95	$19.95	$54.20
30 hours	$83.70	$44.45	$39.95	$29.95

*Standard plan; Windows 95 only

online services and Internet providers support that higher speed.

And although your link to the outside world requires just one phone line, we believe that families who are serious about home learning should install a second line, because you can't be online and on the phone at the same time. That second line, devoted but not dedicated solely to the computer, lets kids reach out and touch information without worrying about cutting off the family (and them!) from friends and the phone.

Online Services Do It All

Information drawn into the house through the phone lines comes from a bewildering array of sources. The easiest place to start,

however, is with what's typically called an *online service.*

These companies offer a one-stop-shopping approach to information; they publish a wide range of information such as news, sports, reference materials, electronic mail, and kid-appropriate content within a self-contained virtual community. They also bring together people in interest-specific areas or forums in which online discussions and chats take place. They charge for the time you're connected and provide specialized software necessary to connect to the service when you subscribe. The most popular online services include America Online, Prodigy, CompuServe, and The Microsoft Network.

Okay, you want to use an online service.

Which one is best for your family? Not all online services are equal, and when it comes to homework help, kids' stuff, and a connection to the Internet (more on the Internet in a moment), we think America Online (AOL) is the one to pick.

Of the major online services, AOL's interface — the way it presents its information — is the most attractive. A recent revamping of its homework help areas (for details on this part of AOL, check out "Using Online Services for Research," in Chapter 7) makes it easier for kids to do research, while its Kids Only Online section carries cool content for children between the ages of 5 and 14.

Other great kid places on AOL include Disney Adventures, the Cartoon Network, and Blackberry Creek, a child-oriented creativity piece of cyberspace. And although its Internet Web browser can't match some of the competition, we think the integration of the Web with AOL's own material is first-rate. (Once again, don't worry if Internet lingo such as *Web browser* is new to you. In the next section, we describe all of the tools you need for connecting to, and then accessing information on, the Internet.)

Spinning an Info Web with the Internet

Online services may be the place to start, but at some point you'll want to leap from the security of services such as America Online to the wild and woolly World Wide Web.

This part of the Internet — which is a global collection of computers and computer networks at businesses, schools, government agencies, and homes — is graphics packed and looks a lot like what you see on a computer running a CD-ROM.

But it's not the way-cool look of the Web that makes it so useful for kids doing homework. The Web's most useful feature is something called *hotlinking* — the capability to get anywhere you want by just clicking on an image or a piece of text. The best Web pages (each screen of information on the

Every major online service, including AOL, connects you to the World Wide Web and provides a Web browser so you can view its information.

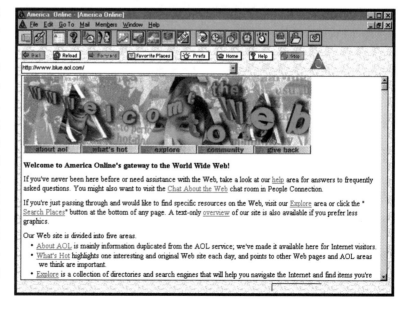

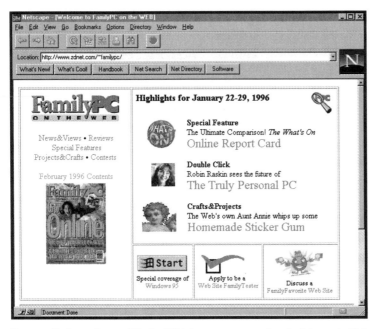

Netscape Navigator is one of the best Web browsers you can buy. A click on a hotlink — shown here by blue-colored text — takes you to another Web page.

Web is called a *page,* in Web-ese) have hotlinks that take you to related information. For example, a Web site that concentrates on the Civil War might have hotlinks to Web sites about national parks and monuments (because most battlefields are administered by the Federal government), to archives of photographs from the Civil War period, and even to Web sites devoted to military history in general.

To access the resources of the Web, you need two things: a connection to the Internet and a piece of software called a Web browser. The simplest way to get both is through an online service; all the major services — America Online, CompuServe, Prodigy, and the Microsoft Network — offer connections to the Web and Web browsers

(although Prodigy's and MSN's browsers are for Windows only).

Unfortunately, using the Web can quickly consume hours of online time. Cruising from one page to other related pages is often loads of fun, however, it can take minutes to download each graphics-loaded Web page to your computer's screen. As a result, the monthly charges from your online service can easily skyrocket past those from your utility company (for cost comparisons, see the sidebar in this chapter titled "How Much Does It Cost?").

The answer for heavy-duty Web users is a separate Internet access account with an Internet Service Provider (ISP). Many ISPs charge a reasonable flat rate each month, so no matter how much you use the Web, you know how much you're spending.

If you think you and the kids will use the Web extensively — say, more than 10 hours a month — we suggest you purchase an all-in-one, get-on-and-go Internet kit that includes a good Web browser and a single-step sign-up from a list of ISPs. Two excellent kits are Netscape Navigator Personal Edition (Netscape, 800-528-6292, $40, for Windows and Mac) and Larry Magid's Essential Internet (Quarterdeck, 800-354-3222, $20, Windows only).

Chapter 3

The Magic Words
Reading and Writing

READING AND WRITING — WITHOUT A good grasp of those skills, your child will be lost in school.

Homework rarely involves *only* reading — some sort of written work usually accompanies the reading assignment. However, you can get young prereaders and early readers excited about turning pages by using the home computer. In this chapter, we show you how.

Writing is a different story: Kids get writing assignments as homework throughout their school years. Whether your kids are working on a simple project — for example, a first book report — or one packed with complexity, the family PC or Mac can help out immensely. That help comes, not so much in the creative process itself (though you shouldn't totally discount the family computer there, as you find out in the section "Tell Me a Story," later in this chapter), but in the mechanical aspects of writing,

editing, and publishing.

In the following sections, we show off the home computer's capabilities for readin' and writin'. As for 'rithmetic, well you have to wait for that — but not long. We tackle math in the next chapter.

Reading Is FUNdamental

Reading is a lifelong pursuit that, like riding a bicycle, once learned is never forgotten. Of course, it's an important part of every child's education.

Helping your preschoolers and early-elementary-school-aged children learn to read may not be homework per se — at least, it's not the same as launching your kids into a specific project — but reading *is* an important skill you can foster outside the classroom.

Although you can find scads of reading-related software programs in the stores — many of them with highly structured activities that duplicate the kind of learning that often takes place in preschools and kindergartens — we think an interactive storybook offers the best way to use the home computer for reading.

Why? That's simple: because interactive storybooks make reading *fun*.

GET SMART: *Interactive storybooks aren't the only way you can teach reading to your youngsters. You can also choose programs that focus on prereading exercises and reading readiness, such as Knowledge Adventures' JumpStart series (JumpStart Preschool, Jump-Start Kindergarten, and JumpStart First Grade).*

Interactive Storybooks — Why Kids Love 'em

Electronic storybooks grab kids' attention and just won't let go. But why? What do computerized books have that in-their-lap paper books lack?

When *FamilyPC* sent out more than a dozen different electronic storybooks for hands-on testing by nearly 600 parents, teachers, and kids, the answers came back, loud and clear.

First, computer-based books *talk* to kids. Hearing words pronounced fosters early reading skills. Even more impressive, many of the best storybooks narrate their tales in several languages (Spanish is the most popular, which makes sense, because it's the second-most-used language in the U.S.), giving a big boost to the educational impact of these titles.

But it's more than a talking computer

that excites kids about interactive storybooks. The lure of interactive books (regardless of whether we like to admit it) is the same as TV's: color, photos, illustrations, animation, sound effects, video, and music. All of these characteristics draw kids in *and* keep them coming back for more.

Increasingly, interactive storybooks match the quality of TV in nearly all these departments. (Video is the one exception; developers still must leap major hurdles before interactive storybooks offer video capabilities equal to TV.) To top it off, many interactive storybooks weave reading activities into their storytelling. For example, Chicka Chicka Boom Boom includes several fun exercises, one of which sounds out silly alliterative sentences as the kids go through the alphabet.

GET SMART: *Worried that interactive storybooks are nothing more than digital baby-sitters? You can avoid this by doing the same thing with an electronic book that you do with a regular book: Spend time reading the book with your child.*

When it comes to interactivity, however, electronic storybooks win hands down over TV and movies. Kids sit and passively absorb TV and movies (as any parent on a Saturday morning knows all too well). With interactive storybooks, kids can take control and make things happen. They can start and stop the story and play games and activities. And, because kids see it all as *fun* while parents think of the whole experience as *educational*, everyone wins.

Interactive Storybooks — The Winners Circle

FamilyPC keeps its finger on the pulse of computer-equipped families by working with an extensive, nationwide network of parents and children who review and rate dozens of PC and Macintosh programs each month. So when *FamilyPC* tells you which books kids like (and which ones they don't), you know that information comes straight from the source.

Most interactive storybooks are aimed squarely at the early reader, making them great picks for parents with preschoolers and early-elementary-school-aged children. Older children hooked on reading and writing should be steered toward other computer activities, such as creating their own stories from scratch. For more information, see "Tell Me a Story," later in this chapter.

Here are three of the best interactive storybooks available.

Chicka Chicka Boom Boom
Ages 3–6
Chicka Chicka Boom Boom makes learning the alphabet as easy as ABC and do-re-mi. Based on the award-winning book of the same name, Chicka Chicka Boom Boom is narrated by blues great Ray Charles (kids can also choose to have the story read by a female voice). In addition to the CD-ROM, kids get a paperboard copy of the book, and the music plays on an audio CD player.

***

GET SMART: *After you install Chicka Chicka Boom Boom, make sure you double-click on the Parents Tips icon. This provides several nifty off-computer activities, as well as a page of letters you can print for coloring or fiash-card-making projects.*

***

The CD-ROM contains five activities related to the story line. Videos of kids — collectively known as the Multimedia Players — introduce the activities and provide help. Words are highlighted as the story is read, making it easy for children to follow along. In the Jump and Jingle activity, the video kids sing cute rap songs for each letter of the alphabet. And if your computer has a micro-

Video clips of real kids introduce the activities in Chicka Chicka Boom Boom and give the program a decidedly fun feel.

phone, your children can record their own 15-second songs.

Dr. Seuss's ABC
Ages 3–7

Based on the popular book of the same name, Dr. Seuss's ABC helps kids learn their ABCs by interacting with Dr. Seuss's delightfully zany characters. Each letter of the alphabet gets its own page, and this CD-ROM includes nearly 600 words your child can learn.

On the page for the letter *b*, for example, your child sees words and animated pictures representing *barber*, *baby*, *bubbles*, and *bumblebee*. When your child clicks on the characters that represent these words, they produce new *b* words. Everything is accompanied by animation, sounds, or music.

When your child clicks on the barber, for example, he plays a boogie-woogie bass by using the single strand of hair sticking up from a baby's nearly bald pate.

When your child clicks on any word, the storybook highlights the word and reads it aloud. By clicking on a noun, he sees a picture; clicking on a verb sets an action in motion. This is a great way to introduce kids to the simplest parts of speech.

The disc also plays on audio CD players and comes with a book to read away from the computer.

Winnie the Pooh and the Honey Tree
Ages 3–8

In Winnie the Pooh and the Honey Tree, your kids get to join the willy-nilly silly old bear as he hunts for his favorite nectar. Along the way, your children learn about words, play games, sing songs, and even pick up a little bit of Spanish.

Children can read this animated storybook or they can listen to it. Like most interactive storybooks, Winnie the Pooh and the Honey Tree highlights the words as they're spoken.

In addition to the story, the disc features five sing-along songs,

Dr. Seuss's ABC shows letters and then actions or objects that begin with those letters.

Winnie the Pooh liked to do his stoutness exercises every morning because exercise made him hungry and being hungry meant that it was time for breakfast!

Winnie the Pooh and the Honey Tree is a straightforward digital storybook with a strong cast of recognizable characters, as well as sing-along songs and fun learning games.

including the popular "Winnie the Pooh" theme song, as well as four games that introduce kids to basic learning skills. In one game, Piglet asks your child to help find toys that Christopher Robin wants to play with.

GET SMART: *For some sneaky vocabulary building, show your young readers how to click on the dictionary, and then on one of the highlighted words to hear a definition of that word.*

The animations that kids activate by clicking on objects change with subsequent clicks (most interactive storybooks associate only *one* animation with each object). For example, one click causes a troop of ants to march into Pooh's honey jar. Click again, and smoke from Pooh's campfire changes into a cloud that drenches the marching column, causing the ants to abandon their sticky mission.

For other interactive storybook picks, see Chapter 14, "Homework Software."

★ TRY THIS! ★

Build Alphabet Power with Colorful Flash Cards or Trading Cards

Reading may be FUNdamental, but you can help your kids go beyond the basics of their interactive storybooks by spending an hour or so creating alphabet flash cards or character trading cards on the computer. You can use almost any storybook. Here's how:

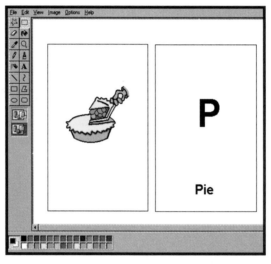

Make the main letter on your flash cards — and any other text, such as the word *Pie*, shown here — large enough to see from across a table.

1. Look through the storybook for interesting pictures of the characters or, if the program teaches the ABCs, one of the letters and its associated image(s).

you snapped the screen. By default, the Macintosh names these files *Picture 1, Picture 2*, and so on.

4. For the flash card, you want a picture of the object or character only, not of the entire screen. Select the object or character with the art program's selection tool and then choose the Copy command from the Edit menu.

2. To snap a picture of the image on the screen in Windows or Windows 95, press Alt-Print Screen. On the Mac, press Command-Shift-3.

3. On a PC, open an art program (Windows 95's Paint program works fine) and choose the Paste command from the Edit menu. The screen you captured is pasted on the page. On the Mac, open your art program and then insert the file created when

5. Open a new document in the art program and choose Paste.

6. From here, you simply have to use your imagination. For example, you can draw two boxes to represent the outlines of the front and back of a flash card. Then, place the picture inside one box and the associated letter in the other. Next, print the page, cut out the cards, and paste them back to back. With your flash cards completed, you can show your child the picture side and ask her to identify the word and the first letter in that word.

Writing a Book Report

A book report? Do I *have* to?

Heard that one before? When kids pull their first real-life writing assignment in school, it usually comes in the form of a book report. The chore, they would like you to believe, is as onerous as straightening up a bedroom.

We aren't about to write your child's book report for her, but we *can* steer kids toward computer-based tools that simplify the mechanical part of the process — the organization, the writing, and the proofing. Along the way, we outline how to assemble a book report with a pair of programs, and we shower young writers with some kid-quality tips and online writing resources.

Book Reports for Beginners

You can tell your kids, "It's not your father's word processor."

Several new writing packages offer good alternatives for children who find their parents' word-processing programs too big, too confusing, and just too much for the job at hand. Writing programs for kids now address the needs of various age groups, offering fun interfaces, lots of colorful graphics, and a bag full of ideas to help young writers get started.

Two of the top-ranked writing programs

What to Look for When Shopping for an Electronic Storybook

Just like paper books, interactive storybooks come and go. Some become classics — the three we highlight here are likely candidates, especially Dr. Seuss's ABC and Chicka Chicka Boom Boom — but you need to know what to look for when you're shopping for a top-flight electronic storybook. Here's our checklist:

✓ **Recognizable characters:**
Kids are most likely to give a storybook the thumbs up when the characters — if not the story itself — are name brands.

✓ **Activities included:**
The best storybooks do more than simply read a tale to children. They offer additional activities, such as games or puzzles, that keep the kids coming back for more.

✓ **Ever-changing animations:**
Kids get bored like everyone else, and books can hold their interest longer by providing multiple animations for each on-screen object.

✓ **Audio CD capabilities:**
You get more for your money if you can pop the disc into the family's stereo system, so your children can listen to the music or the soundtrack.

Go Online!

On the Internet, The BookWire contains lots of children's classics you or your child can read at the computer, or — better yet — print and read together. Here's the address for this Web site:

http://www.bookwire.com/links/readingroom/ echildbooks.html

Hans Christian Andersen's classic fairy tales dominate the list, but you can also find other popular books such as *Treasure Island* and *The Adventures of Tom Sawyer*.

for kids are The Learning Company's Student Writing and Research Center and Broderbund's The Amazing Writing Machine. Both provide the essential word-processing tools — easy editing, the capability to insert graphics, a spell checker, and lots of fonts and text styles — in forms that kids can pick up without lots of learning time.

The Student Writing and Research Center is the more straightforward of the two programs. This package's strongest features are its report template and the gobs of clip art bundled with the program — kids can easily drop these images into their reports.

The Amazing Writing Machine is a bit more playful — its interface leans toward the cartoonish at times

— but it's still a solid writer's tool. Its ready-to-use templates range from layouts suited for essays and stories to formats appropriate for poems and letters.

The Amazing Writing Machine includes two nifty features for helping anxious young authors overcome writer's block: Spin mode and the Bright Ideas tool. Spin mode presents kids with a prewritten letter, story, poem, journal, or essay outline, with buttons the kids can click to add words or phrases. The Bright Ideas tool gets kids thinking by offering quotations, jokes, facts, and even vocabulary words appropriate for the type of writing project.

The Learning Company also offers The Ultimate Writing & Creativity Center, a program for kids ages six to 10. This package stresses the creative aspects of writing (rather than researching). It's a great tool for beginning writers who might otherwise have

Don't let the crazy look of The Amazing Writing Machine fool you. This is a powerful word processor for elementary-school-aged writers.

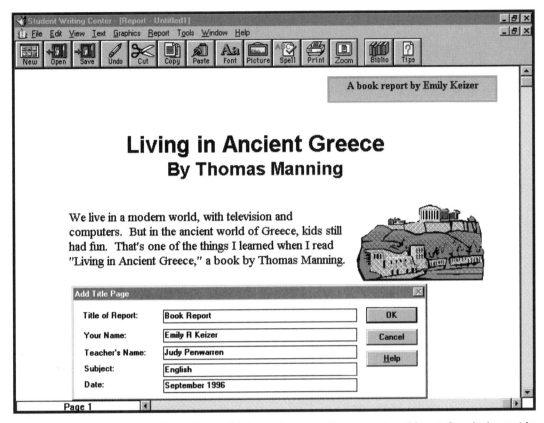

The Student Writing and Research Center is a straightforward program. You can create a title page for a book report by simply filling in some blanks.

a hard time getting past the blank screen. The Ultimate Writing & Creativity Center also includes a paint program and a multimedia presentation module.

Starting the Book Report

Both The Student Writing and Research Center and The Amazing Writing Machine can be used to churn out credible book reports, even if the kids simply sit down and start typing. But to get a "Wow!" out of the teacher, your kids should follow the simple steps we describe in this section.

The Student Writing and Research Center

Pick the Report layout from the screen the program displays when you create a new document. This one-column format works well for book reports.

At the top of the page, type the title of the book and the author's name. Choose a large font for this information and center it by choosing Set Alignment from the Text menu. Press Enter once or twice to move the cursor down and then choose another, smaller font — say, 12 or 14 points — for the main

Go Online!

What's writing without someone to read the finished work? Fortunately, kids can easily expand their book report readership by publishing on the Internet. Using the family's Web browser — or an Internet-capable online service such as America Online or Prodigy — take your children to The Book Nook, which you find at the following address:

http://i-site.on.ca/Isite/Education/
Bk_ report/BookNook/default. html#Nook

The Book Nook posts dozens of kid-written book reports, with sections devoted to writers' grade levels and further divided by subject area (such as science fiction). Your at-home writers can share critiques of books they've read by e-mailing a text file to the site (show them how to use their word processor's Save As command and select Text as the document type) or by filling out a book report form while they're online.

If your child can't decide which book to read for her report — and you want suggestions to help you steer her toward a top-notch title — check out the University of Calgary's resources on the Internet:

http://www.ucalgary.ca/~dkbrown/
awards.html

You'll find several lists of award-winning books, including Newbery Award winners all the way back to 1922. For additional recommended reading lists from organizations such as the American Library Association and the Internet Reading Association, enter the following address in your Web browser:

http://www.ucalgary. ca/~dkbrown/lists.html

At the Book Nook, kids can add their own book report to the library by filling out a form.

Netscape - [Submit a book review]
File Edit View Go Bookmarks Options Directory Window Help

Location: http://i-site.on.ca/Isite/Education/Bk_report/BookNook/About/bkr_form.html
What's New! | What's Cool! | Handbook | Net Search | Net Directory | Software

TITLE of the book:
Secrets of the Shopping Mall
Name of the Author:
Richard Peck
Name of the Publisher:
Dell
Date of printing:
1979
ISBN Reference #:
0-440-40270-0

How much I liked this book .

One Thumb UP
Two Thumbs UP
One Thumb UP
Ok - No thumb   d in ?
Boring .... Thumb DOWN

My Book Report

-- not more than 2 pages please !
Don't give away the ending -- you don't want it to ruin it for others !

Document: Done

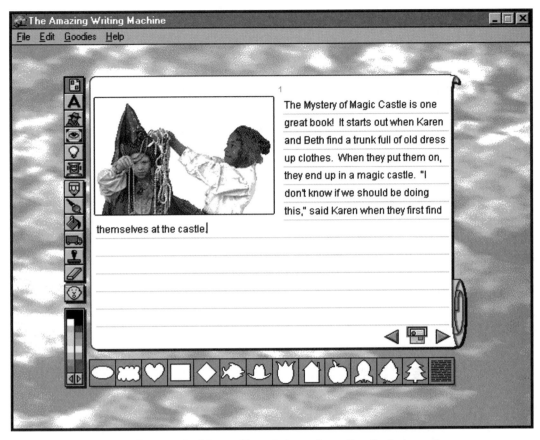

The Amazing Writing Machine lets you mix pictures with words to create an attractive book report.

text of the report. (Before you start typing the body of your report, remember to reset Alignment to *Left*.)

GET SMART: *If your children know how to insert pictures into a document, they can easily punch up a book report on the computer. Show your budding wordsmiths how to add art to their book reports, walking them through the procedure once or twice. For practice, use the program's clip art (if it has some) or download an image from your online service or the Internet.*

The Student Writing and Research Center lets you add artwork to spice up the report. To add a piece of clip art, pick Choose Picture from the Graphics menu and select the picture you want. Once it's on the page, you can move it around and drop it down wherever you want. Notice how the text automatically *wraps* around the picture!

The Amazing Writing Machine

Although the Essay and the Story formats both work for writing book reports, we prefer the Essay format. It doesn't junk up the page with predesigned spaces for pictures (although you can easily add an image in an Essay-style page).

GET SMART: *If your son or daughter keeps a computerized journal using a word processor that lacks such privacy features, the document can be saved to a floppy disk rather than the computer's hard disk. (For more details on journal writing, see "More Writing Projects," later in this chapter.)*

You can use the first page of the Essay as a title page for listing the name of the book, the author's name, and your name. On the second page (you change pages by clicking on the arrow in the bottom-right corner), begin writing the report. To add a piece of

---

★ TRY THIS! ★

Keep a Journal

Writers write, but assigning at-home book reports probably isn't the best way to convince your kids that writing is not only a good idea, but fun, too. Instead, let them develop their writing skills by keeping a daily journal.

Both The Student Writing and Research Center and The Amazing Writing Machine include journals in which children can record their secrets, write an account of their day, or just jot down random thoughts. More important for families sharing one computer, both programs let kids *lock* their journal with a secret password, keeping their private thoughts really private.

---

clip art from the program's collection, all you have to do is click on one of the picture designs at the bottom of the window, position the design, and then choose Import Graphic from the File menu.

Get Serious about Research Papers

Every student's academic writing career eventually progresses from straightforward book reports and simple paragraph-long assignments to more complicated papers. Regardless of whether the teacher calls them *research papers* (and many do, even in elementary school, though they might not require footnotes or a bibliography), these projects are just that: written assignments that rely not on opinion, but on information the student collects from outside sources.

GET SMART: *To spell check or not to spell check? You have to decide whether your children should use their word processor's spell-checking tool, and, if so, how much they should use it. On the plus side, spell checkers let kids concentrate on writing, not spelling. On the minus side, they can easily become a crutch and remove a responsibility — correctly spelled text — that writers have carried for centuries. And remember, spell checkers aren't always right! For example, the spell checker doesn't find anything amiss if your young writer types of when he means or. If you let your kids use the word processor's spell-checking tool, urge them to look carefully at words identified as misspelled and at the suggested replacements.*

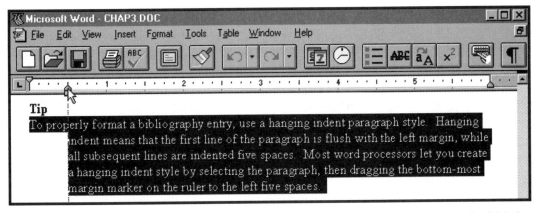

Tip
To properly format a bibliography entry, use a hanging indent paragraph style. Hanging indent means that the first line of the paragraph is flush with the left margin, while all subsequent lines are indented five spaces. Most word processors let you create a hanging indent style by selecting the paragraph, then dragging the bottom-most margin marker on the ruler to the left five spaces.

You can create a hanging-indent style for bibliography entries by dragging the ruler's bottom margin marker 0.5 inches to the right.

But if *research* is the first word in preparing a research paper, writing should come into play just as quickly. When equipped with a solid word-processing program, the home computer mutates into one mean writing machine — a tool your kids can use not only for typing text, but also to organize and present information in the clear, concise fashion that teachers want. (For how-tos on researching from your home computer, don't forget to read Chapter 7, "Wading into the Information Pool.")

When your child is ready to tackle research papers, make sure you have the right home-learning tools at the ready, too.

Work Research-Paper Wonders with Microsoft Works

The budding researcher can write papers with any word processor and probably turn out work worthy of a good grade. But the best family writing tool we've seen for the job is Microsoft Works 4.0 for Windows 95. You can also find Works in versions for the Mac and Windows 3.1, but

The Microsoft Works Task Launcher opens dozens of different documents, including one suitable for research papers.

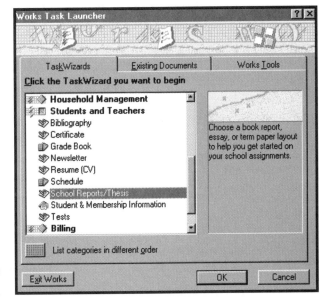

we're smitten with the Windows 95 edition, because it goes the extra mile for students who are wrestling with at-home, for-school writing chores.

GET SMART: *To properly format a bibliography entry, use a hanging-indent paragraph style. This style aligns the first line of the paragraph flush with the left margin and indents all subsequent lines 0.5 inches. Most word processors let you create a hanging-indent style by selecting the paragraph and then dragging the bottommost margin marker on the ruler 0.5 inches to the right.*

Works gets these high marks for the way in which it automates some of the tedious aspects of writing a paper. Several of its word processor Task Wizards — robot-like document designers that quickly create properly formatted pages — aim straight for the needs of middle- and high-school students writing research papers.

When you start Works, scroll down through the list shown in the Works Task Launcher, double-click on the Students and Teachers heading, and then click on the School Reports/Thesis line. You can pick from three common types of school docu-

---

★ **TRY THIS!** ★

Create a Book Report Checklist

You can prepare a prereading checklist in order to help your children focus on the information that is most commonly included in a book report. You can save this file on the computer, and then your kids can call it up and print a copy any time the teacher assigns a book report.

The checklist should include spaces for the following information:

✓ The title of the book

✓ The author's name

✓ A one-sentence description of the book's subject

✓ The name and a one-sentence description of the main character

✓ The name and a one-sentence description of another important character in the book

✓ A brief description of the setting — that is, where and when the story takes place

✓ A one-sentence description of what happens to the main character in the story

✓ A one-sentence description of the story's ending

✓ The grade you give this book (on a scale from 1 to 10, or just "thumbs up" or "thumbs down")

Kids can use this checklist to take notes (either on the computer or on paper while they read), and then expand the notes into a full-length report.

ments: a book report, an essay, and a term paper. Each Task Wizard is programmed to automatically build a particular document for you.

Another useful, school-specific Task Wizard in Microsoft Works 4.0 assembles a bibliography. A bibliography, or list of the references you use in composing the research paper, usually requires a very specific style of formatting. This Works Task Wizard shows all the possible types of reference works and the correct format for the bibliographic listing of each type.

For kids writing research papers, other useful Works features include a good spell checker and easy insertion of tables and charts. For more information on how to use an integrated program's spreadsheet,

Movin' On Up

Works packages can handle most school jobs your kids can throw at them. But if your older children hunger for more power, you should consider movin' on up to an *office suite*, a package of feature-rich applications. For example, Microsoft Office contains Microsoft Word (a word processor), Excel (a spreadsheet), Powerpoint (a presentation program), and a scheduler. The extra power you gain comes at a price, however: The Standard version of Microsoft Office costs $499 (as opposed to $80 for Microsoft Works 4.0 with Bookshelf) and requires as much as 89MB of disk space (Microsoft Works needs 25MB).

But how do you know when it's time for your kids to make the switch?

• If your children create any collaborative documents (some technologically astute middle- and high-school teachers accept papers and reports on disk, enter their comments in the file, and then return it to the student for another draft), the revision-marking capabilities of a stand-alone word processor such as Microsoft Word can make working together easier and more efficient. Revision marks, which show all changes to a document, make it possible for both the student and the teacher to see how the report or paper has been edited and rewritten.

• If your child does a lot of writing, particularly long documents, he'll want a dedicated word processor that automat-

ically creates tables of contents and indexes and has powerful outlining and style sheet functions. Works' word processor lacks an outliner, but Word includes one.

• If your child needs to do more than basic number crunching, you might consider a more powerful spreadsheet with such features as the capability to have multiple sheets in one file, the capability to link spreadsheets, and tools for grouping and outlining data. For example, a high-school student could put data from several science-class experiments on separate worksheets in an Excel file and then use another worksheet to link the worksheets together and calculate totals.

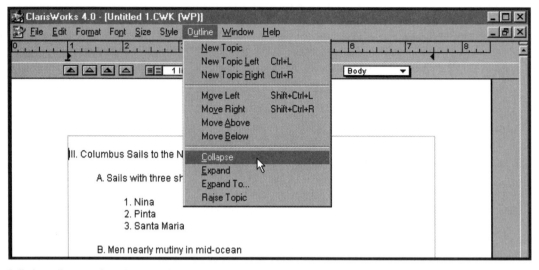

Built-in outliners such as the one in ClarisWorks let you collapse or expand the outline's items, so you see just the main points or everything in the outline.

graphics, and writing tools in combination, check out the hands-on project, "Try This! Use Tables in a Research Paper," later in this chapter.

Go Online!

Okay, your kid is in panic mode. It's Friday night, the paper is due Monday morning, and she can't even remember what a research paper is. Tell her to calm down and head to Purdue University's On-Line Writing Project (OWL):

http://owl.english.purdue.edu/

Packed to the brim with writing tips, OWL's most appropriate page for panic-stricken report writers is "Writing Research Papers: A Step-by-Step Approach":

http://owl.english.purdue.edu/Files/94.html

Outlining

Outlining? Ugh! Few parts of the research-paper-writing process bring frowns faster than preparing an outline.

However, outlining *does* serve an important purpose. To help your child write the paper, and more importantly, organize his or her ideas, your young researcher needs an outline. The process of creating an outline also helps writers brainstorm new ideas.

Some word processors offer integrated outliners that let you create an outline, click on outline items to move them around, and even turn an outline into a more or less finished document. Microsoft Works doesn't offer one, but

ClarisWorks (another good integrated package) does. Many professional-quality word processors, such as Microsoft Word, include an outliner — one reason why your kids might want to make the switch from an integrated package to a word processor.

Even if your word processor doesn't have a built-in outliner, it can still handle the job. Develop the outline, using tabs or spaces to indent the entries, and then save it as MYDOC.OUT. To rearrange items in the outline, use the program's Cut and Paste commands. Before writing from this outline, open the MYDOC.OUT file and use the Save As command to name a new file as MYDOC.DOC. This retains the outline file,

★ TRY THIS! ★

Use Tables in a Research Paper

Sometimes, you can pack a lot of information in a small space by organizing it in rows and columns. You *can* create such a table by using tabs or the spacebar to line up everything, as we all did years ago with a typewriter. However, today's word processors can do most of the work for you.

Look for a Table command in the program's menus. In Microsoft Works 4.0, you find it in the Insert menu.

Select this command, and you can specify the number of columns and rows, and in some cases (such as Works 4.0), even the formatting style of the table.

Just fill in the boxes — called *cells,* in a table — with your information. Everything stays nicely aligned. When you're done, you can usually resize the table by simply clicking on a corner and dragging it into its new dimensions.

Microsoft Works offers lots of different table styles, just the thing for spicing up a science report.

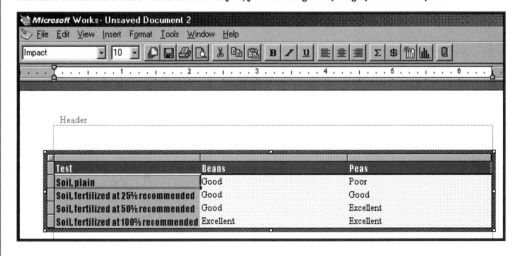

in case you need to revert back to the original version.

Footnoting

The home computer gives a boost to another element of research writing: *footnotes* (sometimes called *endnotes,* when they appear at the end of the paper rather than at the more traditional spot at the bottom, or *foot*, of the page).

A word processor makes adding foot-notes easy, because the program automatically puts them at the bottom of the correct page and automatically adjusts the page breaks to make room for them. As a result, research writers don't have to manually calculate how much space to leave at the foot of the page. Another advantage of using a word processor? When you insert a new footnote between two existing footnotes, the word processor automatically renumbers them for you.

★ TRY THIS! ★

Add a Chart to a Research Paper

One of the biggest advantages of using an integrated package such as Microsoft Works or Claris-Works (as opposed to a word processor) for writing research papers is that you have more than just a writing tool. The integrated program's spreadsheet and chart-making modules can be lifesavers for kids composing papers that must include references to testing results (such as science class papers) or can benefit from illustrative charts (such as history or business class papers).

To add a chart to a

An integrated program such as Microsoft Works or ClarisWorks can easily turn spreadsheet numbers into an informative chart.

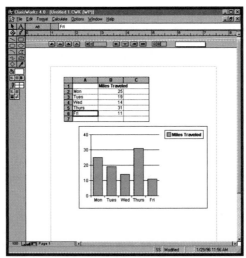

ClarisWorks document (you use a similar process in Microsoft Works), click on the spreadsheet tool (the one that looks like a plus sign) and then drag an outline of the small spreadsheet. Enter the numbers and any text labels, select the range of numbers that you want to chart by clicking and dragging, and then choose the Make Chart command from the Options menu. You can choose from a wide variety of chart types and styles and then position the chart anywhere that you wish in the Works document.

GET SMART: *If your kids find it tough to compose at the computer, encourage them to do first drafts there and then proofread and edit on paper, before entering the changes in the electronic document. That minimizes the time they spend at the PC or the Mac, but makes the most of the time they spend in front of the machine.*

Almost all word processors include a Footnote command. In Microsoft Works, for example, you find it in the Insert menu. A click on the Footnote command adds the footnote number and opens a space for you to type the footnote reference.

GET SMART: *Your children should check with the teacher to find out how they should cite electronic references — from a CD-ROM encyclopedia, for example — in their research papers.*

Tell Me a Story

Storytelling is as old as fire and language. Long before someone scratched the first marks on a clay tablet, people were telling stories the old-fashioned way: by talking.

Our kids certainly have stories to tell — we've all heard some whoppers over the years — but they don't have to actually *tell* them. With some help from the home computer, they can write, illustrate, and publish tales of mystery, adventure, suspense, humor, or whatever strikes their fancy. Storytelling is a super at-home activity, and it's often part of a from-school homework assignment.

We decided not to call this section "Cre-

ative Writing," because a) the phrase is somewhat stuffy, and b) some kids hear alarm bells when teachers use those words to describe the next homework project. "I have to *write* something? On my own? From the beginning?"

GET SMART: *Before your child starts writing a story, he should have some idea of how the story begins, what happens in the middle, and how it ends. First, of course, he has to decide what kind of story he'll write. Will it be a mystery, a scary story, or a sad tale? Will it be a true story?*

Rather than scare them off by referring to *creative writing*, urge your kids to let loose their creativity by telling stories in a new way — to the home computer.

Creative Software for Creative Writers

A good writing program for early-elementary-school-aged kids — ages six through 10 — must provide three things: an easy-to-use word processor; illustration tools, including the capability to add clip art *and* create original artwork; and getting-started help. When teachers assign open-ended creative writing projects as homework, these tools help kids to make up stories. Because most kids in this age range like to draw as much as they like to write (if not more so), they find the combination of illustration and writing tools on the computer more compelling than an all-text word processor. And because staring at a blank page is often the scariest part of the writing process, an effective writing

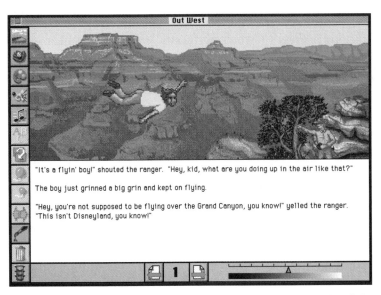

Out West

"It's a flyin' boy!" shouted the ranger. "Hey, kid, what are you doing up in the air like that?"

The boy just grinned a big grin and kept on flying.

"Hey, you're not supposed to be flying over the Grand Canyon, you know!" yelled the ranger. "This isn't Disneyland, you know!"

Kids can resize any Storybook Weaver clip art; here, we bumped up the size of the flying boy with a couple clicks of the mouse.

tool must offer young writers a way to jump-start their ideas.

GET SMART: *Great stories don't have to be big stories. They don't need a complicated plot. In other words, urge your child to think of a simple idea and build the story around that. (Story starters in programs such as Storybook Weaver Deluxe and KidWorks Deluxe are helpful, because they're so simple.)*

Many of the software programs that meet those requirements are called *storybook makers,* because they put younger kids — say, ages six to 10 — in the creative mood by letting them write, illustrate, and print book-like stories. We like two storybook makers as creative-writing homework helpers: Storybook Weaver Deluxe and KidWorks Deluxe.

Storybook Weaver Deluxe

Storybook Weaver Deluxe lets kids ages six to 12 create their own stories with pictures, words, and sounds, either from scratch or using one of approximately 40 story starters.

Starter titles — which include "Why I Want a Dog" and "The UFO" — usually offer a picture and a story opening. For example, "The UFO" opens with a scene in which a boy points to an object in the sky and says, "It sure looked like a space-ship ..." From there, it's up to your child to kick her imagination into high gear and make up the rest of the story. The program also includes a spelling checker and a thesaurus.

GET SMART: *Tell your kids to write the way they talk. Their characters will sound more believable.*

Kids can illustrate stories with backgrounds and can choose from a collection of 1,600 stamps (small, predesigned pieces of art that kids can *stamp* on the page with a click of the mouse). The clip art, which can be resized, flipped, and recolored, is sorted into such categories as vehicles, animals, and storybook people. The program includes background music (such as jungle music and fairground music) and sound effects (such as a barking dog or a bomb exploding) that kids can add to the pages of their books.

KidWorks Deluxe

Suited for even younger children than Storybook Weaver (ages four to nine), KidWorks Deluxe includes writing and drawing tools, as well as a slew of story starters such as "Strange Flying Things" and "A Moving Portrait." The included clip art isn't up to the standards of Storybook Weaver, but with more than 450 stickers, 130 backgrounds, and 100 sound effects, kids can easily produce multimedia-style stories by using this program. KidWorks can also read the story aloud (Storybook Weaver Deluxe does that, too), and if you have an Internet connection (not one through an online service such as America Online, unfortunately), kids can publish their stories there and retrieve other kids' tales.

To find additional program choices for the writers in your family, head to Chapter 14, "Homework Software."

Artwork and text are well-integrated in KidWorks Deluxe. For example, click on the artwork, and the bottom of the screen changes to show only the drawing tools.

★ TRY THIS! ★

Create Electronic Heirlooms

The first stories your children hear are probably tales straight out of the family tree. Remember the time Great-Granddad managed to collide with another car while driving in the Dakotas (where you can see forever and there are more cows than people), or the way Grandma made extra spending money by selling the eggs she collected from hiding places all around the farm?

You can continue that story-telling tradition and spark your young child's interest at the same time by encouraging him to tell you a true or fanciful story that the two of you can then write and illustrate on the family computer. When you're finished, you have a special story you can read to your child — and the whole family. Of course, children in elementary school often spend time studying family trees — perhaps as a personalized introduction to history — so this activity has some serious homework potential, too.

You can use basic desktop publishing or word-processing software for the job, but programs such as Storybook Weaver Deluxe and KidWorks Deluxe make even better tools for writing, illustrat-

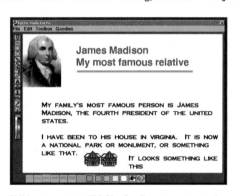

**James Madison
My most famous relative**

MY FAMILY'S MOST FAMOUS PERSON IS JAMES MADISON, THE FOURTH PRESIDENT OF THE UNITED STATES.

I HAVE BEEN TO HIS HOUSE IN VIRGINIA. IT IS NOW A NATIONAL PARK OR MONUMENT, OR SOMETHING LIKE THAT. IT LOOKS SOMETHING LIKE THIS

Children can use Kid Pix Studio to compose picture-filled family histories. If you have a scanner, they can digitize their favorite family photos to add to the stories.

ing, and publishing family stories.

Ask your storyteller to tell you a story out loud. Discuss how much more fun the story would be if you were to write it down, illustrate it, and have it available to read at any time. Spend some time with your child and look at a few favorite children's books to get a sense of how words and pictures interact to tell a story.

Design a cover for your book, including a title, an accompanying illustration, and the author's name. When you design the interior pages, consider the reading level of your audience: Use an illustration and two or three sentences (in large type) per page for prereaders, and more text for older siblings (early readers). When you design pages, keep in mind that less is more — a simple design is easier to create, and it's easier for your child to read.

When you've written the story, designed the pages of your book, and saved the document, print it. To make it even more like a real book, glue the covers to heavy tagboard or cardboard. Add any coloring or painting to your various illustrations and then bind the covers to the pages — use a three-hole punch and then tie the pages together with lengths of yarn. The final product is a custom-written family storybook that makes a great bedtime story and a wonderful family keepsake.

More Writing Projects

Every Kid's a Critic

Ages 8 and Up

Kids have few qualms about stating their likes and dislikes, from movies to software to books, or even what's for dinner. You can introduce your children to critical writing (teachers often assign such essays as homework, even in the early elementary grades) by urging them to write reviews of movies, TV shows, or software products.

With a computer and a flexible program such as Microsoft Works, ClarisWorks, or their own kid-special word processor (perhaps one of the programs touted in this chapter), your children can manipulate fonts and layout to create reviews with headlines, bylines, and graphics. In the end, your kids will produce polished, one-page critiques they can share with family and friends and exchange with fellow reviewers.

To help your child get started, look at a few movie reviews together in your local newspaper. Make a list of the kinds of things reviewers discuss — story line, characters, action, special effects, audience reaction, and so on. (Your child can create this list in a word processor, save the file, and then call it up each time he writes a review.) Next, look at how the reviewers present their opinions. They don't merely say, "The film is great." They go on to say *why* they think the film is great. Of course, the *whys* your child comes up with will differ from those of professional reviewers (maybe your child finds a movie great because he thinks the heroine is cool). Again, it's *his* project — let him explore his own voice and his own tastes.

If your child wants to review soft-

What Every Story Needs

Rookie writers sometimes need a bit of a push. How about jotting down this list of story must-haves on a Post-it note, so kids can keep it by the monitor while they write?

Almost every story includes these things:

✓ **Characters:**

The people, animals, or things in the story.

✓ **Setting:**

Where the story happens.

✓ **Opening:**

The event that starts the story

✓ **Antagonist or troublemaker:**

A character who doesn't always agree with the main character.

✓ **Problem:**

Writers call this *conflict*.

✓ **Solution:**

Most stories eventually solve the problem (but that doesn't mean all stories must end happily).

ware or games, convince him to focus on the things he thinks kids his age like — the quality of the graphics or the intricacy of the plot, for example.

Next, use the computer to create a format for the review. Give the layout a fun name (for example, "Cris's Cool Critiques") and put it at the top of the page, like the masthead of a newspaper. Below that, leave room for a headline, a byline, and the body of the review (this looks very professional in a two-column layout, which you can create in an integrated program or the Student Writing and Research Center). You might also want to leave room for a box of key information, such as the movie title and a rating expressed graphically — for example, five smiley faces, toucans, or stars (flip through the stamps available in your program and look for your favorites).

For the first review, choose a movie or a software program your child has seen or

Go Online!

From storytelling tips to places where kids can publish their writing for millions to read, the online world offers lots of creative writing resources. Here are two of the best.

The Story Resources on the Web has dozens of links to other storytelling-related Web pages, including those spotlighting children's stories, stories *by* children, tales from various cultures (such as Native American, Russian, and Scottish), interactive stories on the Internet (cool!), familiar folk tales, and much more. Here's the address you need in order to take advantage of this great resource:

http://www.swarthmore.edu:80/~sjohnson/stories/

If you subscribe to America Online, send your budding writers to Blackberry Creek (keyword **Blackberry**), where they can submit their own stories (directions for doing so are available online, but you may want to help them out by sending the story for them, at least the first time) and can also read dozens of stories that other kids have posted.

AOL's Blackberry Creek is a super online destination for kids, especially those interested in sharing their writing (or artwork) with other children.

uses over and over again. It should be one you've heard him talk about often, because you may need to prompt him quite a bit at first.

When you're both ready, write a headline under the masthead that sums up his feelings about the movie ("*Toy Story* more fun than a trip to Toys R Us"). Next, put a byline on the piece. He can use his name, a nickname, or an entirely made-up name. The body of the review should include his general impressions of the film or software, what it was about, its good points, its bad points, and whether he recommends it as a film other kids should see (or a game or program other kids should buy).

When the review is complete, he can print one copy to keep in a three-ring binder (with an appropriate label affixed to the front) near the VCR or the computer, and others to send off to his friends, who just might be inspired to get a little critical about things themselves.

Get Personal about Writing
Ages 6 and Up

Writing in a journal is among the most satisfying (and habit-forming) types of writing you can encourage in your older elementary-school–aged children. And on a computer, it's easy to do.

Any basic word-processing program lets your child copy files, scrapbook-style, into a journal — including stories, poems, dreams, letters, and school projects. Your child can create a folder on the computer, in which she can record bits of her journal for you to read, as well as retrieve your responses. She can save her journal on floppy disks, to ensure that the journal remains her personal sanctuary, a place where she can write about her grandest dreams and greatest fears, her hatred of lima beans, and her love of race cars.

Reading back through her journal, she can look at problems she has solved and great days she has enjoyed, a process that confirms the importance of everyday events.

A journal can begin with anything that interests your child: animals, sports, music … even computers. Encourage your child to write every day or at least once a week (when she's hooked, she'll probably increase the frequency herself). In either case, it's important to reserve a time for journal writing and make it a family ritual much like story-reading time.

At first, your child's entries might read, "Scored a goal in soccer today," or, "My rabbit's nose looks funny when he chews." Encourage her to try other kinds of writing: What if she were the only kid playing on the U.S. World Cup soccer team? What if her rabbit suddenly grew to 100 feet tall?

If she writes letters on the computer, encourage her to save parts of her favorites in the journal. Or trade dreams with her each morning and suggest that she record her dreams in the journal. She can use clip art or a computer drawing program to illustrate her thoughts, creating a pictorial diary that shows what she thinks and feels.

A benefit of using a computer for the journal is that your child can share with you only those parts that she wishes to share, while keeping the rest private. To share her thoughts, she can simply create a file (for example, "Journal stuff for Dad") in which she copies only those sections of her journal she wants to share. She might want you to simply read what she has written, or she might want you to comment on it. Talk beforehand to determine how much interaction she wants.

A journal correspondence is a great activity for both you and your child, but don't try to rush it. She might want you to read everything she writes, or none of it. Ultimately, a journal is a personal record, and most journal writers opt to keep at least some of what they write locked away, for their eyes only.

Chapter 4

Numbers
Are Cool
Math

1 + 1 = 2. 2 + 2 = 4. AND MATH + SCHOOL = homework.

Kids have homework in math more often than in any other subject. Once they hit the middle stretches of elementary school, the math work starts coming home almost daily. You're sure to hear about it, too. Although your children may be silent partners in class, they will demand your help with their math homework.

You can do your part, but so can the family's computer. It may be best equipped to serve up computational drills that help your kids sharpen math skills, but with the right software, it can also mutate into an excellent tutor of everything from elementary math concepts to sophisticated numerical modeling.

In the four sections of this chapter,

we cover software for elementary- and middle-school-aged children, show you why a spreadsheet is an essential mathematics tool for older children, and aim our Web browser at some useful online math resources.

Math and the family computer... now *that* computes.

Math Gets Going

Imagine teaching your preschooler or early-elementary-school-aged child the value of numbers by building an electronic bug on your family computer. Your child chooses a buggy body part and a number from 1 to 10, and the computer says aloud the number and the body part, and then pastes the correct number of eyes, legs, spots, ears, or feet on a blank bug's body. Or, how about an entertaining introduction to spatial relationships and scale recognition with a cartoon character named James? Or a complete math curriculum for grades 2 and 3 that covers everything from calculation to geometry?

Today's best math software teaches the fundamentals of mathematical ability: number sense, patterns and relationships, geometry, and problem solving. In the process, it turns your family PC into a patient, energetic, creative, and flexible teacher your child can turn to whenever the math bug bites.

Kids in this age range — that is, preschoolers through third-graders — rarely have math homework, and when they do, it typically comes in the form of worksheets they complete after school. Even though the teacher doesn't always assign homework, you can still beef up your kids' math skills with some after-hours homework of your own design.

In the following sections, we outline the fundamental mathematical principles you should stress, and we make software recommendations to point you toward some of the top math programs on the market. We also include several away-from-the-computer games you can create on your family PC to further animate and illustrate the lessons of early math.

Ready to get cracking on math?

Four Fundamentals of Early Math

In school, math class often gives kids the impression that solving math problems leads only to harder problems (with more com-

plex solutions). You can give your kids a different impression — that math can be fun — with the family computer. By providing your kids with the best early-math software, as well as neat math games you create with your PC and a simple draw and paint program (see the sidebar "The Tangram Game," in a later section), you can emphasize real-world applications of math skills and encourage children to connect math basics with real-life objects and situations.

Number Sense

You should encourage your children to join, separate, and compare objects in sets long before they understand (or need) the abstract concepts for doing this numerically. *Counting* is not the same as *number sense* — many children can count correctly before they understand the meaning of the numerals 1 to 10.

You don't even need any special software to create an enticing math environment for your children. You can create a fun number-sense game by using stamps from a simple drawing program such as Kid Pix. The stamps should fit into classes of objects — such as vehicles of various types, or zoo, wild, and domestic animals. Make your stamps as large as your program allows, and print them on heavy stock paper. Color them (if you don't have a color printer), sandwich them in contact paper, and then cut them out.

Using small bowls, boxes, a doll's house, or egg cartons, make up stories that require your child to classify and combine the objects. For example, suggest that your child

Slap down a category of Kid Pix stamps for a simple classification and sorting game with preschoolers.

put into the doll house all the animals that usually live with people and put the other animals in a shoe box (the zoo). Or have him make suggestions for sets — all the pink ones, the ones that go fast, or the ones that he likes best.

After your child classifies the objects, ask him questions about the quantities in each set and use them as a basis for comparison. (Which place has more animals when we classify them this way: the house or the zoo?)

Patterns and Relationships

Mathematics is the study of patterns and the rules that explain regularities in the physical world. Patterns can be simple (such as day and night) or more complex (such as the pentatonic musical scale). By helping your child recognize patterns and relationships, you give her a head start on problem-solving tasks, logical sequencing, and understanding number patterns such as base 10 and place value.

You can use the sorting sets from the preceding section to play simple pattern-matching games. Lay out a simple alternating pattern — for example, car, truck, car, truck; or pet, zoo animal, pet, zoo animal — and let your child complete it by choosing what comes next.

Geometry and Spatial Reasoning

Geometry is all about the properties and the relationships of flat and three-dimensional shapes. Your child needs geometry to plot out a baseball field in the backyard, build a log bridge, or paint a portrait with natural-looking proportions.

In a drawing program, create an equilateral triangle (all sides of equal length) and copy it several times. Create other shapes, such as hexagons, rhombuses (diamonds), and trapezoids. Do the same with squares and rectangles, matching all sides of the square and two sides of the rectangle to the length of the sides of your original triangle. Print on heavy paper, sandwich this in contact paper, and cut out the shapes to create

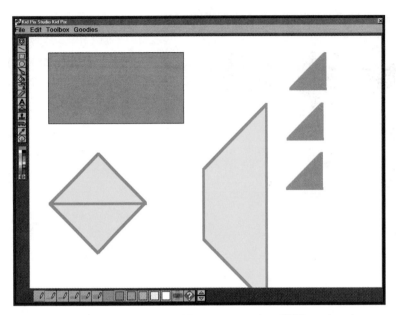

Spend a few minutes drawing shapes with a program such as Kid Pix, and you have an inexpensive set of geometric building blocks.

(quite literally) the building blocks for this geometry game.

Now use these shapes to build symmetrical shapes, combine the smaller shapes to build larger ones, or fill a long rectangular shape with as many (or as few) smaller shapes as you can. Discuss with your child what happens when you combine the shapes (show her how a rectangle or a square is made up of two triangles) and compare the components of each shape (length, width, angles) and how they make the shape unique.

Problem Solving

Logical thinking is essential to problem solving. It involves remembering sequences, generating alternative solutions, and predicting outcomes. One way to introduce

preschoolers to problem solving is with tangram puzzles. These puzzles differ from simple geometry and spatial-reasoning games because they ask the child to put shapes together in many imaginative ways, all of which are correct. (Because tangram puzzles require patience and planning, they're best suited for children older than three years.)

Use your draw and paint program to divide a large square, as shown in the sidebar, "The Tangram Game." Save the drawing as a template and print several copies on heavy paper. Sandwich each sheet of shapes in contact paper and then cut out the shapes.

The rules of the tangram game are simple: use all pieces to make each figure, and all pieces must lie flat. Now set the goals for the game — make a pattern that your child needs to copy, or name a figure such as a horse, a person, or a bird and have your child use the shapes to build it. Better still, challenge your child (and yourself) to reconstruct the original square.

Math Software Gets an *A*

Walk into a software store in search of an early-math program, and you're bombarded with choices. All profess to match the type of math learning that takes place in school. For preschoolers and first-graders, that means clearing the way for math by mastering counting, shape recognition, and sorting. For kids in grades 2 and 3, it means diving into the mechanics of arithmetic (addition, subtraction, and in many classes, multiplication as well). But of all the programs on the store shelves, which ones *really* do the math?

The Tangram Game

An ancient Chinese puzzle could be the solution to your child's math problems. Creating the pieces to play the tangram puzzle game is itself an exercise in problem solving, geometry, and shapes.

Follow these directions to create your own tantalizing tangram using Kid Pix Studio or another paint or draw program:

1. Choose the rectangle tool and make a square by holding down the Shift key as you drag the mouse. Make your square as large as you can.

2. Use the straight-line tool to draw a diagonal line from one corner to the other. Then repeat, dividing your square with a large X.

3. Use the Eraser to remove the upper-right portion of the X.

4. Use the straight-line tool to draw a line from the middle of the X, straight to the top of the square.

5. At the point where that line meets the outside edge of the

The tangram puzzle should look like this on your computer's screen.

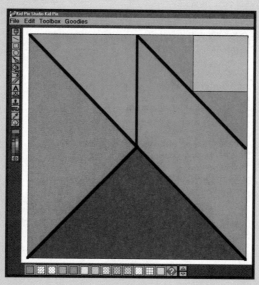

square, draw another line at a 45-degree angle to the middle of the right side of the square. (This forms a triangle in the upper-right corner.)

6. Choose the rectangle tool and, starting in the upper-right corner, draw a square extending out from the corner to the edge of the small triangle. (This forms two more triangles.) If your finished drawing looks like the figure shown here, you're ready to print, color, and cut out your puzzle pieces. To make this game more interesting, you and your child can time each other while building and naming different figures, or see who can construct the most figures in a given period of time.

We think these five programs are tops in the topic.

Millie's Math House
Ages 2–5

With a parent's notebook (to track your child's progress in six different math activities) and parental help screens that explain the mathematical principles underlying each game, Millie's Math House is well worth a visit. Millie, your host, is a creative cow with lots of friends intent on teaching your child about numbers, patterns, geometry, and introductory problem solving. You meet a cool caterpillar in Build-A-Bug, Millie's horse friend Harley in Cookie Factory, and a family of friendly mice in Mouse House. Always, there are the voices of children.

Unlike other early-math programs, Millie's Math House doesn't have multiple levels of difficulty. Instead, parents (or children) can set two modes of operation: an unguided Explore and Discover mode, or an interactive Question and Answer mode. The Explore and Discover mode lets your child explore the games on her own; Question and Answer mode is directed by various hosts, such as Frank Lloyd Mouse in the Mouse House game.

Math Rabbit
Ages 3–6

Math Rabbit, which rated tops when *FamilyPC* first FamilyTested early-math programs, uses a trip to the circus in order to teach kids skills in counting, number recognition, and basic addition and subtraction.

Each activity in Math Rabbit has three levels of difficulty, so kids can challenge themselves by using either bigger numbers or more complex equations. In the Balloon Matching Game, the Tightrope Show, and the Sea Lion Show, you can even change the mix of math problems, choosing just addition, subtraction, or multiplication, or a mixed bag. Math Rabbit also has an activity that teaches spatial concepts, but this program is most useful for stressing numerical skills.

Kids practice basic addition and subtraction in Math Rabbit's Sea Lion Show.

Children ages three to five will enjoy numerous fun math learning activities and a storybook in James's kitchen.

James Discovers Math
Ages 3–6

Another highly rated math program for young children (it scored an almost-unheard-of 91 out of 100 in *FamilyPC*'s most recent FamilyTested exam), James Discovers Math offers 10 skill-building activities. Filled with animated sing-alongs, activities, puzzles, and a fun story about James himself, this CD-ROM includes games such as Fruit Shop, in which kids fill orders with the right combination of objects; Blockes, an addition and subtraction game; and Face, in which kids put features on a blank face as they learn about spatial relationships.

JumpStart First Grade
Ages 5–7

JumpStart First Grade isn't strictly a math tutor, but it includes plenty of practical math instruction. And the program is hard to ignore: *Fami-lyPC*'s testers gave it (and its siblings, JumpStart Kindergarten and JumpStart Preschool) the coveted *FamilyPC* Recommended software seal of approval.

Designed with the help of educators, JumpStart First Grade gives kids ages five to seven a head start on their elementary-school education by providing a complete digital curriculum that covers math, reading, geography, science, and music. More than 90 skills are taught through 18 learning modules, and the program automatically adjusts the level of difficulty as your child learns more.

On the math front, JumpStart introduces kids to math, fractions, and measurement skills with games that involve Ms. Pickles, the lunch lady. In one game, your child must fill lunch orders by placing food on trays divided into fractions. Other games teach kids how to count money, tell time, and perform complex logic tasks.

JumpStart First Grade is a complete digital curriculum, and it includes plenty of practical math problems and tutorials.

Adi's Comprehensive Learning System 2nd & 3rd Mathematics

Ages 7–9

Adi the extraterrestrial is one of the most effective math tutors we've seen. Parents agree; they awarded the program the vaunted *FamilyPC* Recommended seal in a recent roundup of math titles aimed at elementary-school-aged children. Adi's understanding of the subject is impressive, and so is his ability to communicate this knowledge to kids.

Packed on two CDs, this thorough exploration of math topics typically studied in second and third grades covers everything from numbers and calculation to measurement and geometry. For example, the second-grade numbers section lets kids choose questions about Writing Numbers, Counting, or Place Values. Each category contains several levels of instruction. Adi is a particularly good choice as a bridge between the glut of math programs for preschoolers and kindergartners and those that address a broader range of skill levels and ages — such as Math Workshop, which we describe in the next section.

Looking for other outstanding math programs? Check out Chapter 14, "Homework Software," for more suggestions.

Growing Up with Math

Children in elementary and middle school usually tackle math on a daily basis. That means they have math homework almost every day.

For the most part, math homework orig-inates from a textbook and consists of a specific set of problems your child must solve. So what can the family computer do to help kids in this age group with their math homework?

Plenty. You can steer kids toward specialized math software — and you have lots of choices — for additional practice and drills involving the mechanics of math. You can aim them to online math aids, which range from conversion tables and calculators to math experts who answer the questions you can't. And you can point them toward a draw program when the teacher asks them to produce graphs or design geometric shapes.

First, we recommend a pair of math programs we believe should be in the software library of almost every family with school-aged children.

Math Workshop

Ages 6–12

Math Workshop, a colorful, animated program, lets kids ages six to 12 hammer away at a range of math problems that require reasoning, computational, and problem-solving skills. *FamilyPC*'s testers — parents and kids alike — gave Math Workshop a big thumbs-up and a *FamilyPC* Recommended seal of approval. In fact, Math Workshop was one of five math programs — and the only one for this age group — to receive the magazine's *FamilyPC* FamilyTested Award in 1995.

Math Workshop features seven activities, but its purest math challenge is Bowling for Numbers, which lets kids test their skills in addition, subtraction, multiplication, division, equivalencies, and estimation. With equivalencies, for example, the program displays a grid, and your child has to figure out how many squares are displayed and select that answer from the four choices offered (all questions in Bowling for Numbers are multiple choice).

The disc also includes a Parent's Video Guide, which discusses current teaching strategies and how parents can get involved teaching their kids math. The Parent's Video Guide includes a list of math-based activities that families can do together.

Math Workshop doesn't finish your kids' homework, but its entertaining approach will keep them interested long enough to sharpen their skills. We highly recommend this program for elementary-school-aged kids in grades 3 through 5.

Alge-Blaster 3
Ages 12 and Up

When kids hit middle school, math starts getting *really* interesting. By this time, they should have the basics under their belts.

And in middle school, kids usually encounter algebra for the first time. Remem-

The Rhythm Shop, one of Math Workshop's activities, teaches the concept of fractions by using music.

Electronic Graph Paper

Kids draw countless graphs in algebra class. Although inexpensive graph paper, a pencil, and an eraser work fine for this task, the family computer can make the chore even easier.

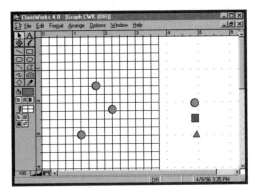

How? By letting kids easily make changes. When they use graph paper and a pencil, correcting graphing mistakes takes time. On the computer, kids can create and modify a graph faster than they can on paper.

To make graphing even easier, create stock objects — such as the three colored shapes on the right — and then copy and paste them onto the grid.

GET SMART: Advanced-level math classes may require some writing — to document a proof, for example. Unfortunately, the word processors found in integrated programs aren't cut out for mathematical tasks. Instead, turn to a program such as Microsoft Word. Using Word's Equation Editor, your kids can easily create and print even the most complicated mathematical expressions.

To make some electronic graph paper, you need a *draw program*. A paint program won't do, because you want each graph element to be a discrete object that you can move or delete with a click of the mouse. (In a paint program, a circle is actually dozens or hundreds of small dots; in a draw program,

that same-sized circle is a single object that you can easily manipulate.) We use the Draw module in ClarisWorks, and we recommend it for jobs like this. Create a new Draw document and make sure that the rulers are visible (select Rulers from the Format menu). These rulers serve as guides while you make the graph paper.

To create the graph, draw horizontal and vertical lines. Spacing is up to you, but we recommend 1/2-inch between adjacent lines. To speed up the process, you can make a small patch of the grid by creating several lines, group those lines together (hold down the Shift key while you click on each line and then choose Group from the Arrange menu), and then copy and paste additional patches to complete the grid. Save this file to disk, using a name such as *Graph*. This is your blank graph paper.

Each time your child needs to draw a graph for a homework assignment, she loads this document, then immediately saves it under a new name by using the Save As command in the File menu. Now she can create small circles to mark numbers on the graph, place text to label the graph (including the axes), and after erasing some of the grid, even enter the equations represented on the graph.

ber algebra? Remember integers, factoring, polynomials, solving quadratic equations, or making graphs? No? Then you're not going to be much help when your kids start asking questions, are you?

GET SMART: *Because Alge-Blaster 3 covers the subject so thoroughly, we don't hesitate to recommend this program to families who home-school their children.*

One way you can compensate for your memory loss is by giving your kids a copy of Alge-Blaster 3, our favorite math program for middle-school-aged kids. This program is sometimes a bit too cute for our tastes, but it's the best at-home algebra support tool we've found.

Alge-Blaster 3 includes a school-year's worth of algebra content, wraps much of it in entertaining activities and games, and most importantly, clearly explains how to solve algebraic problems in both equation and word formats. The Video Chalkboard visually demonstrates how to solve each type of algebra problem, the program presents sample problems, and then kids can turn to the 20-some practice problems. It's a very effective way to teach the topic.

Other areas of Alge-Blaster 3 are more

Go Online!

The online world isn't as flush with math resources as it is for other school subjects such as history or science, but you can go modeming to some useful places when math is on your mind.

We highlight some of the best math resources here. To find others, use one of the Internet's search tools (you can get started by entering the keyword *math* in Yahoo! or Yahooligans!) or look through your online service's educational areas.

Steve's Dump: Math Sites on the Internet
http://forum.swarthmore.edu/~steve/steve/mathlevels.html
If you bookmark any page on the Web for math help, bookmark Steve's Dump: Math Sites on the Internet. This site is the best place to go —

and one of the first Web resources you should visit — when you want help with math. Steve's Dump (don't let the name fool you; this is a well-organized site and *far* from dirty) categorizes math links by school level (elementary, middle, secondary, and college).

Ask Dr. Math
http://forum.swarthmore.edu/dr.math/
You have a math question, but no teachers are in sight. So you head to Ask Dr. Math, a Web site where you can e-mail math masters (actually, math students at Swarthmore College) any question you want. Before you ask your question, though, search Ask Dr. Math's archives, which list questions others have asked (and the

Continued on page 68

answers), organizing them into categories for elementary-school, middle-school, high-school, and college students. Want to know why we need decimals? To find the answer, just ask Dr. Math.

21st Century Problem Solving

http://www2.hawaii.edu/suremath/home.shtml

"The sum of the ages of David, Tom, and Jim is 34. David is three years older than Jim, and Tom is five years younger than Jim. Find the age of David." Does that sound familiar?

For many children, solving word problems is one of the most difficult jobs in math class. (Coming up with an algebraic expression to define the problem is tough for many adults, too.) This site, sponsored by a University of

Hawaii math professor, offers dozens of example word problems in algebra, chemistry, and physics; shows how to solve those problems (and word problems in general); and provides an encyclopedia of solved word problems for additional study.

Although many of the problems offered at the 21st Century Problem Solving site are best suited for high-school students, some are appropriate for middle-school-aged children exploring word problems.

Helping Your Child Learn Math

gopher://gopher.ed.gov/00/publications/full_text/
parents/math.dos

Parents looking for some math guidance should turn to Helping Your Child Learn Math, an all-text document from the U.S. Department of Education. Filled with tips you can pass along to your kids to bolster their math confidence, it also includes lots of good at-home activities for exploring math.

Word problems get a workout on the 21st Century Problem Solving Web site.

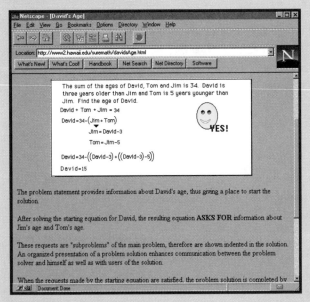

Online Calculator

http://www.math.scarolina.edu/
cgi-bin/sumcgi/calculator.pl

If you don't have a top-notch calculator in the house, you can always turn to the Online Calculator. Just enter an expression (this page also lists the keyboard characters for such things as cosines and square roots) and the answer appears in the box at the bottom of the screen. What's 25^3? Easy! 15,625.

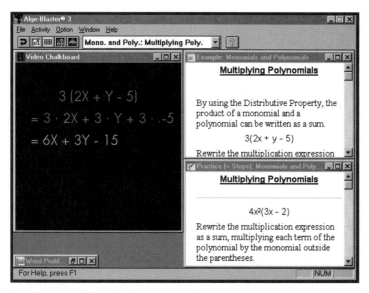

Alge-Blaster 3's Video Chalkboard tutors kids in the intricacies of polynomials and other algebraic concepts.

gamelike. For example, Decoder lets kids translate words into algebraic expressions, and Simulator familiarizes children with slopes and points in an alien shoot-'em-up game.

Chapter 14, "Homework Software," lists other top-ranked math programs that you might want to consider.

Money *Is* Math

Math isn't just about adding and subtracting. In the real world, most math happens in business — counting money, tracking income, watching expenses, and so on.

Kids like to be entrepreneurs. Teachers often use that desire — and in the meantime get children to apply math skills — by creating miniature businesses in the classroom, by following the stock market with a pretend portfolio, or even by creating products and marketing them to the outside world.

When armed with a simulation or two, your home computer can help kids use their business sense without risking a dime of the family's (or the school's) fortune. In just a few hours, a computerized simulation can provide young venture capitalists with a year's worth of business experience, quickly showing them a bit about how the real world *really* works. At the same time, such programs can slip some practical math under kids' learning-is-boring radar.

In the following sections, we recommend a trio of business-oriented simulation programs, outline some great ideas your kids can use to create several out-of-the-ordinary homework projects, and point you toward an excellent online resource in the kids-doing-business vein.

Captains of industry? *Your* kids? You better believe it!

Biz Sims for the Beginning Tycoon

To provide your kids with some computerized business — and thus, practical math — experience, you should look into three simulation programs (okay, one really isn't a biz sim *per se*, but it's such an all-around outstanding simulation that we *had* to squeeze it into *The FamilyPC Guide to Homework*).

★ TRY THIS! ★

Keep a Business Journal

One way your child can use these business simulations as the foundation for a homework project is by keeping a journal. While playing the simulation, your child can take notes using a word processor. He should record the major decisions he makes to start the business and keep it operating.

Have your child refer to the following checklist as he takes these notes and crafts his report:

- The decision
- My choices
- What I did
- Why I did that

Take screen shots of the simulation — perhaps at some of the most important decisions — to help your child illustrate the decision-making process. By adding these screen shots (and appropriate captions) to the word-processor document, your child can create a visual as well as a textual record of events.

___

GET SMART: To take a screen shot in Windows or Windows 95, press the Alt key and the Print Screen key at the same time (to capture the currently active window) or just the Print Screen key (to capture the entire screen). On a Macintosh, you take a screen shot by pressing the Command, Shift, and 3 keys simultaneously. (This captures the entire screen.)

DinoPark Tycoon
Ages 8 and Up

Your kids have watched *Jurassic Park* a zillion times, so getting them interested in running their own dinosaur theme park shouldn't be a problem. DinoPark Tycoon, a simulation perfect for capitalists ages eight and up, offers an excellent introduction to the world of business.

In DinoPark, kids start with a grub stake of $5,000, which they use to buy real estate, build fences, add dinosaurs, hire workers, and stock up on food. Then they wait for the crowds to come. The challenge lies in keeping the park running — and expanding it. More than anything, little CEOs learn that they have to manage money. They can adjust ticket prices, but they quickly find that higher prices mean fewer visitors. Another eye-opener is labor costs, which can quickly spiral out of control if kids go into a hiring frenzy without the income to support those salaries (if employees aren't paid on time, they quit). Good theme park operators keep an eye on the books, reviewing the income and the profit their park generates.

___

GET SMART: *Be patient; you don't need to spend money all the time. Sometimes it's best to sit back and just watch the crowds come and your income grow.*

Gazillionaire
Ages 10 and Up

Nothing beats Gazillionaire for teaching budding business types ages 10 and up a lesson in the oldest capitalist trick in the book: supply and demand. Kids race from planet

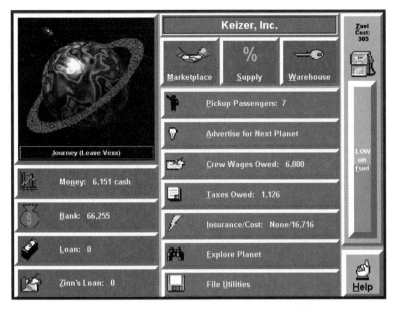

Gazillionaire's main screen is your space shipping-control panel. Click on one of these buttons, and you're faced with more business decisions.

— such as taxes, crew salaries, insurance, and loans — make the task tougher.

Gazillionaire brings the theory of supply and demand to life. Your pint-sized profiteers must learn to buy goods at a low price (on planets where those goods are in plentiful supply) and then sell them elsewhere at a high price (on worlds where the goods are in great demand). Spotting a good deal is crucial to success. Kids must manage other business practices, such as paying back loans quickly (interest, calculated weekly, can be a killer), upgrading equipment (the spaceship), advertising (to attract more business), and monopolizing a planet's docking facilities.

to planet, building their space-based shipping company to the magic one-million kubar mark, buying and selling, and wheeling and dealing like space-happy Wall Street brokers.

GET SMART: *Try to put some money in the bank — where it draws interest — so you have a down payment ready when you're offered a new, and bigger, spaceship.*

Kids start with a spaceship, a debt of 100,000 kubars, and seven planets on which they can conduct trade. As many as six kids can play, and six computer-run competitors are ready to run the human traders out of business. Everyone hops from planet to planet, buying goods here and selling them there (for a profit, they hope). Other details

SimCity 2000 Special Edition
Ages 10 and Up

A city *is* a business of sorts. It must make ends meet, keep its customers happy, and grow without going bust. SimCity 2000 Special Edition, the premiere city-building simulation, can be used to explore how business works. We include SimCity 2000 in our simulation roundup because, frankly, it's one of the most popular games around. You may already have a copy in the house.

Pint-sized public servants begin with a

clean slate, laying out a city with residential and commercial (business) zones, putting in streets and power lines, and placing services such as police and fire stations in strategic locations. Kids don't plant individual buildings; the city grows those on its own. However, children must mess with money in the form of taxes, which they levy on the SimCitizens.

GET SMART: *First-time mayors should select the Easy level; it gives them more money to begin their town.*

Although your kids will think they're playing mayor, they're actually racking up some virtual corporate experience when they play SimCity. When they start planning how to spend the city's money — for example, how much they should allocate to transportation, safety (police, fire), various ordinances (such as city beautification or an antidrug campaign in the schools), and health and welfare — they're doing the same thing business people do when budgeting their company's resources.

SimCity also emphasizes another important element of business: managing the unexpected. Fires break out, natural disasters make the earth quake or tornadoes whirl, even monsters make an appearance. Just as important, though, are the interconnected aspects of SimCity: high taxes may make businesses move out of town (just as high prices can keep away customers), and a lack of transportation angers the citizens (just as poor service sours customers).

Go Online!

If you don't want to clutter your computer with CD-ROM business simulations, send your children to America Online's KidzBiz (keyword Kidzbiz), one of the best places we've found for kids interested in learning more about business and money. From the main menu of Kidz-Biz, children can head to Get Bizzy, an area dedicated to young entrepreneurs.

If the profit motive intrigues your kids, point them to America Online's KidzBiz area.

They can find tips about starting a real business, chat with other money-making kids, and dig up information about future careers. Check out KidzBiz even if your child isn't interested in business; its other sections cover everything from inventions and money-saving tips to a stock market game for the classroom.

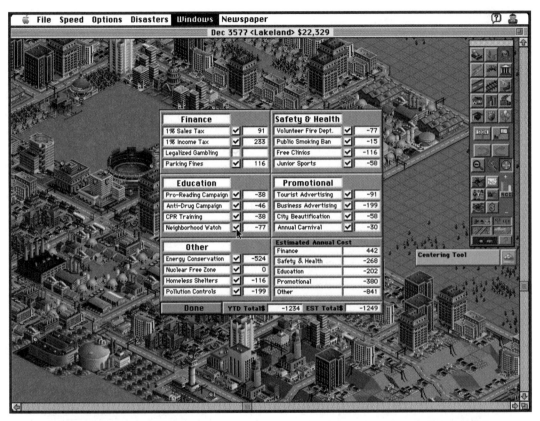

You use various charts, tables, and graphs to manage finances and other businesslike aspects of SimCity 2000.

Be a Business Consultant

Everyone likes to give advice. Why not use these business simulations to turn your child into a make-a-business advisor?

After playing one of these simulations, your child can craft a report that outlines some of the things she learned about business. The report can take various forms, but here are three suggestions to get her started:

• **Top 10 List.** What are the top 10 things you learned about how to start and grow a business?

• **Time Line.** Using a paint or draw program, create a time line that highlights the crucial steps for running a business. (For details about how to design a time line, check out " Time Line Tango," in the "Ancient History" section of Chapter 6.)

• **Math Makes It.** For a math-related report, your child can outline the math concepts she applied while playing these simulations. In Gazillionaire, for example, she used multiplication to calculate the total cost of goods she purchased (price x number of items = total cost).

Tipping Is Allowed

Simulations invite experimentation. That's their charm: you can do anything without risking life, limb, or lots of real money.

Still, it's a good idea to have some tips handy when your kids plunge into a digital business. Not only does this get you involved in the activity — think of yourself as a silent partner or an out-of-sight financial advisor — but it may mean the difference between an easy entry into the simulation and a quick exit from the program.

Some Sim Tips

• Start younger children or kids who haven't spent much time playing computer simulations on the easiest level; give them a reasonable chance of success.

• In simulations, you always have a second chance. To prevent total disaster — and to keep kids at the computer — remind kids to save the game often. When the worst happens, they can load the game from its last position and try a different approach.

• Encourage your kids to be creative. They shouldn't be afraid to experiment, even go crazy. That's what simulations are for.

• Emphasize the fun — the gamelike parts of these programs — when pitching them to your kids. If you describe these programs as games, kids are more likely to stick with them.

Some Biz Tips

• If you know a lot about business, don't overwhelm your kids with exotic details. When giving advice, stick to the most elementary business principles.

• *Profit* is the difference between income and expenses. In business, the idea is for income to be larger than expenses. In the real world, a profit of 10 percent ($110 in income for every $100 in expenses) is usually considered

excellent. In these simulations, the profit margin may be much higher, letting players work with more.

• Real businesses track the bottom line with accounting software or spreadsheets. These simulations usually offer some sort of report that lists expenses and income. Encourage your kids to check such reports frequently for updates on how they're doing.

• In simulations *and* in real business, *the customer is always right*. Make sure kids know that business success depends on meeting their customers' demands and desires.

• Some of these simulations let players borrow money from a *bank* to fund the business and its expansion. This is a great way to teach kids a bit about credit, loans, and interest. One tip that you might want to share with your kids is to pay back loans as quickly as possible to reduce interest payments.

Real-World Math

For most of us, math comes in two varieties: school math and real-world math.

School math is what we remember studying in class and what our kids are tackling today. Packed full of isosceles triangles, square roots, polynomial equations, and algebraic functions, school math sometimes seems far, far removed from real-world math. We use *real-world math* to balance checkbooks, calculate square footage for the new addition to the house, and compare prices in the store.

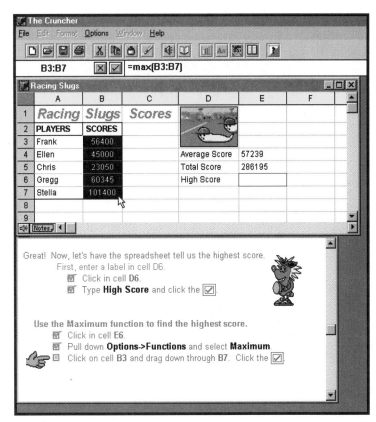

Cruncher's interactive tutorials make complicated spreadsheet concepts easy enough for anyone to understand.

One of today's most popular real-world math tools is the *spreadsheet*. More than just a digital calculator, a spreadsheet lets businesspeople model profit projections, calculate the break-even point of advertising, and generally keep track of the company's bottom line.

But a spreadsheet can also be used by kids for both homework assignments and fun with numbers. At the same time, they learn the basics of spreadsheet manipulation, an important skill many will use in college and later, when they land a job.

You probably don't even need to buy an-

other piece of software to let your kids work with spreadsheets. If you have an integrated program such as Microsoft Works or ClarisWorks, or an office suite of applications, you already have a spreadsheet in the house.

Spreadsheets Can Be Fun... Really!

Although spreadsheets are excellent real-world math tools, they rarely come ready for kids. One exception is Davidson's Cruncher, a fully functional spreadsheet that includes several kid-specific tutorial projects

The Cruncher - [Untitled - 3]

File Edit Format Options Window Help

N5 | Show | =(E5+G5+(2*H5)+(3*I5))/D5

BASEBALL STATISTICS

HITTING

Name	Pos.	G	AB	H	R	2B	3B	HR	BB	SO	Avg.	OBP	SLG
Casey A. Thebat	C	148	565	170	84	8	3	29	22	20	0.301	0.327	0.480
Gregg the Slugge	RF	142	587	240	102	10	5	32	15	19	0.409	0.424	0.606
											DIV/0	DIV/0	DIV/0
											DIV/0	DIV/0	DIV/0
											DIV/0	DIV/0	DIV/0
											DIV/0	DIV/0	DIV/0
											DIV/0	DIV/0	DIV/0
											DIV/0	DIV/0	DIV/0
											DIV/0	DIV/0	DIV/0
											DIV/0	DIV/0	DIV/0
											DIV/0	DIV/0	DIV/0
											DIV/0	DIV/0	DIV/0
Team Totals		1152	410	186	18	8	61	37		39	0.356	0.376	0.544

WOW!

PITCHING

Name	G	IP	BB	SO	H	R	ER	W	L	Pct.	ERA	SO/BB
Rand Arnold	35	260	100	300	320	162	100	20	12	0.625	3.462	3.000
Nolan Ryan	27	157	69	157	138	80	65	5	9	0.357	3.726	2.275
										DIV/0	DIV/0	DIV/0

Notes

Cruncher includes 20 ready-to-try spreadsheets fit for kids. This one calculates baseball statistics.

and a slew of predesigned spreadsheet templates aimed at kids' math interests and school needs.

GET SMART: *Cruncher's six interactive tutorials provide kids with an excellent introduction to spreadsheet terminology, concepts, and practices. In fact, these outstanding tutorials make the price of Cruncher worthwhile for parents who have trouble explaining how spreadsheets work.*

Like all spreadsheets, Davidson's Cruncher uses a column-and-row arrangement to hold numbers, lets you enter complicated mathematical functions by clicking on a menu item and dragging the mouse pointer through the cells in the spreadsheet (the term *cell* is spreadsheet lingo for the column-and-row location of an entry in a spreadsheet), and automatically changes the results of those mathematical functions when you enter new numbers.

Because Cruncher so closely resembles the spreadsheets found in integrated programs or office suite collections, your children can easily make a smooth transition from Cruncher to another spreadsheet — perhaps the one in the family's integrated package, so they can use its word-processor and charting capabilities to create polished reports and projects.

Cruncher's 20 spreadsheet templates (which it calls *projects*) also help introduce kids to spreadsheet mechanics and, more importantly, they introduce kids to some spreadsheet applications. Ranging from spreadsheets that calculate baseball statistics to worksheets that compare the price of popcorn, several of these templates can be used as the basis for unique math-related projects. And your kids can modify any of these templates so they exactly fit the requirements for a homework assignment.

However, budget-minded families can forgo Cruncher and send kids ages 10 and up directly to the family's spreadsheet (with some help from parents). We recommend

Making the Link Between Numbers and Words

To forge even stronger links between a spreadsheet and a word-processor-based report, you can connect the two files so that any changes you make in the spreadsheet are automatically reflected in the report.

Why bother? Because then you don't have to manually copy and paste numbers from the spreadsheet each time you make a change. In other words, you ensure that the numbers in the report — whether they're values from a science class experiment or population figures for a social studies report — are *always* up to date.

In Microsoft Works for Windows 95, you create this type of link by using the Paste Special

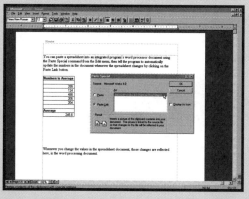

Click on Paste Link in the dialog box, so that the report automatically updates these numbers if you change the original spreadsheet.

command in the Edit menu. With both the spreadsheet and the word-processor document open in Works, select the part of the spreadsheet you want to link to the report by clicking and dragging. Then pick Copy from the Edit menu.

In the word-processor document (your report), choose Paste Special from the Edit menu. Click on the Paste Link button and then click on OK. Works pastes the spreadsheet into the report.

You can check to make sure the link is active by returning to the spreadsheet and changing one or more of its numbers. Switch to the report; the new values now appear in the linked spreadsheet section of the word-processor document.

★ TRY THIS! ★

Putting Your Spreadsheet to Work

Just Average

Spreadsheets are cool. Not because they perform calculations faster than the speediest pencil, but because once you set up a calculating formula, it works with any numbers you enter. Think of a spreadsheet as a word processor for numbers: Rather than re-type the entire formula to use a different set of values, you simply enter new numbers and immediately see the answer.

You need to emphasize this important point to kids working with a spreadsheet for the first time. To reinforce this concept, show your kids how to create a simple formula that calculates the average of a series of numbers. (We picked averaging because the concept is often introduced in elementary-school math class.)

GET SMART: To change the column width, put the mouse pointer at the junction of column A and column B and then click and drag to the right.

Open your spreadsheet program and create a new worksheet by pressing Ctrl-N. (For this demonstration, we use the spreadsheet in Microsoft Works for Windows 95, but the directions fit virtually any spreadsheet.) You see a blank worksheet. In column A, row 1 (in spreadsheet terminology, that's *cell A1*), type *Numbers to Average* and then press either Enter or Return.

Next, enter a series of five numbers in column A, starting in row 3. Press Enter or Return after typing each number. Type the label *Average* in cell A9. Click on cell A10 and then select Function from the Insert menu. From the list in the dialog box that appears, double-click on AVG. Click on cell A3 and, while holding down the mouse button, drag down through cell A7. The five cells containing numbers should be highlighted (that is, they appear in black). Notice that the function in cell A10 now reads =AVG(A3:A7). That's the formula the spreadsheet uses to calculate the average of the five

Click and drag the mouse pointer to select a range of numbers in a spreadsheet's formula.

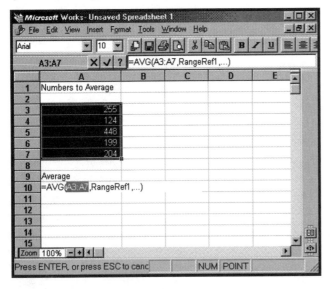

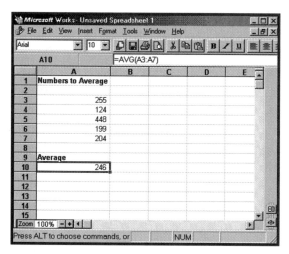

No matter what numbers you enter in cells A3 through A7, the spreadsheet automatically calculates their average and places the result in cell A10.

numbers you entered in cells A3 through A7. (Delete any characters that appear between *A7* and the final parenthesis.)

GET SMART: Microsoft Works makes the process of creating the most common formulas even easier. After entering the numbers you want to calculate, choose Easy Calc from the Tools menu. The program walks you through the procedure for completing the formula.

To demonstrate the flexibility of a spreadsheet to your children, change any (or all) of the numbers you entered in cells A3 through A7 and watch as the resulting average of those numbers automatically changes in cell A10. Nifty, huh?

Charts and Graphs

Your kids can also put a spreadsheet to work for homework by tapping its chart- and graph-making capabilities. Charts and graphs are required for many math class assignments (particularly in elementary school and middle school); your kids can also use them to spice up assignments in other subjects whenever numbers are involved. If your kids use an integrated package such as Microsoft Works or ClarisWorks to create reports, you'll find that adding number-based charts and graphs is especially easy.

Assume that your kid is assembling a report on France for her language or social studies class. As part of the report, she wants to show how France's geographic area and population compare to that of the United States. She can easily do that by using a spreadsheet.

You don't need to enter functions or create a formula to build simple charts and graphs with a spreadsheet.

She first digs up the appropriate numbers (we used the Microsoft Encarta 96 electronic encyclopedia), and then she enters them in the spreadsheet. With no formulas or functions to worry about, she simply types labels for the columns — *France* in one, *United States* in another — and the rows: *Area* and *Population*.

To create a chart comparing the sizes of the two countries, she selects the Area row (making sure to select the values for both nations) and then picks Create New Chart from the Tools menu. After selecting the type of chart (most spreadsheets, both stand-alone and those included in integrated programs, offer a variety of chart types, ranging from bar charts to pie charts), she clicks on the OK button to create the chart.

With the chart completed, she copies it from the spreadsheet and pastes it into her report (probably a word-processor document).

Instant graphs and charts!

Microsoft Works for Windows 95 shows you a preview of the chart, in the style you select.

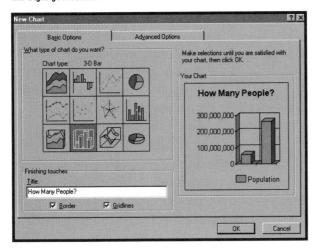

the spreadsheet modules within the integrated packages Microsoft Works and ClarisWorks. These spreadsheets are powerful enough for almost any homework assignment, but kids can easily handle them because they don't include the high-end features found in stand-alone programs such as Microsoft Excel.

People and Places
Geography and Other Cultures

TEACHERS START ASSIGNING GEOGRAPHICAL homework early in kids' school careers, usually through map-making projects and other-lands research assignments. You need to be ready to help out with project ideas and tips for doing research.

With a computer near at hand, kids don't need a passport to study other peoples and other places. But you need to make sure your family's PC or Mac is ready to take your children on some globe-trotting field trips.

In this chapter, we show you how to send your kids on round-the-world expeditions using the family computer. You learn how to help them connect with electronic pen pals, use digital atlases to work with maps, and step into the virtual shoes of people who live in faraway places.

Get ready to help your kids travel and see the world.

Getting to Know You...

What better way to learn about other places, other cultures, even other countries, than by going to the source — people who actually *live* in those cultures and locales?

That's not as hard as it sounds. All your child needs is a pen pal, or two, or three.

When you were younger, maybe you wrote to Annie in Australia or Gunnar in Germany — posting letters with *lots* of airmail stamps. However, today's wired-up kids can use the family computer to contact and communicate with children around the globe or as close as another state in the U.S. or province in Canada.

Several traditional pen-pal organizations can link up kids with similar interests. By using the home computer, a modem, and an online service or the Internet, you can offer your kids a faster and equally rewarding ex-

Japanese pen pal wanted for school project, ages 10-12
I'm Ashley and hoping to talk to someone in Japan around my age range relating to different cultures. I'm into fastpitch softball, soccer and watching movies.
Ashley

Keyboard pal listings on the Internet and commercial online services usually include just a few facts about the boy or girl — but enough to get the conversation started.

perience: correspondence with a *keyboard pal*. And even if you don't have a modem, your child can use the family's word processor and art programs to create great-looking letters the old-fashioned way.

E-Mail Keyboard Pals

Putting pen to paper or tapping on a keyboard is the easy part; finding a pen pal or a keyboard pal can be a bit daunting. How do you go about helping your child find a friend halfway around the world?

Sending and receiving e-mail ranks as the most popular activity on every major commercial online service. Each service delivers hundreds of thousands of messages every week, with many from established keyboard pals, and many others requesting new keyboard pals. Following are some suggestions for helping your child find a keyboard pal.

GET SMART: *Spend a few minutes showing your kids how e-mail works on the family's online service or Web browser.*

First, most online services let you search the member directories for subscriber interests. For example, you could use the directory-searching function to find a person from a city, state, or country that interests your daughter, or look for someone who shares her interests in sports, travel, and the like. Searching the directories is a cinch. With America Online, for example, pull down the Members menu and choose Search Member Directory.

GET SMART: *Want to send something snappier than a plain message? How about surprising your child's keyboard pal with a digital postcard? Using your Web browser, go to The Electric Postcard (**http://postcards.www.media.mit.edu/Postcards/**), pick a postcard (you can choose from lots of famous paintings), type your message, and off it goes. However, your child's keyboard pal must have Internet access to retrieve your card.*

Electronic bulletin boards offer another great means for finding keyboard pals. Because online services provide so many opportunities for people to form communities of interest, you and your daughter could browse a bulletin board that fits her interests. By participating, she can get to know the regulars and maybe begin an online friendship.

You can find some of the most popular bulletin boards for kids on the commercial services in America Online's Kids Only (keyword **kids**), Blackberry Creek (keyword **blackberry**), and Electronic Schoolhouse (keyword **ESH**) and in Prodigy's Just Kids (jump **Just Kids**).

The Internet is also chock-full of keyboard pal possibilities. The Mail Office at Kids' Space has lots of keyboard pal listings (grouped by ages) for kids in the U.S., some from Canada, and a few from other countries such as Great Britain and Singapore:

http://plaza.interport.net/kids_space/ mail/mail.html

For keyboard pals outside North America, try the Heinemann Keypal List:

http://www.reedbooks.com.au/heinemann/ global/keypali.html

or the Rigby Keypal List:

http://www.reedbooks.com.au/rigby/ global/keypal.html

Break the Ice

Once your child finds an interested keyboard pal, he may be a bit shy about what to say. KidLink — a large-scale, classroom-based keyboard pal project on the Internet — has connected 50,000 children from 80 different countries since 1990. To help break the ice, KidLink requires students to start their correspondence by answering four questions:

1. Who am I?

Have your child say a little about himself — his name, age, interests, hobbies, and anything else he considers special about himself. For example, he might mention that he loves animals, collects comic books, enjoys playing the piano, or is looking for a keyboard pal from a specific country or region. He should include the region where he lives (but *not* his street address or telephone number) and the name of his school.

2. What do I want to be when I grow up?

Encourage your child to share his vision of the career he thinks he might like to pursue. He should also explain why that particluar career interests him.

3. How do I want the world to be better when I grow up?

He should describe how he would improve life on Earth.

4. What can I do now to make this happen?

Have him describe the steps he would take to realize his personal goals and his vision of the world.

You can check out KidLink for yourself by pointing your Web browser to the following address:

http://www.kidlink.org/home-std.html

Sponsored by Australian educational publishers, both of these sites list scores of *keyboard-pals-wanted* requests from children around the world. Your kids can add their keyboard pal request to any of these Web pages, or answer mail directly from the listings by using their Web browser.

Offline Keyboard Pals

Even without an online link, your family computer still offers a versatile tool for staying in touch with keyboard pals. With a word-processing program, your child can choose fun fonts, type sizes, and type styles to fit her moods.

GET SMART: *A modem isn't the only means for staying in touch with keyboard pals. With Print Shop Deluxe Ensemble II, your kids can create snappy-looking cards for sending to offline keyboard pals.*

Creative writers can use the column functions in a more advanced word-processing

---

Keys to Safe Keyboard Palling

A few commonsense precautions can help your kids enjoy a safe online experience:

• Remind your kids that it's *names only* and that they should check with you before giving out personal information such as their address or home phone number.

• Prohibit face-to-face meetings with keyboard pals unless you know about them.

• Steer your children toward online areas designed for them and monitor their online activity to ensure they don't stray into inappropriate places.

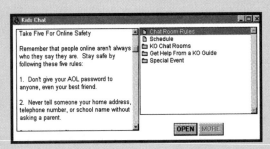

Your kids should follow America Online's smart chat safety suggestions. Remember, in the online world, not everyone is who they seem to be.

• Check to ensure that adults monitor the online areas your children visit to guard against obscene language and offensive behavior.

• Use your online service's parental controls or a Web-based blocker to prevent your child from accessing inappropriate areas. In America Online, for example, you can lock your child out of all but the Kids Only area (which offers plenty of opportunities for communicating with keyboard pals).

• Tell your children to check with you first before they post a personal picture online. (They can put a drawing on instead.)

program to imitate a newspaper layout (with a picture of the author glued into a space under the headline). Kids can produce newspaper-like stories that highlight their most recent sporting event, a family trip, or a make-believe adventure.

Using draw and paint programs, your child can add a new twist to the tradition of exchanging pictures. Have her create a caricature of herself as part of her letter (maybe she could include caricatures of her parents, siblings, and pets, too). If she is particularly artistic, have her send a *rebus* story (a story told with pictures instead of words) to her pen pal or keyboard pal.

For real high-tech keyboard palling, suggest that your child and her new friend exchange computer disks packed with their favorite shareware, stories, images, puzzles, and games.

Snail-Mail Pals

If your child decides to look for an offline pen pal, groups devoted to linking enthusiastic pen pals will help match him with a companion. Two large pen-pal organizations for finding nonelectronic (*snail mail*) pen pals are World Pen Pals and Gifted Children's Pen Pals International. World Pen Pals is a program of the United Way and the International Institute of Minnesota (612-647-0191); Gifted Children's Pen Pals is a service of MENSA (212-355-2469).

GET SMART: *Scanning software usually lets you choose from among several file formats for saving the images you scan. If your scanning software doesn't let you save the image in a file format that your keyboard pal's computer can read, you have to find a utility program that translates your image*

★ TRY THIS! ★

Create E-Mail Postcards

One of the neat things about using the computer to communicate with faraway friends is that your kids can send more than just words. By trading photos — perhaps of your city or your house — your children and their keyboard pals can get a better feel for each other's home and way of life. One simple way the keyboard pals can begin is by trading postcards of

their cities or photos of their homes or their hobbies.

You need a way to digitize the photos or other images. We recommend the EasyPhoto Reader (see Chapter 2, "The Bare Necessities," for details about this petite scanner), but there are many copy shops that scan photos for a fee. Scan the photo or postcard (a scenic shot of your

fair city or state would be perfect) with the scanner and then save it as a graphics file.

It's best if you know what kind of computer your child's keyboard pal uses. If she's using an IBM PC or compatible (the standard not only in the U.S., but around the world), save the image as a BMP file. If she has a Mac, save it as a PICT file.

*files to a format that your keyboard pal's computer can handle. For Windows-based PCs, we like Paint Shop Pro, a shareware program you can obtain from CompuServe (go **JASC**) and on the Web at **http://www.jasc.com/index.html**. On the Macintosh, the premier shareware conversion utility is GraphicConverter. You can find this program on most online services and on the World Wide Web at several different sites. We found it at **ftp://mirrors.apple.com/mirrors/info-mac/_Graphic_%26_Sound.Tool/grf/graphic-converter-24.hqx***

You can attach any type of file to an e-mail message and send both at the same time. In America Online, for example, you click on the Attach button in the e-mail window to *clip* a file to your message.

Attaching a graphics file to an e-mail message is simple when you use a commercial online service, such as America Online. Sending files over the Internet is more difficult and is best left to older children or adults.

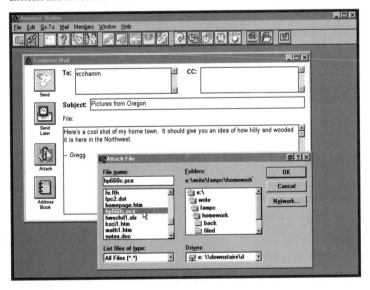

Where Are We?

When you want to know where you are — or where you've been — you usually consult a map. And when you need lots of maps, collected for your convenience, you want an atlas.

Today's digital atlases not only give you maps — tons of maps, in most cases — they often include a wealth of information about geography, history, and different cultures.

Maps are important elements of any electronic encyclopedia, but to really get answers to "where are we?" questions for school- and home-based learning, you should consider adding a software-based atlas to your library.

In the following sections, we point you to three great atlases — and online maps, too — that can help your children add some snap and sizzle to their reports and projects.

Atlases at the Top

Rand McNally may be the most familiar name in the paper atlas world, but kudos are up for grabs in the world of PC- and Mac-based atlases. Fortunately, *FamilyPC*'s network of family testers helped us narrow the list to a quartet of top-ranked CD-ROMs. (If you want to play pick-the-cartographer on your own, use

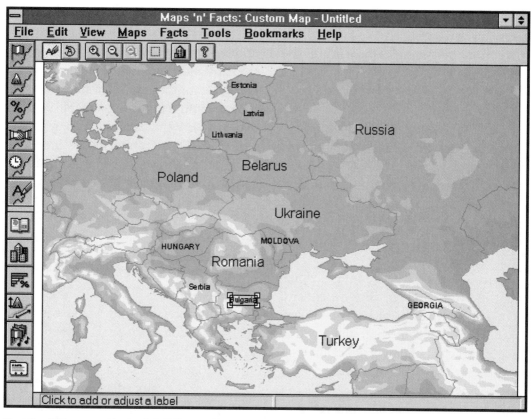

More than 300 maps and loads of statistics provide a detailed world view in Maps 'N' Facts, but this program really shines when kids use it to create custom maps for homework assignments.

the sidebar "A First-Rate Atlas Includes…" as a guide.)

PC Globe Maps 'N' Facts

PC Globe Maps 'N' Facts, which our testers stamped as *FamilyPC* Recommended, is a program that is especially effective in creating maps for homework assignments. The program features detailed information about 227 different countries, with more than 300 maps, including political, physical, and statistical maps, as well as an interactive time-zone map. Naturally, you can click on any map to zoom in for greater detail.

One of Maps 'N' Facts' strengths is its custom map feature, which provides the outline of a country and lets you add place-name and other labels. It makes almost any map-production chore a snap. Just as important for schoolwork needs is the program's capability to separate a country from its neighbors, making it easy to print exactly — and only — what you want. You can also view the flag of each nation, listen to its national anthem, and calculate point-to-point distances on maps just by clicking the mouse.

PC Globe's facts are as impressive as its maps. You can compile custom lists of countries and instantly compare them in over 200 categories.

3D Atlas

A *FamilyPC* Recommended exploration of Earth, 3D Atlas focuses on geography and environmental issues. This CD-ROM features a 3-D spinning globe, nine zoom levels of detail, shaded topography, and thousands of satellite images. You can look at the Earth from environmental, physical, or political perspectives.

To access information about individual countries, your children click on either a list or the country on the globe. This displays the country's flag, some vital statistics, and three or four color photos of key landmarks.

3D Atlas can also take your child on some fascinating 3-D flights over various biomes — savanna and rain forest, for example — and over impressive landscapes, including the Alps and the Himalayas. The program is notable for the amount of statistical data it contains and the striking graphical ways you can view the data: as shading on the globe (which you can rotate), by individual nation, and in various chart forms. Kids can print out much of this data.

GET SMART: *For the sharpest-looking printed maps, use coated paper made especially for ink-jet printers.*

Cartopedia

Beautifully designed and replete with useful information, Cartopedia has 600 colorful maps of the physical and political world, and 500 photographs and video sequences. Cartopedia garnered a *FamilyPC* Recommended seal of approval when it was reviewed by the magazine's family testers.

The heart of Cartopedia is its abundance of multimedia country articles. Each of these contains a map, a brief text description of the country, photographs, video clips, and pop-up windows accessible from the Navigation Panel. From the Navigation Panel, you can access detailed information on various aspects of a country, such as climate, the political parties in power,

3D Atlas uses thousands of satellite images to portray the real world.

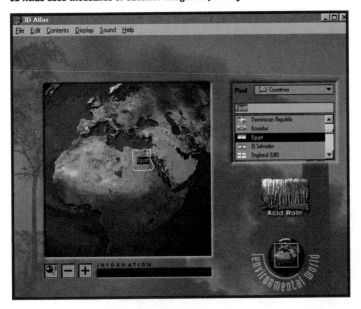

the amount of GDP spent on health and education, crime rates, world rankings in several categories, and a brief chronology of the country's history.

From Cartopedia's articles, you can view a country's flag and listen to its anthem. You can print and copy most of the information on the disc. However, the package doesn't include a printed manual, and its articles lack depth.

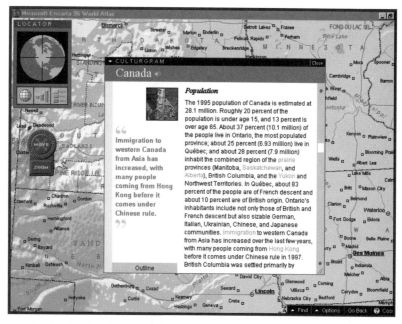

Encarta 96 World Atlas shows more than just maps. Its Culturegrams are self-contained articles about countries, with plenty of hypertext links to other points of interest.

Microsoft Encarta 96 World Atlas

Too bad the Microsoft Encarta 96 World Atlas works only on PCs with Windows 95; Mac and Windows 3.1 users miss out on one of the most stunning atlases ever.

GET SMART: *If you have access to the Internet, check out three activities you can do with World Atlas at* **http://www.microsoft.com/ewa/investigate.htm.** *All three activities can be used for interesting school reports and projects.*

You navigate by using a sliding compass to focus on a part of the globe, and then the zoom tool to get as close as though you were orbiting the Earth from a mere 120 miles. It takes a bit of practice for young children, but the animated guide Cosmo does a good job of explaining and demonstrating how the program works.

With more than one million place names, 3,000 color pictures, 4,000 audio clips, and even a series of satellite photos, World Atlas has plenty of reference possibilities. The Culturegrams — one for each of 118 countries — provide fodder for reports, with information on everything from eating habits and health to history and customs. You can even listen to greetings in each country's primary language!

World Atlas also makes the best attempt to show kids how a digital atlas can be used for schoolwork. Cosmo, the guide, steps you through the process of gathering information and maps from the CD-ROM, then copying them to a word-processor file to build a report.

Who Are You?

If you look at only maps, you might think all rivers are blue, all deserts are yellow, and borders are marked with dotted lines. You might also get the idea that the world is a big, empty place.

Of course, nothing could be further from the truth. People — millions in every coun- try, and billions spread across the globe — live in the real places that are marked by all those outlines and colors on maps. To get a grasp on the diversity of humanity and to better understand how other people live, your kids have to step away from an atlas and take virtual field trips with the family's computer.

Even with the best software and the most complete online information, the experi- ence isn't as rich as actually being there. However, a well-planned electronic jour- ney *can* be an eye-opener.

A First-Rate Atlas Includes...

CD-ROM atlases are great sources of geo- graphical information. A good electronic atlas should include the following:

• Maps
Does the atlas provide a variety of perspec- tives, including topographic and demograph- ic ones?

• Zoom controls
How closely can you zoom in (to the region, country, city, or street level)?

• Sound
Does the atlas include music, languages, and sounds?

• Video and photographs
Can you view video clips of unique rites of pas- sage, busy streets, or exotic customs?

• Statistics
Does the atlas provide a variety of useful statis- tics, such as data on population, climate, and currency?

• Updates
How often is the atlas updated, and how much does it cost to upgrade from an earlier version of the same software?

• Printing capabilities
Can you print maps in different sizes, orienta- tions, and formats?

• Copying and pasting tools
Can you easily copy material — maps, especially — from the atlas so that you can paste that in- formation into files you create with other pro- grams, such as your paint or draw program or your word processor?

★ TRY THIS! ★

Plot the Path

Although maps can play a part in plenty of subjects, they're used most often in social studies class, where they illustrate key moments in history (quick, in which state is Gettysburg located?) or highlight broader movements of the world's people (for example, when Rome ruled, what exactly *did* it rule?).

Creating a customized map to accompany a social studies report or a history project not only adds color to all those black words on white paper, but can actually allow your kids to explain complex ideas at a single glance. And your kids can easily create such customized maps by using a digital atlas. Here's how.

First, help your child select an appropriate map from the family's electronic atlas—in this case, World Atlas. For this example, assume that your child wants to create a map to accompany a report on Ferdinand Magellan, the Portuguese explorer whose

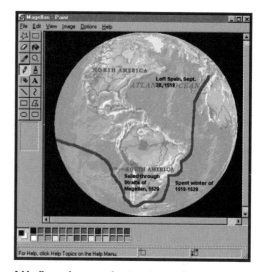

Add a line and some explanatory text, and you have a custom map that shows the world's first globe-trotting expedition.

expedition of 1519–1522 was the first to circumnavigate the globe. Because your child wants to show the entire voyage on one map, set World Atlas to show the globe from 24,700 miles, and rotate the map to show the Americas. Then put a copy of the map in the Windows Clipboard by picking the Copy Map command from the Options menu.

Next, paste the map into your favorite drawing program. Show your child how to add a line to show the path Magellan's ships took — the brush tool works well here. Then your child can add text to describe the most important events from Magellan's voyage. Creative kids can even draw small sailing ships and place them at various points on the map.

Start your map-making project by copying the current map to the Windows Clipboard.

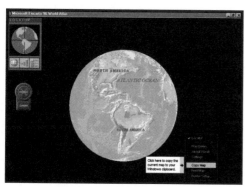

Go Online!

The Internet has many more maps that kids can use for geography projects. So many, in fact, that your best bet is to use one of the Web's search engines to find exactly the right map. Try Yahoo! for starters:

http://www.yahoo.com

When we used the keyword *map*, we found hundreds of map-related sites. Here are three of our favorites:

● Xerox PARC Map Viewer creates a color, computer-generated map of any location on the planet. Using your Web browser, you can copy the map or save it as a file to use in a report. The maps don't include too much detail, which makes them perfect for customized map-making chores. Point your Web browser to the following address:

For out-of-the-ordinary maps, such as this one of the Roman Republic, head to the Internet.

links to Web pages that offer other information about those places). To visit this Web site, enter the following address in your browser:

http://fermi.jhuapl.edu/states/states.html

● Historical Atlas of Europe and the Middle East offers top-notch maps for students who are doing research on periods up to and including the Renaissance (as of our last visit, although this site is adding more maps all the time). This is a worthwhile stop in your cartographic search if your kids are looking for super maps for history class:

http://www.ma.org/ maps/map.html

Recognize this place? It's part of the state of Colorado, as seen from space.

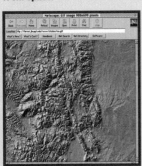

http://pubweb. parc.xerox.com/ map

● Color Landform Atlas of the United States is an excellent U.S. map resource, with relief and county maps for all 50 states (and

Cultural CD-ROMs

Numerous top-flight CD-ROMs can help children understand how other people live, including their customs and their cultures. We have three recommendations for kids who are interested in studying faraway places and the folks who live there.

Material World

Based on the book of the same name, Material World takes your kids on photo- and information-rich visits with 30 families from 30 different countries. Sixteen photojournalists collaborated on the book and this CD,

living with these statistically average families for a week, taking pictures of them and their possessions.

GET SMART: Here's a great research project idea that uses Material World: Grab questions from the questionnaire the families filled out, enter them in a word processor, print copies, and ask classmates, friends, and family members to complete the survey.

Elementary-school-aged kids can easily navigate the CD. By clicking on buttons, they can see a description of each country

Material World's thumbnail shots let you choose which of its 30 families you want to visit.

★ TRY THIS! ★

Map Your Roots

Finding a cultural banquet doesn't always require a trip overseas. Your kids may be able to find everything they need right here in the United States.

Your kids can explore the cultural variety of the U.S. (or North America, for that matter) by combining information from an electronic atlas with some investigative research close to home. This artistic project, which can be accompanied by a research report, is a perfect pick for elementary-school students, though older children can certainly use it, too.

First, your child should compose a questionnaire that asks his classmates to identify — as best they can — which country or continent their families left behind when they immigrated to or arrived in this country. If they can add the year their families reached the U.S., all the better (even approximate answers are fine). Your child can type the questionnaire in a word processor and print copies; an alternative is to simply ask each classmate and jot down the answers at school.

Next, locate an appropriate map in the family's electronic atlas. Depending on the responses from your child's schoolmates, he might select a map of Europe; one that shows Europe, Africa, and the Middle East; or a map of the entire globe. Copy that map, then paste it into an empty page in your art program.

Now, your child can use the data from the questionnaires to create a map that illustrates his class-

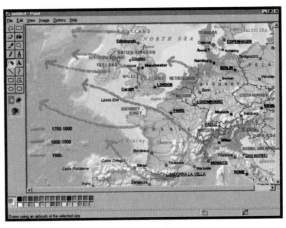

A kid-made map is a snappy way to illustrate a cultural project about the origins of classmates' families.

mates' points of origin. He can decide how to organize this data; one method is to assign each person in the class a number and then place that number in the appropriate spot on the map to show where that family came from. He can add color-coded arrows to show the approximate date that each classmate's family arrived — for example, blue for before 1800, green for 1800–1900, and so on.

GET SMART: To scale down this project, your child can ask classmates where they were born and then use that information to color-code a map of the United States. For example, states with one classmate birthplace could be colored blue, and states with two to five classmate birthplaces could be tinted green.

(from the U.S.A. and Ethiopia to Iceland and India), photo albums of the families, video and audio clips, facts and figures on the countries and their peoples, and the questionnaire each family completed.

Although the photos are terrific — they illustrate the vast material differences among humanity — it's the questionnaires that show our similarities. From Texas to India, families generally think of themselves as "comfortably off," they worship devoutly, and they want the best for their children.

Africa Trails

Based on a real trek by world-famous cyclists, Africa Trails takes your kids on a simulated bicycle journey across Africa. Along the way, kids get a peek at the continent's geography, history, and most importantly, its people and their cultures.

Filled with more than 1,000 photos and two dozen video clips, this disc isn't a passive exploration. Instead, it casts kids in the role of real-life cyclists who must make decisions along the way. They must manage their resources — money and supplies, as well as their own endurance — to successfully bike from one end of Africa to the other. Along the way, players score points by visiting interesting sites and meeting the people who live there. There's even a multiple-choice reading comprehension game that tests kids' attention to details as they peddle across this virtual Africa.

Passage to Vietnam

One of the best multimedia titles around, Passage to Vietnam provides a stunning, informative experience for both adults and children. Like a top-notch TV documentary, Passage to Vietnam presents a wealth of photographs, video clips, and other information about a country most of us don't know, but which is so important to our nation's history. This fascinating disc comes as close to putting you on the spot as any CD-ROMs we've seen.

Although the core of this disc is its photographs, kids can easily move beyond the pictures to listen to audio narration or watch video. A half-dozen topics — ranging from the country's culture to a history of Vietnam's wars — let you explore in detail.

Perfected Geography Projects

"Are we there yet?"

You may find that question annoying when it comes from the bunch in the backseat of the family car, but it takes on a different meaning when you and your children are seated in front of the family computer. By spinning out some unique ideas for projects and reports, you can encourage your children to expand their geographic horizons without leaving the comfort of home.

We've developed three fun geography activities: mapping your backyard, creating a kids' resource map of your state, and making computer postcards from exotic places around the globe. These easy-to-do projects are fit for both home fun and school assignments.

By starting with the most familiar landscape in the world to your children (your backyard), you can encourage them to explore the people and places of the world.

Build a Backyard Treasure Map

You can turn young children into instant geographers — and demonstrate the basics of relative distance and scale — by showing them how to map their own backyard for a personalized treasure hunt. This activity uses a familiar landscape to teach the fundamentals of mapmaking and map reading, including symbols, scale, and direction. Although you can use it as a launch pad to generate ideas for elementary-school projects, it's actually best applied as an at-home learning lesson.

The key to creating maps on your computer is the ease with which your child can graphically display everything in your back-

Go Online!

The least expensive way to step into other people's shoes is by using the online resources of your family's computer. As with almost every other area of study, you can find hundreds of online service and Internet locales for exploring cultures and ethnic groups.

One of the best is NetNoir Online, which is available on America Online (keyword **netnoir**). This area of AOL provides a wealth of Afrocentric content in areas ranging from education to business and includes well-populated message boards and chat areas for person-to-person conversations. Although it focuses on African cultures — including African-American — NetNoir is open to anyone. If your mid-dle-school or high-school-aged children are looking for a first-rate cultural resource, point them this way.

The CIA World Factbook 1995 should be high on your Web browser's hotlist. It may be your tax dollars at work, but in this case, they seem to be well spent. Each country has its own page, with tons of facts about its geography, people, resources, and more. This Web site doesn't offer a lot of cultural life, but kids looking for figures to back up a report should visit this place:

America Online's NetNoir section explores Afrocentric cultures and peoples.

http://www.odci.gov/cia/publications/95fact/index.html

yard, such as the garage (the dragon's lair?), a wild blueberry patch, the tree stump (home plate for T-ball?), Mom's garden, or even your child's favorite climbing tree.

In this activity, you create a personalized unit of measure and translate it to a backyard map by using a drawing program and some clip art or the stamps included in such top-notch art packages as Kid Pix or Kid Pix Studio.

First, come up with a unit of measure equal to one of your child's strides. We called it a *Noah*. You may want to point out that the ancient Egyptians had units of measure based on the distance from a king's elbow to the tip of his middle finger (cubit), the width of his hand (palm), and the width of his finger (digit).

Have your child pace off the distances between objects in your backyard and then record the positions in a notebook. Mark in your notebook the position of objects with respect to each other, measured in Noahs (or Beths, or whatever unit you choose). You may sketch the yard, but it will be more challenging if you simply record the positions of objects with respect to each other. Also, explain to your child what a compass does, and use one to record the orientation of backyard objects.

When you're ready to begin making your backyard map, load Kid Pix or any other drawing program with a stamp or clip-art feature. Find a stamp you can use to represent your Noahs. In Kid Pix, you can use the smiley face, baby face, or footstep stamps (if your child hopped instead of stepping off distances in the yard, you could also use the

bunny stamp). Edit the stamp by inserting your child's name (in Kid Pix, open the Goodies menu and select Edit Stamp).

GET SMART: *To turn this backyard map-making exercise into something more appropriate as an elementary-school classroom project or a free-form homework assignment, switch locations to your child's school. You can take a Saturday morning to step off some of the distinguishing landmarks around the school yard, such as the playground equipment and the bus stop.*

Lay down the scale by stamping Noahs all along the top of your soon-to-be map. Do the same along the left side (for the stamps you use on that scale, open the Goodies menu, choose Edit Stamp, and rotate the stamp).

Now, using the notes you took during your backyard exploration, help your child draw your backyard as though looking down from a tall tree or from the back of a bird. If your child has difficulty with the concept, you might suggest he or she begin by drawing a prominent feature — say, the garage or a flower bed — then the next closest thing, and so on, until the backyard is completely filled in. Talk about what objects look like from above — for example, a tree is just a big, bumpy, green circle.

Once your child finishes drawing the scale and the symbols to represent all the features of your backyard, she can add some directional indicators. Draw a simple compass rose somewhere on the page (be sure it is correctly oriented). Review directions with your

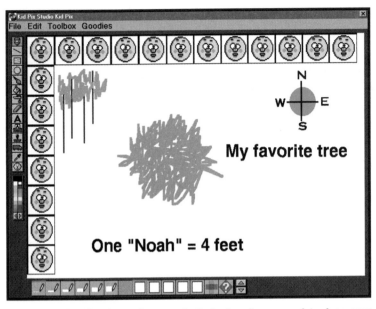

My favorite tree

One "Noah" = 4 feet

By mapping a familiar place — for example, the backyard — you can introduce young kids to basic geography.

child by asking about the relationships among objects in the backyard (for example, is the shed south of the swing set?).

Print your map using a color printer. Or, if you're printing in black and white, have your child decorate portions of the map with markers or colored pencils. Make enough maps for several school-age scavenger hunters.

GET SMART: *Not only is this activity an excellent geographical learning project on its own, but it can also be used for outdoor parties, such as birthdays.*

With your map complete, you can organize a scavenger hunt. Hide treasures in your backyard (plastic award medals that say "Winner" are great and readily available at department stores). Along with each map, provide distance and direction clues. Watch as your child's friends try to convert Noahs to inches, or to the equivalent distance measured in their own strides (if they happen to be the same height). After the kids discover all the treasures, redeem each for a healthy treat.

Mapping Amusements

Geography really comes alive when kids make maps *and* study them. And the best way to launch a cartography career is by showing kids that maps can illustrate things in which *they're* interested. In this section, we outline how children can create a map of kid-hot locations such as amusement parks, favorite playgrounds, or museums in their area. You can easily modify this activity to turn it into a map-making project fit for a state-specific report.

Your child can get a knapsack full of information by calling local or state chambers of commerce or by visiting a nearby travel agency. Phone calls to relatives and friends around the state are another great way to gather data for a map drawn from a kid's-eye view. But one of the best ways to find out the top entertainment sites is by using your family's PC and an online service such as

America Online, CompuServe, or Prodigy.

Your child can leave a message in a travel forum (on AOL, the keyword is **travel**; on CompuServe, enter **GO TRAVEL**; and on Prodigy, jump **Travel BB**). Or your child can search the membership directory by city and state and send e-mail messages explaining that he's looking for contributors to a resource map for kids. (For more information about using pen pals and keyboard pals for gathering this type of data, see the section "Getting to Know You," earlier in this chapter.)

Kids will get excited about geography when they create custom maps that highlight places and things they enjoy visiting.

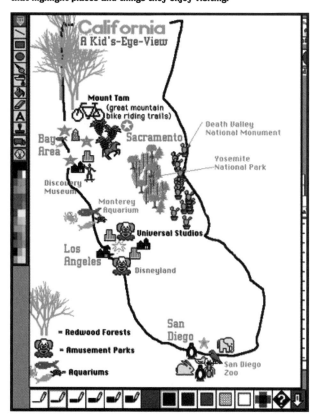

Once your cartographer has the data, she can start drawing the map. She should leave enough space to type the name of the state in the largest font. If you have a digitizing tablet, your child can trace the state outline directly into the computer. (See Chapter 2 for information on our recommended digitizing tablet, the Wacom ArtPad II.)

With the state border on the screen, the next step is to add the capital and the major cities. Use a star for the state's capital and a circle or a square for large cities. Your child should also draw any major lakes or rivers, as well as large mountain ranges.

Next, your child can devise stamps to use as symbols. Include a legend that links the symbols and the resources. She can even make an arrow pointing off the map to a box with information such as the name of the amusement park and its location (and, if it was recommended by a keyboard pal, her name and e-mail address).

To go beyond the just-for-kids stuff, add information about the state's agriculture and industry from an electronic atlas such as 3D Atlas or World Atlas.

Imagination Destinations

Using your family PC, a drawing program, and reference information from an electronic world atlas, your child can create personalized postcards from faraway places, complete with drawings, pictures, and wish-you-were-here information about the climate, the people, the food, and the sights. By assembling several such postcards on locales studied in school — say, a handful from one country or one for each of a half-dozen U.S. states — your child can create a unique project fit for filing with the teacher.

Begin by talking to your child about your family's native country, countries you've visited, or your own dream destination. Or keep a globe near your favorite reading chair and point out worldly destinations in his favorite storybooks. Using a simple art program or a word-processing program with graphics capabilities (such as Microsoft Works or ClarisWorks), your child can design colorful postcards with a scene on the front and information about that destination on the back.

Open a file in the family's art program, and use the Square tool to draw the largest rectangle that comfortably fits on your screen

Go, Go, Go with Geo Games

If the homework is done and your kids are still clamoring for more exotic places to visit, try turning them on to the Carmen Sandiego series of geographic detective games.

In all Carmen Sandiego titles, Carmen and her gang of thieves commit crimes that range from stealing a glacier from Alaska to nabbing a valuable shadow puppet collection from Jakarta. Kids solve each mystery by following clues the crooks leave behind. A clue leading to a town in Montana may read, "He said he planned to follow the route of Lewis and Clark to the source of the Missouri River", a clue pointing to Egypt may say, "She wanted to see examples of Bedouin weaving."

If you're not sure who Lewis and Clark were or you've never heard of Bedouin weaving, don't worry; you have some help. Where in the World is Carmen Sandiego? comes with the King Fisher Reference Atlas; Where in the USA is Carmen Sandiego? includes a copy of Fodor's USA travel guide.

As your young sleuths solve more and more cases, they move up the ranks in the detective agency, encountering more difficult cases and more obscure geographic clues. The ultimate prize, of course, is to capture the wiliest thief of all — Carmen Sandiego, geo-gang leader extraordinaire.

Kids must use good geographic sense to thwart the crooks in the Carmen Sandiego series. In Where in the USA is Carmen Sandiego?, children can use the included reference work to help solve the crime.

(the largest card you can send for the postcard rate is 6-by-4 inches). Use a rough sketch as a guide, then use the program's Pencil, Paintbrush, or Airbrush tools to complete the exotic scene. (If you're using a stamp-capable program such as Kid Pix Studio, kids can add appropriate artwork from the package's stamp collection.) If your word processor or art program has graphics-importing capabilities, import an image from a CD-ROM atlas or download one from a commercial online service or the Internet.

"Wish you were here" takes on a new meaning when kids use an art program to produce postcards that highlight places they're studying in school.

GET SMART: Kids can create such personalized postcards by using artwork and facts from their country or state, and then send the finished product to a pen pal or an electronic version to a keyboard pal. For details on how to locate a pen pal or a keyboard pal, see "Getting to Know You," earlier in this chapter.

When your child completes the artwork for the front of the postcard, make a new file for the back. Draw the same rectangular border, a vertical line down the center, three or four lines on the right side for the address of the person to whom you're sending the postcard, a box in the upper-right corner that says *Place Stamp Here*, and a short sentence in the upper-left corner describing the image or graphic shown on the front.

*GET SMART: A super resource for postcard-appropriate images is America Online's Pictures of the World area (keyword **Pictures**).*

When you've completed the back and saved it, print both files (front and back), cut around the borders, and glue both sides to a piece of tagboard for rigidity. If you don't have a color printer, your children can hand-color or paint the front of the card.

The Past Is a Blast
History

HISTORY DOES REPEAT ITSELF, IF ONLY IN the repetitive memorization of names and dates that so many of us associate with the subject.

But history should be more than a jumble of 1066s, 1492s, and 1776s. It should be a window into the past, and therefore help us understand where we are today.

One way to put excitement into history — and the inevitable homework assignments — is with the family's computer. In this chapter, we focus on some of the most popular areas of study within the subject of history, help you give your children an instant idea list, and identify the resources they need to complete their history projects and reports.

Thanks to today's technology, history is a blast from the past.

History Gets Personal

Although learning about the history of a country or a culture is important, perhaps the most fascinating to your family — especially your kids — is your own history.

Family history, sometimes referred to as *personal history*, is studied in many classrooms, often as an introduction to history in general. And that means family history can come home as homework.

You may be able to pass along some family history to your children, but your information is probably sketchy and disorganized. Using the home computer, your kids can collect, organize, and present their family history — in as little or as much detail as they want — for a terrific, A+-style report or project.

And along the way, they might give the entire family the history bug.

Gathering Information

First, you and your child need to collect as much information as you can about your family. Here are some ways you and your child can research your personal history:

- Interview family members by letter, telephone, or e-mail.

- Look through family photo albums and identify who's there.

- Use online resources, genealogical libraries and collections, and government information such as Census reports.

For most family history homework projects or reports, your children should gather information by interviewing family members and searching through photo albums. (Online resources, genealogical libraries, and government information are more appropriate for serious genealogical research, when you're trying to dig back more than three or four generations in the family tree.)

Creating an Interview Letter

One way to plumb the depths of your family history is with a simple interview letter, which you and your child can create in your word processor and then mail to as many relatives as possible. When you receive the responses, enter the data into a genealogy program such as Family Tree Maker or use it to embellish a multimedia slide show.

You can customize the interview letter to concentrate on the facts and stories that you want to collect. At the least, however, ask each person to supply the following information about as many members of their family tree as possible:
- Name
- Date of birth
- Place of birth
- Date of death (if applicable)
- Place of death (if applicable)

You should request this information not only for the relative to whom you mail the letter, but for that relative's husband or wife; their children (and grandchildren); their parents, grandparents, and so on. In addition to these basics, ask each relative for a favorite story or two about themselves or someone in their immediate family; such personal anecdotes are often the most interesting part of family history.

GET SMART: *Encourage your relatives to loan you old photographs of themselves and their families. Assure them that you will return the photos as soon as you scan the pictures into your PC or Mac.*

To improve your chances of getting a response, be sure to include a self-addressed, stamped envelope with the interview letter.

Organizing the Information

All this information you collect has to go somewhere. Rather than put it in a shoe box, why not use the computer equivalent, a database?

But don't use just any database. If your family has more than a passing interest in its history, we recommend Family Tree Maker 3.01 as the best genealogy program for families. Family Tree Maker is easy enough for kids to use, produces attractive charts, and allows you to create a multimedia show on your PC, complete with photos, text, video, and sound.

Family Tree Maker's multimedia scrapbook can hold scanned pictures, text, and even audio narration.

GET SMART: *Use a small scanner to digitize photographs you want to include in your family history file within Family Tree Maker. We recommend the EasyPhoto Reader, an affordable scanner especially designed for scanning photos as large as 4 by 6 inches. See Chapter 2, "The Bare Necessities," for more information about this scanner. If you don't own a scanner, phone local copy shops and inquire about scanning services and their cost.*

Family Tree Maker makes entering data (for the most part, this will be names and dates) a snap. However, this program's coolest feature is its multimedia slide show. Each person in the family can create their own *scrapbook* containing photos, sound

bites, text stories, and even video clips with sound.

For more serious study, Family Tree Maker's FamilyFinder Index, which comes on the CD-ROM version of the program, helps you locate long-dead family members among its database of more than 100 million names culled from state and federal records. Although you pay extra for the CD-ROMs that contain details about these individuals, the leads may be worth the money if you or your kids get hooked on genealogy.

Family Tree Maker's charts work well as the final form for family research homework assignments. In particular, the ancestor chart puts your name in a shadowed box and uses brackets to connect your name to those of your parents, grandparents, and great-grandparents.

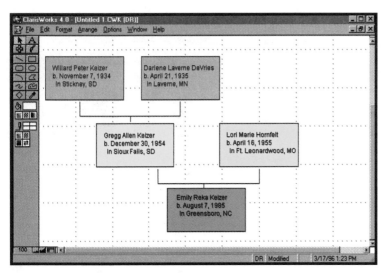

Using any paint or draw program, you can create a family tree from scratch. By coloring the boxes, you can show each generation at a glance.

Presenting the Information

Specialized programs such as Family Tree Maker simplify organizing your family's history and make it possible to easily assemble a multimedia slide show for a super classroom presentation. However, you may want to economize by using software you already have.

GET SMART: *A draw program works better for this task, because you can group text, boxes, and lines into single objects, which you can then easily move around on the screen as you organize the family history.*

You can create a basic family history chart by using a paint or draw program. Because it has an excellent drawing module, we turned to ClarisWorks, one of two integrated packages we recommend.

Start by setting the page orientation to Landscape and then create a small box of sufficient size to hold information about one person (at the minimum, the person's name, birth date, and birth place). To keep the genealogy chart consistent, make several copies of this box. To do this, select the box, choose the Copy command from the Edit menu, and then choose the Paste command several times in succession.

Next, use the text tool to enter the personal data for each person in the family tree. Select the text and drag it into a box.

For each person in the family tree, your drawing has two objects: a box and some text. To keep these two objects together, select each while holding down the Shift key and then pick Group from the Arrange menu. Now you can move the box and its text as one object, positioning them anywhere you like.

Create one box to represent each person in the family tree and then arrange them in an upside-down pyramid shape, with the child's name at the bottom, her parents above that, and their parents above them.

Current Events

Current events *are* history — history in the making. And in many classrooms, current events provide the basis for history and social studies assignments.

Kids can comb through the daily newspaper (no matter what futurists say, print is far from dead), looking for the news and information they need to complete a paper or a report. Or they can turn to the ever-growing world of electronic news presented on the family computer's screen via online services and the Internet.

The difference between newspapers and online news involves more than just presentation — that is, print versus pixels on the monitor. Although a newspaper is high-ly portable (and inexpensive), it doesn't let kids search for the news they want to use. With online news, on the other hand, they can easily find the stories that best match their needs. Is your daughter looking for political news about the Middle East? She can search through online news for just that topic. Does your son need more than just yesterday's stories? He can cull articles from any number of news databases and retrieve dozens of articles to give his report the Big Picture perspective.

In the following sections, we help you point your children toward some superb

Go Online!

To research family history beyond a few generations, you may want to turn to available online resources. You really can't dig deep into family history research with a modem yet, but several sites are worth exploring.

America Online's Genealogy Forum helps family history beginners by providing some solid research tips and hints.

genealogy software, and message boards and chat sessions that let you connect with other family history researchers, America Online's genealogy forum is the place to begin if you subscribe to AOL.

Name Search

http://www.census.gov/ ftp/pub/genealogy/www/ namesearch.html

More for fun than anything else, this Web site lets

Yahoo!'s Genealogy Index

http://www.yahoo.com/ Arts/Humanities/History/ Genealogy/

This is a good launching pad into the Web's genealogical sites.

America Online's Genealogy Forum (keyword: Roots)

Packed with plenty of information, shareware

you enter your family's last name (or your first name) and then see how it ranks in popularity. Keizer is *way* down the list; Smith (1), Johnson (2), and Jones (4) rank near the top of the chart. See how you rate.

★ TRY THIS! ★

Collect Online News Clippings

Collecting current-events stories is only half the battle. Your kids also need to organize and present the information they gather.

Instead of slicing up the newspaper, today's kids can gather news and publish it in a newspaper-style format. All it takes is a little electronic cutting and pasting. The results look snappier than a pile of newspaper clippings —

By assembling the news in an electronic document (rather than simply printing it on paper), your child can search through his or her collection of stories.

which is important when your child must hand the current-events assignment to the teacher. And, when the clippings are in digital form, students can search through those clippings in a flash.

Assume that your child's assignment is to follow national political news during an election year; she must compile at least 20 clippings of stories that outline the candidates' stands on the ecology. As she digs through an online service or a Web-based paper, she uses keyword combinations such as *ecology AND presidential election* and finds one or two articles each day that

seem to fit. Rather than print out each news story, she can copy the text by using the Copy command in the online service or the Web browser. But where should she put the text she copies?

GET SMART: Your family — or better yet, kid-specific — word processor can produce newspaper-style clippings if it lets you separate a page into two or more columns.

That depends on the family's software library. If you have a desktop publishing program such as Microsoft Publisher, your child

can create cool-looking newspaper-style pages in just minutes by using the template included with the program. Missing a publishing program? An integrated package such as ClarisWorks or Microsoft Works can serve almost as well. Use the program's newsletter document template, if it has one.

No matter which program your child uses as a clipping repository, once a document is open on the screen, she selects the program's Paste command to lay down the text she grabbed from the news service. Finally, she adds some pithy headlines to the page and saves the file on the computer's hard disk.

Because she stored the text in digital form, she can later call up the clipping file and use the Find command to search for any word or phrase. That comes in handy when the assignment goes beyond simply collecting news stories to include using them for reports or short research papers.

digital news resources. We also provide suggestions for showing them how they can feed the information they find into their homework.

Get the News

No matter which online service the family uses, your children can access an amazing amount of news (enough, it sometimes seems, to fill a dozen Sunday-sized newspapers). Not only does the online service itself provide hour-by-hour coverage of important events, its Internet connections provide access to even more information on what's happening around the world, across the country, or in your home state.

But how can your kids best use this news? We show you by taking a spin through the news section of *our* favorite online service, America Online (AOL).

From the main menu display of AOL, click on the Today's News button. In a moment, you see the front page for this part of the service. (Remember: Online services frequently change the look of their information; the following description may differ somewhat from what you see on the screen when you reach AOL. However, the procedures we outline should remain basically the same.) A multipanel display appears, showing such categories as US and World, Politics, Sports, and Business.

GET SMART: *Skimming the online news? Use the headlines to locate the stories you want to read, just as you do when you look at a printed newspaper.*

Browsing through online news is similar to flipping through a newspaper. You start by turning to the most appropriate news category and then you open individual articles (or sometimes folders that contain multiple news stories).

But you open the real power of AOL's online news by using its Search command. Click on the Search button (found on virtually every news-related screen), type one or more keywords, and you're rewarded with a list of recent news stories on the subject you're exploring. When we entered the keywords *china* and *war*, for example, we got a list of more than 100 stories about an escalating crisis between China and Taiwan that flared up in early 1996. Try doing that with a daily

America Online provides a colorful, well-organized interface to its electronic news service, letting you choose from various major news categories.

Go Online!

We recommend the Web editions of two newspapers for starters:

● The New York Times

You can read articles, search for news, and even see a digital duplicate of the front page on this top-notch newspaper's Web site. Steer your middle-school- and high-school-aged children here if they're looking for national and international news, two areas in which this newspaper really shines:

http://www.nytimes.com/

● USA Today

Almost as colorful on the Web as it is on paper, USA Today is a super online newspaper pick for

Electronic newspapers such as the New York Times Web site usually offer a search tool so you can dig through old stories as well as current news.

Bright colors and short, easy-to-digest articles make the USA Today Web site a good news source for the younger children in your family.

almost any child older than 8. Many articles are summarized in a paragraph or so (but you can click the mouse and read the full text of the story if you want). A slick search tool lets kids dig through the paper's databases. To visit this site, point your Web browser to the following address:

http://www.usatoday.com/

Of course, you can find hundreds of other newspapers on the Internet — you must pay for some, though most newspaper sites are still free. To help your children dig up additional news sources, head to Yahoo and search using the keyword *newspaper*:

http://www.yahoo.com

newspaper, or even a stack of them at the public library, and see what you get!

Famous Faces

To give history lessons an extra spark, teachers sometimes transform kids into actors portraying the lives and times of famous people. Maybe that's why biographical reports are such popular homework assignments.

The family's computer can help your kids research notable men and women of the past (or the present), as well as spice up the presentation of that information. With a bit of biographical digging, your kids may just hit pay dirt.

Doing the Research

The family PC or Macintosh can't bring famous people back to life (wouldn't *that* be a trick!), but it can be the conduit to first-rate biographical information. As in any computerized research project, your kids do their biographical digging with two types of tools: CD-ROM encyclopedias and on-line information. (For lots of tips on how to research almost anything with your computer, head to Chapter 7, "Wading into the Information Pool.")

If an assignment involves famous figures in history, your kids will probably have better luck using an electronic encyclopedia (although online services and the World Wide Web have biographical gems that you

Because your kids can quickly search electronic news files for exactly the news they want to use, they'll finish their current-events homework faster than they could with a print newspaper.

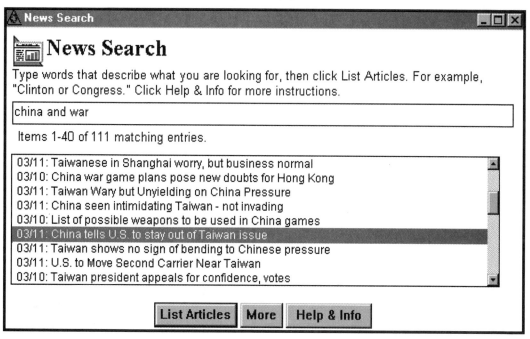

The Biographical Checklist

If your child can't decide on a biographical target, this checklist makes the process easier and gives him a research head start. You can type this list into a word processor, save the file, and then call it up for viewing or printing.

When a teacher assigns a paper or project that involves some biographical research, your child should complete the checklist for each prospective subject and then compare the checklists to make his final pick.

✔ Name

✔ Date of birth/death

✔ Place of birth/death

✔ What this person did (pick his/her main occupation)

✔ What is this person most famous for?

✔ What are this person's most famous words (if any)?

✔ What was the world like *where* this person lived (just a sentence or two)?

✔ What was the world like *when* this person lived (just a sentence or two)?

can find tucked away here and there.)

While they research, remind your kids to take notes using a word processor (or, if they work in Encarta 96, using that program's Notemarks feature). They can also collect information by using the Copy command in the encyclopedia or the online software, and then the Paste command in their word processor. Then they can save the word-processing document on the computer's hard disk.

GET SMART: *To help your children really root out biographical information, show them how to search using the person's first name and last name — for example, Julius AND Caesar.*

Digging Deeper

Encourage your young biographer to dig below the surface. (Professional biographers

---

After just a few minutes of searching the World Wide Web, we found this informative article about Julius Caesar.

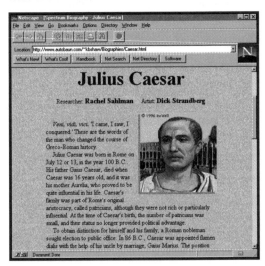

certainly don't stop at the surface; instead, they write entire books about even the most obscure historical figures.)

Unlike basic biographical research, digging deeper is easier on the computer than with books at the local library. Here's why.

As your kids research a person, they'll come across related facts that they can quickly explore in an electronic encyclopedia or an online information resource. For example, while researching Julius Caesar, you might come across the term *Gaul* (which refers to what we now know as France). To follow that thread, you simply look for the keyword *Gaul* by using the encyclopedia's Search or Find command.

You'll be amazed at what your kids find during this type of nonlinear research. When we dug deeper into Caesar's life, we found maps of the world as he knew it, photos of

---

★ **TRY THIS!** ★

Hey, It's My Birthday!

Famous people have birthdays, too. And you can help your kids create a custom calendar that notes the B-days of as many personalities as they want, for any month of the year. This out-of-the-ordinary project may look like it took weeks to research, but with just a bit of Internet time, you can pull it together in less than an hour.

Using your Web browser, head to the Britannica Online site:

A free service provided by the electronic version of Encyclopedia Britannica, Britannica's Lives lists famous birthdays.

Britannica's Lives — Biographies by Birthday is free to all, all the time.

Click on it to see a long list of the famous people who were born on today's date. The listing includes short biographies of each person, but for more details, you have to head into Britannica Online itself. Even cooler, you can easily change the date to show other birthdays.

After selecting one birthday to represent each day

http://www.eb.com:84/cgi-bin/bio.pl

Although you have to pay to use this online version of the well-respected *Encyclopedia Britannica* ($150 per year for a subscription), the item marked

— and taking a few notes about the person's life — your child can transfer these names and facts to a paper calendar or, if you have a draw or paint program, to an electronic calendar form you've created with grid lines and numbers for the dates. Print it out and he can hand it in.

★ **TRY THIS!** ★

Résumés of the Rich and Famous

Nobody likes a boring report. Teachers hate reading them, kids don't like to write them, and parents feel guilty because they haven't pointed their children in a refreshing direction.

One way you can help your kids beat the biography blues is by showing them how to present the profile as a résumé. (This is a nifty idea, because the project not only takes care of a biographical assignment, it gets middle- and high-school-aged kids accustomed to a document essential in later years.) By definition, famous people are... well, famous — usually by virtue of their accomplishments. If anything, it's tough to squeeze all their exploits into a one-page résumé.

If you have an integrated program such as Microsoft Works or ClarisWorks, your kids have a predesigned résumé template at the ready. They just have to fill in the blanks. In the following paragraphs, we take you through the process using Works for Windows 95.

After collecting facts, quotes, and details about the biographical subject, start Microsoft Works, choose Resume from the TaskWizards list (that's what Works calls its automated document makers), and click on the Yes button that appears in the next dialog box.

You then must pick from three types of résumés. Go with Chronological; it makes the most sense for a biography. The next screen lets you select such options as the fonts you want to use, which résumé components the page should include, and how many *jobs* the biography will list.

With the template finally on the screen, you can start entering the information your child collected. Use your imagination and creativity here. For example, the résumé template in Works has places to detail several *jobs*. You can use these to describe the person's notable deeds. (To stay in the résumé spirit, list them in reverse chronological order; in other words, the first item you list should be the last important exploit before the famous person died.)

If you grabbed a photo or an image of the person from a CD-ROM encyclopedia or an online service, you can add that to the résumé, too. We clipped an illustration of Caesar, stuck it under his name, and then centered it on the page for a classy look.

For an even more realistic touch, dress up your biographical resume with an illustration or a photo of your subject.

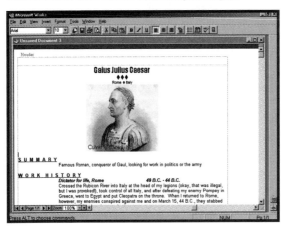

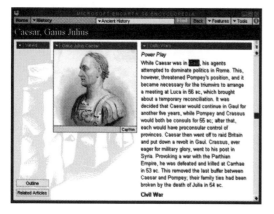 

The hypertext links within most electronic encyclopedias make it easy to research not only a famous person, but also the world in which he or she lived.

statues said to be in his likeness, and more information about his enemies and conquests than we could possibly fit into a five-page report.

America's Civil War

The most painful period in American history gets plenty of attention in school, and for good reason. Not only did casualties during the Civil War exceed those in any other of our many wars, but this was a defining moment — some would say *the* defining moment — in our country's history.

Kids study the Civil War in every level of school — starting sometime in elementary school and usually ending in 11th grade — and your kids can expect related homework several times during their educational careers. By combining the family computer, one or two pieces of software, online information, and a couple of ideas from you, you can hand your kids the keys to a time machine that takes them back — way back

— to the days of Fort Sumter and Appomattox Court House.

In the Shoes of Soldiers

One great way to gain perspective on historical events is by putting yourself in the shoes of people in history, gathering the facts available at the time, and asking yourself what *you* would do. With some CD-ROM software and a connection to the Internet, kids studying the Civil War can do just that, and produce a unique project or report that stands out from the crowd.

For children ages 10 and up, Gettysburg Multimedia Battle Simulation makes a good starting point. This *simulation* — a game that tries to replicate a period in history by letting players make some of the same decisions that the real participants faced — allows your kids to step into the shoes of the actual commanders.

Gettysburg is often mentioned as *the* turning point of the Civil War. Gettysburg Multimedia Battle Simulation lets your kids

★TRY THIS! ★

On the Battlefield

Here are a couple of project ideas for creating history reports that stand out from the crowd.

What If?

Gettysburg Multimedia Battle Simulation can be more than just a computer game. It can also serve as the foundation for a unique, you-were-there report. Here's how.

Choose the free play option in Gettysburg Multimedia Battle Simulation. As each day of the three-day battle begins, take one or more screen shots of the battlefield (which shows the positions of the two armies). After taking each screen shot, open a new page in your paint or draw program and then use the Paste command to copy the image from the Windows Clipboard. Save each screen shot as a separate file, using names such as DAY1, DAY2 and so on.

GET SMART: To take a screen shot in Windows (or Windows 95), press the Alt and Print Screen keys simultaneously (this captures the currently active window) or just the Print Screen key (this captures the entire screen).

At the end of the third day, take one or more shots of the field to illustrate the armies' final after-battle positions. (You can snap additional screens to document crucial moments in the battle.)

As the battle commences and contin-ues, take notes about your decisions (for example, why did you attack where you did?), the casualties inflicted, and what the computer-controlled general on the other side did in response. Use these notes and a word processor to produce a running commentary about this What-If? version of the Battle of Gettysburg. Young generals may end up with only a short paragraph, while older commanders might generate a page or more.

To produce the report, print each screen shot, print the word-processor document containing the commentary, and after alternating the pages — screen shot of the first day, commentary of the first day's fight, screen shot of the second day, and so on — staple them together.

By combining a map copied from an electronic atlas with an art program, your kids can create custom maps tailor-made for their reports or projects.

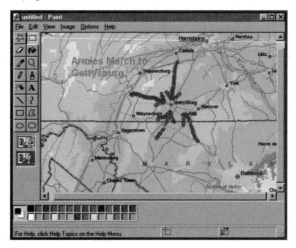

Making Battlefield Maps

If your home learning library includes a digital atlas, your child can easily enhance a more traditional report. Mapmaking, a task often assigned as homework, can be accomplished in less time on the computer than with colored pencils and paper. (Check with the teacher to make sure this is acceptable.)

With an atlas such as Microsoft Encarta World Atlas 96 or the maps found in the family's electronic encyclopedia, you can choose the scale of the map. For maps that illustrate entire campaigns, pull back so that you see several states on the screen; for maps of individual battles, however, you should zoom in tight.

Copy the map and then paste it into a new file you create in an art program. Using the art program, add arrows to show the movement of armies, or color the states to show which were for the Union and which were within the Confederacy.

GET SMART: For electronic atlas recommendations and tips on how to use them to create custom maps, check out Chapter 5's "Where Are We?" section.

answer the question: What would *you* have done if you were commanding Union or Confederate troops? This simulation gives you a view of the action from the field. You can choose historical play (which accurately follows the plans of action during the epic, three-day battle) or free play (in which you control the action). In free play mode, you control artillery, troop movements, weaponry, and tactics as the Army of the Potomac battles the Army of Northern Virginia.

As field commander — General Meade for the Union side, General Lee for the Confederacy — you have access to antique-style or realistic terrain maps you can overlay with troops, planned troop movements, and field notes. The game automatically calculates casualties, combat action or

zones, and battle summaries. The on-screen characters are cartoonish, but the simulation provides historically accurate information on the units that participated and the effects of different strategies.

With Gettysburg Multimedia Battle Simulation, you can listen to Lee's surrender speech.

Go Online!

Although the Civil War ended more than 130 years ago, today's technology can make it seem as though it happened only yesterday. To get started, use one of the Web search tools to find Civil War sites. For example, entering the search phrase *Civil War* produces scores of good choices when you use a Web search tool such as Yahoo:

http://www.yahoo.com

To help you explore some of the best Civil War–related Web sites, we collected some addresses you can enter in your online service's Web browser.

The 76th Ohio
Volunteer Infantry
http://www.infinet.com/~lstevens/civwar/
March along the battle trail with the 76th Ohio Volunteer Infantry as it fights in 44 skirmishes and loses 351 soldiers. This site provides a text-heavy, blow-by-blow description of the trials and travails of the 76th, following them from Fort Donelson, Tennessee, in February 1862 to Bentonville, North Carolina, in March 1865.

The Valley of the Shadow: Living in the Civil War in Pennsylvania and Virginia
http://jefferson.village.virginia.edu/vshadow/
vshadow.html
For an outstanding, you-were-there view on the Civil War, dig into this huge Web resource, which uses thousands of digitized pages of period newspapers, census returns, and army rosters to illustrate what two towns went through during the conflict. You can even track the wartime activities of individual residents of Chambersburg, Pennsylvania and Staunton, Virginia.

The Gettysburg Address
http://lcweb.loc.gov/exhibits/G.Address/ga.html
Head to the Library of Congress Web site to see digitized images of the actual speech. The original is under glass — and one of the country's most important documents — but your family computer lets you bring it home.

The Letters of Captain Richard W. Burt
http://www.infinet.com/~lstevens/burt/
Get a perspective on life in the field by reading the letters of Captain Richard W. Burt. Find out how Captain Burt received a gunshot wound to the mouth but kept the missile as a memento. You can even read the captain's obituary as it was printed in the Coshocton (Ohio) *Age*, the paper he edited after the war.

The Civil War Home Page
http://funnelweb.utcc.utk.edu/~hoemann/cwarhp.html
Find links to hundreds of other Civil War–related Web sites, ranging from specific battles and unit rosters to personal accounts and picture files containing photos from the Library of Congress.

The Gettysburg Multimedia Battle Simulation CD-ROM also provides plenty of background on the momentous battle, including clips from a documentary film, Lincoln's Gettysburg Address, and Lee's less-famous address to Confederate troops. Your young history scholars can also get reference information on the strategic situation, Civil War weaponry, and news updates of the battle.

Go West!

Another period in American history studied extensively in schools — and in related homework assignments — is the Wild West. Not the version that Hollywood and television portray, but the years during the 1800s when hundreds, then thousands, then millions went west. The fascinating story of America's expansion — and the price paid by emigrants and Native Americans alike — demands attention from school children of all ages.

To provide a touch of reality and a clearer perspective on the period, point your children toward the home computer. It wasn't around when Wyatt Earp ruled Tombstone, but with the right software it *can* put your kids on the scene.

Events in Oregon Trail II force young simulation players to make decisions just like the real pioneers.

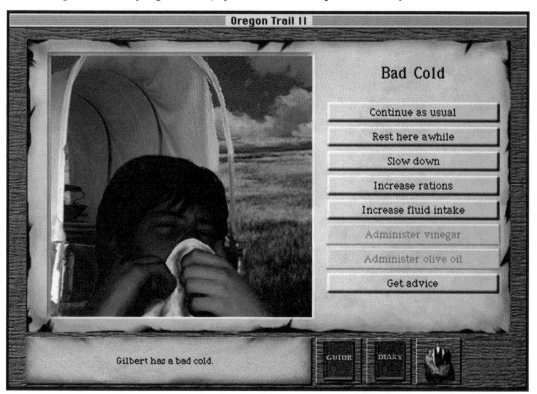

★ TRY THIS! ★

Take the Personal Approach

We have a couple of project ideas that bring a personal touch to reports about the Old West.

The Trials and Tribulations of Emily the Emigrant

Kids take to Oregon Trail II faster than the snow flies in the Sierra Nevadas during December (just ask the Donner Party!). But this simulation is fit for homework duties, too. The program includes a diary, which automatically adds highlights of each day's travels. The program also lets you record your own observations in the diary.

Many people who traveled the Trail kept a journal; your kids can duplicate the process, recording their pretend trip across the country. They should click on the Diary icon frequently. Encourage them to use their imagination and creativity when writing entries in the diary. They should try to stay in character (here's a hint: if they do not use contractions, the entries will sound a bit *stiff*, like the writing of the period).

They should be inventive, too. When the digital travelers consume food, your kids can write about what the food tastes like. They should try to record feelings they think a real pioneer would have. If it rains for several days in a row, wouldn't she complain or remark about how her shoes always feel heavy in the mud?

After they complete the simulation (even if they don't *survive* the trip), tell them to choose Export Diary from the File menu and then save the resulting text file on a floppy disk or the hard disk. For a handwritten look, open the text file with a word processor, select the entire document, and then change the font to a script style. To make the journal appear even more authentic, add some hand-drawn illustrations (use pencil; the folks crossing the Great Plains probably didn't have colored pens).

Although Oregon Trail II automatically keeps a diary, your child can add his own comments to turn the diary into a suitable report.

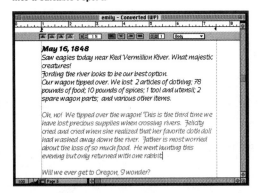

Pairs and Partners in the West

Why pack your kids brains with just facts and figures about the West when you can show them how history involves so much more? This creative project combines our recommended get-personal approach to the subject with a bit of biographical expertise. (For more information on biographical research, take a look at "Famous Faces," earlier in this chapter.) The idea is simple: find a pair of people from the Old West who have something in common and then use an electronic encyclopedia and perhaps some online reference time to create a compare-and-contrast-style report.

To help you get them going, here are four interesting pairings from the period:

- George Custer and Crazy Horse — opponents at the Battle of the Little Bighorn.

- Geronimo and Chief Joseph — two notable Native American leaders.

- Jesse James and Wyatt Earp — a bad guy and a good guy, but which was which?

- Davy Crockett and Santa Anna — one lived and one died at the Alamo.

Your kids can use the family's digital encyclopedia to research each person in the pair. (Encarta 96 has good-sized write-ups on all the examples in the preceding list.) They should try to uncover similarities and striking differences in the background, character, and exploits of each person.

A multicolumn layout works well for presenting the

Head-to-head comparisons of citizens of the American West can quickly illustrate how they were connected in real life.

information, regardless of whether the report compares or contrasts the two people. In your word processor, create a three-column document, with the subject's names (and, if possible, illustrations or photos copied from the encyclopedia) at the top of the middle and rightmost columns.

Use the leftmost column for headings, such as *Born* or *Most Famous For....* Then enter appropriate facts or descriptions in the next two columns so, anyone reading the report can easily compare the two people.

Two Views West

By equipping the family's computer with a pair of software packages, you can give your children a virtual view from two perspectives: through the eyes of emigrants looking for land, and from the standpoint of the Native Americans whose land was taken. These packages provide an eye-opening experience for everyone and set the stage for a pair of intriguing homework projects.

Oregon Trail II

What was it like to be part of America's move westward? When you launch Oregon Trail II, you — and your kids — will find out firsthand. In this decision-intensive simulation (which teachers often use in classrooms, asking kids to work cooperatively in teams), you choose your starting point and destination, set the level of difficulty from greenhorn to trail guide, and then set off in a digital wagon heading west.

Once you decide who you are, where you're headed, and who's going along, you need to load up on supplies. Be sure to check the Guidebook for helpful hints and tips. For example, avoid the Conestoga wagons (they're quaint enough for use in cities on the East Coast, but too heavy for the journey west). And, if you're headed for the Willamette Valley of Oregon or the Great Salt Lake Valley, buy oxen instead of horses.

Your kids can even pick up some interesting trivia. For example, lots of families heading west during this period brought along a couple of cats. Why? The novelty of cats in frontier towns drove up their value (you could sometimes trade a kitten for a horse). The software monitors the weather,

Go Online!

Kids can return to the days when the West was young by going online. This pair of World Wide Web sites takes you on a you-were-there journey to the California gold fields and gives you a huge amount of information about the Oregon Trail.

Diary of a Prospector

http://uts.cc.utexas.edu/
scring/index.html

For a personal, firsthand account of a trip from New York to California during the Gold Rush of 1849, read the memoirs of miner/ adventurer Eugene Ring (1827–1912). He describes everything from bar fights to bears and cholera.

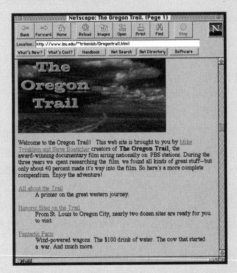

This Oregon Trail Web page may not look like much, but it's one of the most information-packed history sites we've seen.

The Oregon Trail

http://www.isu.edu/~trinmich/
Oregontrail.html

After three years of research, the makers of the award-winning PBS documentary "The Oregon Trail" had so much material that they could squeeze only about 40 percent into the film. This Web site has the leftovers (what leftovers!) and more.

You can follow the real route, read fantastic pioneering facts (such as the hare-brained idea of using balloons instead of wagons to get people west!), and view a list of supporting materials, including a free study guide originally created for teachers. This superb guide has a basic vocabulary list and tons of activities. If your kids are studying this period of American history, make sure they visit this fascinating Web site.

your supplies, and the health and morale of your party as you attempt to handle the daily hardships of pioneer life.

500 Nations

Many people seem to forget that long before the colonists ever arrived, America was a continent of Native American nations. Microsoft's 500 Nations tells about America's indigenous people, presenting information in four different categories: Timeline, Storytellers, Homelands, and Pathfinders.

The CD, narrated by Kevin Costner (of *Dances with Wolves* fame), breathes life into the history of these people with a combination of tours of ancient cities and civilizations, interviews with Native American descendants, and galleries of artwork. You and your kids can visit Mayan and Anasazi cities and villages, go inside longhouses, read historical accounts of encounters between Europeans and Native Americans, and listen to storytellers who offer a variety of different tribal perspectives on a wide range of events, such as the tragedy at Wounded Knee. For example, you can listen to Tall Oak, a Narragansett storyteller, as he gives the Native American perspective on cultural change through history.

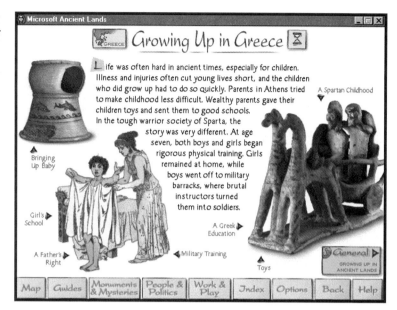

Ancient Lands' colorful interface leads kids on a free-form exploration of how everyday people lived long ago.

Ancient History

Not all history homework involves the United States. Most schools cover world history, too.

One area within that subject that gets lots of attention is ancient history. Exploring how people lived long ago fascinates kids and teachers alike. With some help from the family computer, you can foster that fascination and help your children dream up a new way to present the information they find.

Software That Takes You Way Back

CD-ROM software that can take kids back to the beginnings of recorded history — and then transport them back toward modern times — isn't exactly a growth industry.

Rule and Conquer

CD-ROMs such as Ancient Lands and How Would You Survive? let kids see history through the eyes of individuals, but other programs can give kids a much broader perspective on life in days gone by. In fact, we've found a pair of simulations that let kids take control of entire cultures or exploratory expeditions.

Sid Meier's Civilization

Although it's several years old, Sid Meier's Civilization still gets high marks as an entertaining — and somewhat educational — historical simulation. You take charge of a small tribe of people and try to grow the tribe into a full-blown technological civilization of the 20th century. Like real life, much of this simulation involves warfare, for you must build armies and navies to keep barbarians and other civilizations from destroying your culture. Persevere, and you gradually acquire enough of a technological edge to bring your people into modern times.

Conquest of the New World

Conquest of the New World focuses on the era when Europeans rushed into the Americas. Equipped with ships, settlers, traders, and soldiers, your expedition explores the unknown (the simulation randomly creates a new *world* for each game, so the geography you explore and the dangers you encounter are as unknown to you as the New World was to the explorers of the 15th and 16th centuries).

You can choose from several game styles — for example, concentrating on trading rather than fighting — as well as play the part of explorers from England, France, Spain, Holland, or Portugal, or the Native Americans. And because Conquest is a multiplayer game, you can try your hand against as many as five other explorers by using your modem.

Conquest of the New World sends you and your kids back in time to the days when Europeans explored and exploited the Americas, letting as many as six players venture into new and uncharted lands.

However, a few specialized programs do exist. We found a pair that play well in the home, provide a smattering of hard information, and, most of all, get kids involved, because they approach the subject from a you-were-there angle. Both are good choices for kids in grades 4 through 8.

Microsoft Ancient Lands

Using Microsoft Ancient Lands, an interactive encyclopedia about Greece, Rome, and Egypt (with a bit of additional information here and there about other ancient civilizations in Persia and Central America), you and your kids can delve into the long-ago past. With nearly 1,000 articles — many of them connected by hypertext links — packed with color illustrations and hours of narration and sound, this program describes everyday life way back when. Your children can explore each of the three civilizations on their own or follow any of several guides who walk them through the articles. And the program's picture gallery lets your kids copy illustrations to other documents (perfect for reports) or send them to the printer.

★ TRY THIS! ★

A Day in the Life

Thanks to the CDs and on-line resources we describe in this chapter, your kids have a good idea how people lived during ancient times. Now what?

To show their grasp of the subject, they can re-create a typical day in the life of someone who lived during ancient times. But rather than just slap together a written report, why not put it into a more modern format, such as a daily schedule?

Start your word processor and open a new document. Down the left side of the page, enter the hours of the day in one-hour increments. Place the

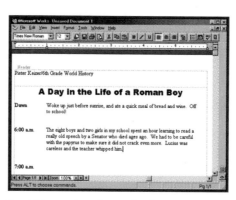

Your kids can show the teacher how much they've learned by creating an hour-by-hour schedule for a hypothetical person from the past.

cursor beside each hour label, press the Tab key once or twice to move the cursor to the right, and then have your child type a short description of what he (that is, the person he's playing) would do during that block of time.

The project will go smoother if your child puts himself in the shoes of someone with a specific occupation, someone from a defined class, or a child his own age from the period. If he assumes the role of a farmer, for example, his day will differ quite a bit from that of the son of a Roman senator.

Go Online!

The World Wide Web can take your kids back to ancient times (long before the invention of the home computer, anyway).

Much of what you'll find by searching the Web for ancient history is better suited to professional historians or college students, but a few sites include colorful kid-appropriate information. We found a trio of terrific Web resources about times long, long ago.

Quick. Can you name the Seven Wonders of the Ancient World? This Web page describes all seven in detail.

Web site. Illustrations show artists' representations of the Wonders (only one, the Great Pyramid of Giza, still stands), a map pinpoints their locations, and descriptions and a brief history of each are provided. Heavily hotlinked so you can explore related topics, this place makes a superb resource for young researchers.

The Ancient World Web

http://atlantic.evsc.virginia.edu/julia/AncientWorld.html

Anyone exploring the Web's ancient history resources should stop here first. With hundreds of sites listed by subject or geographical location, this mega index lets kids easily find Internet resources on everything from ancient Roman recipes to a virtual tour of the Acropolis.

GET SMART: *The Seven Wonders of the Ancient World Web site is so solid that it can serve as the foundation for a top-notch school report.*

The Seven Wonders of the Ancient World

http://pharos.bu.edu/Egypt/Wonders/

A cultural touchstone even today (and, if nothing else, one of the oldest Top Ten–style lists), the Seven Wonders of the Ancient World are described in great detail on this

The Legacy of the Horse

http://www.horseworld.com/imh/kyhpl1a.html

If your child wants to tackle the Try This! project, "Time Line Tango," in this section, send her to this virtual exhibit sponsored by the International Museum of the Horse (there really is such a place!), where she'll find information about how the horse was domesticated, where stirrups originated, and what a day at the track (at Rome's Circus Maximus) was like.

How Would You Survive?

How Would You Survive? let's kids step into the shoes of ancient Egyptians, Vikings, and Aztecs and learn how these people played, what they ate, how they dressed, and how they communicated, all in an active, you-were-there style filled with animation, illustrations, and sound effects. A *survival guide* for each culture includes facts, a map, and a time line to help kids live in the past, and a quiz at the end of the trip tests their newfound knowledge.

★ TRY THIS! ★

Time Line Tango

History isn't just it-happened-once events; it's also about how things change over time. How has the automobile changed? How has it affected the way people work and live? Which objects and ideas have links to the past that we take for granted?

Pick an object and trace it back through time. Most almanacs have lists of inventions and discoveries, and CD-ROM encyclopedias have interactive time lines. Does your child love race cars? Some of the jazziest ever made were from Edison's time. What's the history of bridges, or horses, or money? Remember, you don't need to choose something dramatic or important.

With the research done, your child can create a time line by using a draw or paint program. Open a blank page in the program, and before drawing the line, change the page orientation to Landscape; this lets your young historian fit more time line on one sheet.

Now draw a thick, black line across the middle of the screen.

Using the text tool, your child can enter dates along the line to match the entries. To keep from crowding the time line itself, your child place the descriptive text above and below the line and then use thinner lines to point to the appropriate place on the time line. Place a picture or two — either drawn by your child or grabbed from a clip-art collection, a CD-ROM reference, or an online resource — in strategic positions. Finally, add a title at the top of the page.

Time lines can be used to outline the life of a famous figure.

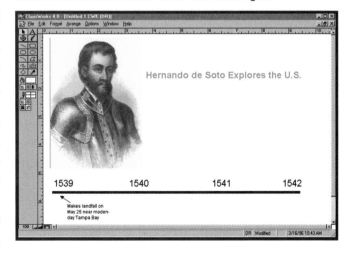

Chapter 7

Wading into the Information Pool

Doing Research with the Home Computer

RESEARCH ISN'T JUST FOR SCIENTISTS LOOKing for a breakthrough or political pollsters aiming for an angle. It's also one of the most important pieces of the schoolwork puzzle.

Without research — even the most elementary research — information is just so many nouns and verbs and numbers. To know something, especially something new, you have to find it. And finding information is what research is all about. In other words, if you skip research, you waste valuable opportunities for learning.

If your home computer doesn't do anything else during its campaign to become a homework helper, it

should serve as the family's information pipeline. Even if you toss out all the drill-and-practice software and the creativity programs that let kids build while they learn, as long as the family computer brings information into the house, it's an amazing tool that pays immediate dividends.

When connected to the outside world with a modem (for more details on modems and connections to online services and the Internet, see Chapter 2, "The Bare Necessities") or when equipped with CD-ROM reference tools, the home computer brings libraries into your house. And it happens instantly.

The information pool is deep — kids

can drown in it if you don't teach them how to swim the data stream — but this chapter shows you how to show them how to research almost anything.

The Searchers

If your kids can't find the laundry basket, how can you expect them to find an account of Amelia Earhart? Or the reason why fish have fins?

The information pool may be a bit like a digital library, but the way you search through each is as different as an abacus is from an electronic calculator. Even though your children know their way around a library, they may know next to nothing about how to do research on a PC or a Mac.

Fortunately, all digital resources — online services, the Internet, and reference CD-ROMs such as electronic encyclopedias — share the same basic search techniques. Learn them and you'll be able to dive right into the information pool.

Words Are the Key

The key to electronic research isn't using an index or looking for a title or an author, as you do in a paper-packed library. Instead, you use *keyword searches.*

Keyword searches are really quite simple. You enter a word, and the program or the electronic service looks through all its text, searching for that word. When it finds an article that in-

cludes the word, it tags the article. Each time the program or service successfully finds your keyword, it's called a *hit* (this jargon is left over from database searches, the root of all electronic search tools). At the end of the search, each article is posted, usually in a list. Click on the name of one of the listed articles — or, in the case of an online service or the Internet, one of the service areas or a Web page — and it pops up on your screen. If the program or service is smart, it displays the first place in the article where your keyword appears.

Here's an example showing how it works. Suppose your daughter wants to know about weather, particularly tornadoes and whether they're somehow related to thunderstorms. She puts Microsoft Encarta 96 in the CD-ROM drive and clicks on the Find button, which makes the program display the Find

To narrow the list of articles, use more than one word during a keyword search, as we do here in Microsoft Encarta.

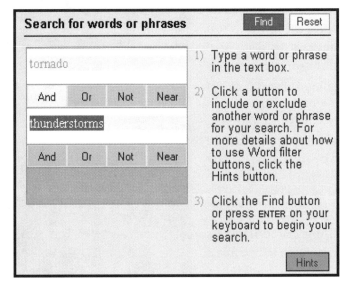

box. To begin the keyword search, she clicks on the Word button, types **tornado**, clicks on the Search button, and waits for the program to post a list of all the articles in which that word appears. When the search is completed, she can click on the title of any article in the list.

GET SMART: *The names of search tools vary from program to program, but they're usually labeled* Find.

Some Slick Search Tips

• Watch your spelling! If you type *dogg* instead of *dog*, for example, you probably won't find what you want.

• Abbreviations may or may not work as keywords. Use a Boolean OR search to look for either the abbreviation or the complete word or phrase. For example, depending on the reference CD or online service, you could use a Boolean OR search with the keywords *NASA* and *National Aeronautics and Space Administration.*

• If you're researching online, create a list of keywords before the kids dial the phone. Not only will that force your children to think about what they want, it should trim time spent online and save you money.

You aren't limited to looking for information using just one keyword at a time. In fact, encourage your children to research by using several keywords in combination. For example, if your daughter uses both *tornado* and *thunderstorms* in her search, only those articles containing both words will appear in the hit list.

In some programs, you may see a reference to a *Boolean search*. No, that's not some alien race from a *Star Trek* episode. It's another database search term, used to describe even more flexible searches. Whether they use the term or not, most programs support Boolean searches. The simplest is an AND search. Surprise! The search for articles containing the keywords tornado and thunderstorms is an AND search. Only those articles that include both words — thus the AND — meet your requirements and are

considered hits. The second most common Boolean search is an *OR search*. That means an article is a hit if it includes either of the two keywords.

GET SMART: *You'll get more hits if you use separate keywords, rather than a phrase. For example, use* fish *and* tropical *rather than* tropical fish. *In some cases, however, using a phrase may cut the list of hits to a more manageable length.*

Depending on the program or service you're using, you may have to enter punctuation marks or special characters — most often, a comma or a space — to separate two words in a Boolean search. To find out the proper punctuation for keyword searches, read the documentation or the help file.

MICROSOFT ENCARTA Intro Edition

▼ Science & Technology   ▼ Earth Science   Find   Go Back ▼ Views ▼ Tools

Cyclone

▼ PINPOINTER   Close

10 Articles   Reset

Wind
Kansas
Lightning
Manitoba
Nebraska
Ohio
Saskatchewan
West Virginia
Whirlwind
Wind
Wisconsin

10

Related Articles

Cyclone, in strict meteorological terminology, an area of low atmospheric pressure surrounded by a wind system blowing, in the northern hemisphere, in a counterclockwise direction. A corresponding high-pressure area with clockwise winds is known as an anticyclone. In the southern hemisphere these wind directions are reversed. Cyclones are commonly called lows and anticyclones highs. The term *cyclone* has often been more loosely applied to a storm and disturbance attending such pressure systems, particularly the violent tropical hurricane and the typhoon, which center on areas of unusually low pressure.

Clicking on hypertext — for example, the word *Cyclone* in the "Wind" article — shoots you right to related information.

Hypertext Isn't Just Hype

The research job isn't finished once you have a list of hits. Not in the information pool.

Most electronic reference works and virtually all the pages presented on the World Wide Web use *hypertext* to cross-reference information. This hypertext, which is usually marked with a different color, is like a fork in the road. When you click on a hypertext word, you're immediately taken to additional, but related, information. It's a bit like browsing, but with a guide to take you straight to something else connected with the original article.

For example, after searching in Encarta for *tornado* and *thunderstorms*, your daughter might select the article about Wind. This article contains several color-coded hypertext connections. When she clicks on *Cy-*

clone, Encarta takes her right to that article.

But this straight-to-the-source guidance isn't the best thing about hypertext. The most useful aspect of hypertext is the serendipitous way it presents information. When children are researching, they don't always know exactly what they want. Hypertext can lead them to an entirely unexpected piece of information — one they wouldn't have thought to look for on their own. For example, after clicking on Cyclone in Encarta, your daughter will find out that this isn't another word for tornado, as she might have thought, but that it more accurately describes hurricanes or typhoons.

Neat, huh?

Saving What You Find

When you uncover information in a real library, you grab a notebook and a pen or head to the photocopy machine. In the digital information pool, collecting and storing information is even easier.

You still copy the information, but you do so using the program's Copy and Paste commands. Every Windows, Windows 95, and Macintosh program — including the online service interfaces and the Web browser you use to surf the Internet — has a Copy command in its Edit menu. To copy text, click at the beginning of the section you'd like to copy, drag the cursor to the end of the section, and choose Copy from the Edit menu. You can usually copy an image by simply clicking on it and then choosing the Copy command.

GET SMART: *The Macintosh offers something called the Scrapbook, which you find in the Apple menu. You can paste several pieces of text or graphics into the Scrapbook, where they remain until you delete them. Unfortunately, PCs running Windows or Windows 95 don't include this kind of electronic notebook. They use the Clipboard, which can hold only one piece of text or one image at a time; when you copy another object, Windows erases the previous contents of the Clipboard.*

Next, open a word-processing document (you can paste the copied information into another type of document, but a word-processing file is the easiest). Position the cursor on the page and choose the Paste command from the Edit menu. The word processor places the copied text or graphic on the page. Save the word-processing document. Later, when you want to view or use the information you've gathered, just open this document. Of course, you can also copy material from this document and paste it into others.

GET SMART: *If you paste a lot of text in a document, choose the word processor's Find command (usually, it's in the Edit menu, too), enter an appropriate keyword, and press Enter or Return. The cursor jumps to the first instance of that word in your document.*

Using Online Services for Research

Using an online service — for example, America Online, Prodigy, The Microsoft Network, or CompuServe — is the quickest way to turn your home computer into a personal reference desk that can meet your kids' research needs. Because the Internet lacks a stable organization, and electronic encyclopedias can't continually stay current, an online service is an essential part of your family's home learning center.

But what kind of homework help can you and your kids expect from an online service? And how well do these services function as research centers?

Admirably, we think. By dialing into online services, your kids can find more than enough information for almost any school

---

Your daughter's tornadoes-and-thunderstorms search might lead her to this article about Kansas. Instead of taking notes, she can just copy the text and paste it into a word-processing document.

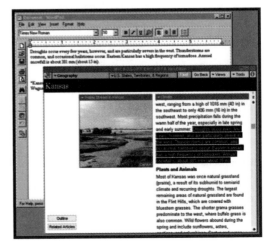

or home project. Your children can find vast amounts of information and reference materials online, including pictures, newspapers, magazines, encyclopedias, atlases, museums, and mountains of reference material from the federal government. And as a bonus, kids learn an important skill for the future when they go online: the ability to use electronic information sources as tools for solving problems.

Homework Helper

Although you and your child can find homework help in many places, the single best place in all of online-service cyberspace is Prodigy's Homework Helper (jump **Homework**) and the Internet's Electric Library:

http://www.elibrary.com/

Although the name changes depending on where you access the information, Homework Helper and the Electric Library are essentially the same. This remarkable compilation of resource material includes information from daily newspapers, radio and television transcripts, books, encyclopedias, maps, and atlases. Better still, it's easy to use. In most cases, your child simply types a question in plain English and then waits for the answer (lots of answers, in fact). Homework Helper/Electric Library is a great resource for children 10 years old and up, though younger children will need help using it.

Homework Helper/Electric Library offers six general sources of information: newspapers, maps, pictures, magazines, books, and television and radio transcripts. It con-

Prodigy's Homework Helper, a huge online library, is the single best place for kids 10 and up to do digital research.

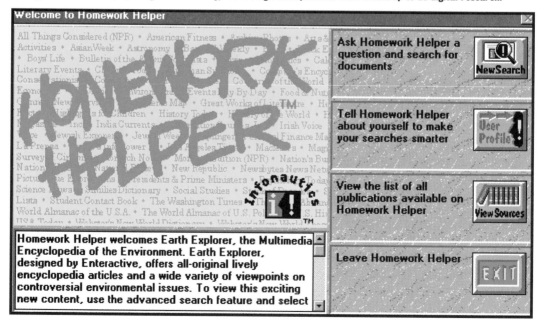

tains information from more than 3,000 books, 800 magazines, and 150 newspapers and journals, along with more than 21,000 photos and maps and transcripts from television and radio shows, including National Public Radio news programs. Newspapers range from major national journals such as *USA Today* to international ones such as *La Prensa* and specialized newspapers such as *Black Enterprise*. Similarly, magazines range from general-interest publications such as *Harper's Magazine* to specialized ones such as *Technology Review* and children's magazines such as *Boy's Life*.

Searching for information is simple. Your child types a

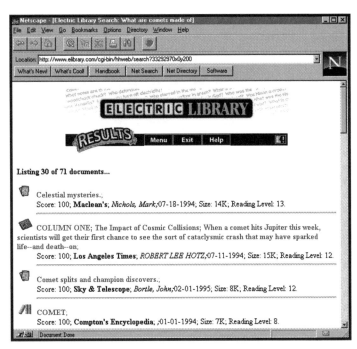

Kids search Electric Library using plain-English questions — for example, "What are comets made of?" — and in return receive a huge list of articles. Double-clicking on any article downloads it to your computer, where you can view it, copy it, or print it.

question using the same language she would use if she were to ask her teacher that question. Homework Helper/ Electric Library automatically extracts only the vital information — at least in theory. In practice, it often needs some help in narrowing searches so that it returns manageable amounts of information. If you get extremely large hit lists, limit the search to maps or photos or even to magazines or newspapers. Or further refine your search by turning on or off general subject categories such as literature, science and technology, or history.

After your child enters a question, Homework Helper/Electric Library returns a list of helpful documents, along with a relevancy score that shows how well each document fits the search criteria. It also identifies the source, the size of the document (which is important, because the larger the document, the longer it takes for the generally slow Prodigy network to download), the publication date, and, most important, the grade level for which the information is written. Your child browses through the list of documents and then double-clicks on any that he or she wants to read. The document is sent to your computer, where your child can print all or part of it or save parts of it to a file. It's that simple.

Homework Helper/ Electric Library is also a great source of pictures for spicing up reports. We entered the word *comet* and found six pictures, including one picture of Halley's Comet that made a dandy addition to our science report.

Homework Helper's built-in dictionary and thesaurus are easy to use and useful in a pinch. You can also do multiple searches at the same time, reading the results of one search while another runs in the background; this saves you

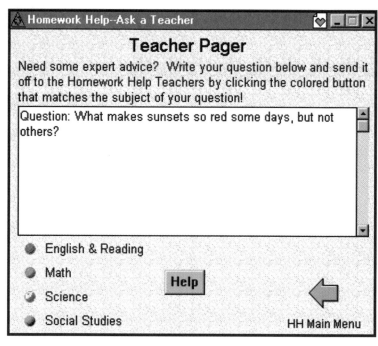

With the Teacher Pager on America Online, children can ask teachers questions, and they actually get answers.

research and online time (and online money).

Homework Helper comes at a price: $9.95 per month in addition to Prodigy's normal monthly fee of $9.95. The $9.95 Homework Helper fee gets you 50 hours of use. If you exceed 50 hours, you pay $2.95 for each additional hour. For those without a Prodigy membership, going directly to Homework Helper costs a bit more: $11.95 per month for 50 hours. The Electric Library's prices are similar — $9.95 per month, above and beyond what you pay to access the Internet from home.

Homework Help on America Online

If you don't want to pay the additional charges for Prodigy's Homework Helper or the Internet-based Electric Library, then America Online is the best overall place for your kids to get help with schoolwork. In *FamilyPC*'s most recent family-based tests, America Online got an A grade as a homework helper.

For fast access to homework aids on AOL, just use the keyword **Homework Help** and then click on either Homework Help for Kids, Homework Help for Teens, or Academic Assistance Center. If you click on the button for either Homework Help for Kids or Homework Help for Teens, AOL lists the following options:

- Look It Up (reference)

- Ask a Teacher (one-on-one academic assistance)

- Discuss It (academic-assistance classrooms)

- Explore (other reference material)

The most helpful option is the Teacher Pager, which pops up when your child clicks on the Ask a Teacher button. With the Teacher Pager, your child can fill out a form, asking a question and picking a subject area of expertise. What happens next is as close to an electronic personal tutor as you can get: A teacher responds with either an invitation to a live chat or an e-mail message containing the answer to your child's question. This is one of the more remarkable and useful ways in which your child can receive help, and it's more personal than any other place you'll find online.

Your child can also get live help from an educator by choosing Discuss It. This chat area offers regularly scheduled tutorials and lessons on a wide range of academic subjects. In order to find out the best time to go online for homework help, you and your kids should check the weekly schedule that you'll find posted here.

GET SMART: *The keyword **AAC** takes you to America Online's Academic Assistance Center, where all the school resources of the service are collected in one easy-to-find spot.*

The Reference Desk (keyword **Reference**) provides links to sites within America Online that offer help on everything from politics to the environment, as well as encyclopedias and other reference tools. Basically, it places a huge reference library at your fingertips. You can even get to America Online's Web browser from here (click on the icon for Internet reference sites). America Online has done a superb job of collecting top sites on the Internet that can help with your child's homework.

Older children who need help with book reports should head to Barron's Booknotes (keyword **Barrons**), which has the familiar study notes and guides to dozens of books, from the *Aeneid* to *Wuthering Heights*. Your child can read the guides online or download them and read them using a word proces-

The Reference Desk on AOL is another good spot for research work. Here, kids can connect to various research tools, including an encyclopedia, a dictionary, and the Internet.

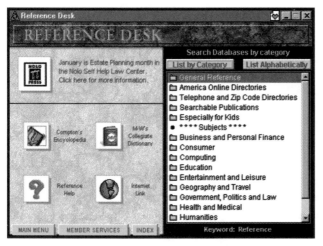

sor. And the online version of *Scientific American* (keyword **Scientific American**) is a good place for finding science-related material.

If your child's homework has anything to do with environmental matters, the Environmental Forum (keyword **EForum**) is worth a visit. Most useful is the Search the News Wires area, which finds articles your child wants on any subject having to do with the environment. For information about the White House and the government in general, the White House Forum (keyword **White House**) has press releases, memos, and information on the presidency and the federal government. Your kids can even drop a letter to the president while they're visiting this area.

Online Homework Help Elsewhere

Other online services such as CompuServe and The Microsoft Network aren't as school-oriented as Prodigy and AOL and so don't have as much homework help available. If your family currently subscribes to one of these services, we recommend you switch to Prodigy or America Online.

For more general homework help, CompuServe does have a pair of encyclopedias — *Grolier's Academic American Encyclopedia* (go **Groliers**) and the *Hutchinson Encyclopedia* (go **Hutchinson**), which includes pictures you can view online or download and use in reports.

And although The Microsoft Network is still a half-empty place, the online version of the Encarta encyclopedia is nearly as useful as the CD-ROM version.

Research on the Internet

You've heard about the Internet — the Net, to those in the know. You can't avoid it, what with the constant barrage of newspaper headlines and magazine articles describing this vast pool of information that spans the globe and contains everything from the Library of Congress to weather forecasts in Finland.

Truth is, the Internet isn't just for grown-ups who use it for business. Kids can use it — at least, the graphical part of it, which is called the *World Wide Web*, or simply the *Web* — to do some incredible, right-to-the-source research.

But if you think the library is a tough place to find facts, wait until you start surfing the Internet. It's a hodgepodge, with information scattered across continents, and no single, centralized index that lists everything. (Frankly, that's not even possible — not with the Web growing by thousands of pages every month.)

As in all electronic research, you can use keyword search techniques and hypertext to root out the right information. But unlike an encyclopedia or an online service, the Internet doesn't have a Find command. Or, then again, does it?

In the following sections, we take you and your children on a brief tour of the Web spots you can use for doing research. We don't show you what's on the Web — that would take a dozen or more books — but we do show you where to go and what to do when you're searching for information on the Web.

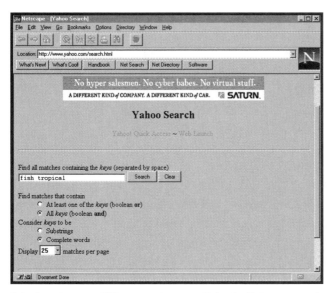

Yahoo's options let children search more efficiently. If they want only the words themselves to count — for example, only *fish*, not *fisheries*, they should click on the Complete words button.

Yahoo!

When you're trying to find the information needle in the Internet haystack, the first place you should head is Yahoo!. The name may sound like a hillbilly yell, but it's just the offbeat title for one of the premier where-is-it? listings on the Web. Yahoo claims that it can locate more than 10 million(!) Web addresses.

You find Yahoo at the following address:

http://www.yahoo.com

Enter that address into your Web browser, and in a moment Yahoo's front page appears, showing categories and subcategories of Web pages and information. You could browse for the category that seems to fit your interests, but that could take days.

Instead, type a keyword (or words) in the Search box and press Enter. Even better, click on Options, and Yahoo displays a more powerful Boolean search tool. Once there, enter the keywords and choose between a Boolean AND or OR search. (Remember, AND means that a Web page must contain both keywords to qualify as a hit, while OR means a hit occurs when a Web page contains either word.) For this example, we use *fish* and *tropical*.

In a moment, Yahoo posts the pages in its directory that match your keywords. We got 12 matches, or hits, on our two-word search.

Hypertext now comes into play. On the Web, hypertext — that is, cross-ref-

Yahoo posts the pages that match your search. From here, you have to decide where to go next — a tough job because Yahoo's descriptions are so short.

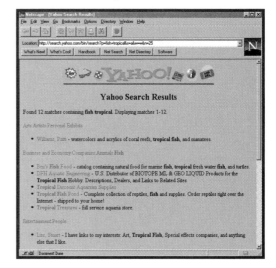

erencing words that take you to other in-formation — are typically called *hotlinks*. Hotlinks are connections to other Web pages, and they appear in most Web pages. That's the great thing about the Web (and a problem, too); you can spend hours zip-ping from one page to another. After brows-ing through our list of a dozen hits, we de-cide to try out **Liss, Stuart**, a personal page that claims to offer lots of hotlinks to trop-ical fish information.

From Stuart Liss's page, we find another hotlink to something called FINS (the Fish Information Service). This sounds like what we want, so we go there. Perfect. This Web site has all kinds of information about trop-ical fish and aquariums and more hotlinks to scientific Web sites dedicated to ocean-ography, fish, marine science, and scores of images of fish we can download.

Open Sesame!

Yahoo is an excellent starting point for searching, but it's not all-encompassing. Al-though its search tools may dig through Web page titles and Yahoo's own descrip-tions, Yahoo won't look at every single word on a site. For example, a child using Yahoo to look for background about the Civil War battle of Gettysburg may miss lots of

---

Yahooligans! Is For Kids

Yahooligans!, a version of Yahoo designed for kids ages 8 to 14, may be a super spot to send your Web-surfing chil-dren, but its search tool isn't as strong as Yahoo's.

You find Yahooligans at this address:

http://www. yahooligans.com

Like Yahoo, Yahooli-gans displays subject categories — Art Soup, School Bell, Science and Oddi-ties, and others — on its front

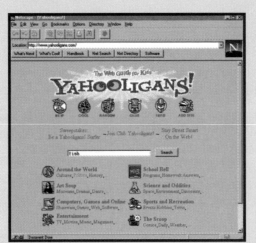

Yahooligans is a searchable index that uses colorful graphics and lists kid-appropriate Web pages.

page and lets you search its di-rectories by entering a keyword.

However, the Yahooli-gans search tool isn't as sophisticated or pow-erful as Yahoo's, and it doesn't search through the entire Yahoo index. (In keeping with its kid-perfect theme, the Ya-hooligans database is limited to sites most ap-propriate for children in its target age range.)

Those caveats aside, Yahooligans is a safe place to send your kids; this handy search en-gine indexes many of the sites and pages we recommend.

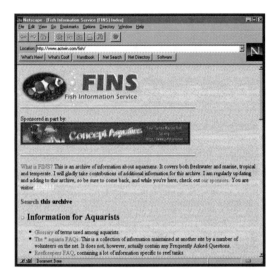

Although the FINS Web page has lots of stuff about tropical fish, it doesn't have to be your last stop on this information-hunting journey. You can continue by clicking on any of the hotlinks at the bottom of the page.

relevant information.

That's why you should also turn to Open-Text, which you find at the following address:

http://www.opentext.com/omw/f-omw. html

OpenText searches through all the words within a Web document or page. If a page contains your keyword *Gettysburg*, OpenText will find it. Like Yahoo, OpenText is a free search service; as long as you have a Net connection, you're set.

To help you harness all that search and research power, OpenText offers three different search techniques: Simple Search, Power Search, and

Weighted Search. You can use one or all to root through the Internet.

Simple Search

Simple Search is much like Yahoo's search tool. You enter one or more keywords and then pick one of the following methods:

- *this exact phrase*. When you use this method, OpenText looks for the entire string of text that you enter.

- *all of these words*. This specifies a Boolean AND search.

- *any of these words*. This specifies a Boolean OR search.

In a moment, OpenText lists the first 10 hits, in descending order of relevance. In other words, the page at the top is the one

OpenText's Simple Search is a perfect pick for younger children doing research on the Internet.

OpenText believes best meets your criteria. Of course, you decide whether that's true.

Power Search

Power Search is more complicated than Simple Search, but once mastered, helps you call up a list of information sources that more exactly matches your needs. This search technique includes several boxes for entering keywords and lets you choose from a wealth of search options that examine specific parts of a Web site, such as its title or the summary. You can also use Power Search to find instances in which one word is near, but not immediately next to, another. OpenText's Power Search is a useful tool for older students who are in middle- and high-school grades.

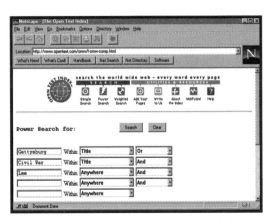

Using Power Search, you can construct a search that examines a broad range of titles — in this case, those including either *Gettysburg* or *Civil War* — but shows only those pages that contain a specified keyword.

Weighted Search

Weighted Search is even more sophisticated than Power Search and takes some practice and forethought to achieve top-notch results. Essentially, you enter keywords, designate where they may appear, and then *weight*, or rank, each keyword. For example, if you want to find Web information about General Lee's part in the Battle of Gettysburg, you might weight the keywords *Lee* as 20 and *Gettysburg* as 10. (The higher the number, the more importance you assign to that keyword.) In most cases, a well-built weighted search returns fewer hits than you would

Other Internet Search Tools

Yahoo and OpenText aren't the only search engines you can use to dig through the digital haystack of the Internet. You can use several others, including

• Lycos
http://www.lycos.com/

This search engine claims to index more than 90 percent of the Web's pages, far more than Yahoo. Despite all those pages in its directory, searches on Lycos are surprisingly fast (sometimes much faster than Yahoo). And its search options, which include Boolean searches, are very flexible.

• Infoseek
http://www.infoseek. com/

Like all the other search engines we recommend, Infoseek is free. And its category organization and search tool are solid. In our experience, however, Infoseek is among the slowest of the available search engines.

obtain from a Simple Search or a Power Search, but those hits usually offer a much closer match with the information you're seeking.

Bookmarks Mark the Spot

The Web may seem like anarchy compared to an organized library, but once you and your homeworking children find the Web sites you need, you can easily return to those sites whenev-

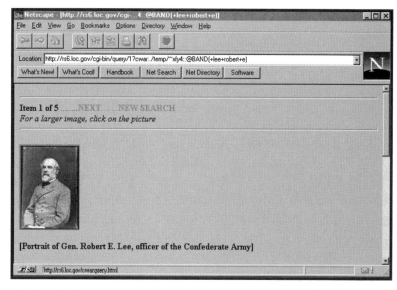

Using OpenText's search tools, we were able to find and download this photograph of General Robert E. Lee in less than 5 minutes. It makes a perfect art addition to our report on the Battle of Gettysburg.

er you want. Using a feature — most often called a *bookmark* — in your Web browser, you can note the Internet address of any page and even file it away in a digital fold-

er. To return to the page, you simply click on the bookmark title. It's like having a personal librarian who always remembers where you can find the good books.

Show your children how to bookmark Web sites they like; it makes Net navigation a lot easier. To keep everyone's favorite sites separate, you should also create personal bookmark folders for each child who uses the Web browser.

Bookmarking a Web page is easy. In Microsoft's Internet Explorer — one of the Web browsers for Windows 95 — you choose the Add to Favorites option from the Favorites menu when you're on the page you want to mark. Of course, you can change the name of the

Remembering Web pages is a snap when you use the browser program's bookmark feature. Internet Explorer calls them Favorites rather than bookmarks, but they perform the same function.

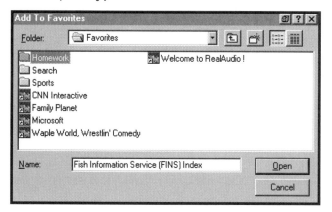

Safe Surfing

You can control where your children go on the Web as well as what kind of material and information they find. You might want to investigate one or more of the parental control programs for Web-surfing families, such as

- Surfwatch (800-458-6600)
  http://www.surfwatch.com

- CyberPatrol (800-489-2001)
  http://www.cyberpatrol.com

- NetNanny (800-340-71770)
  http://www.netnanny.com/netnanny/

These tools use various techniques, from blocking out sites inappropriate for children to restricting access to certain times of the day (perhaps only those hours when a parent is home to monitor the places kids go.)

page or stick it in one of the folders you've created for storing bookmarks.

Digital Encyclopedias for Research

Although online services and the Internet contain mass quantities of school-suitable information, an electronic encyclopedia offers the most cost-effective means for getting your children research-ready. Pay for the CD-ROM — all digital encyclopedias come

on CD-ROMs these days — and you don't have to lay out another dime. (At least, not until next year's update, and then only if you feel the need to stay current.) You don't have to worry about any online charges or Internet-access fees.

Even if your home computer is online and Internet-ready, you should still have an electronic encyclopedia in the house. It's an essential part of any child's learning library, just like a printed encyclopedia was when we were kids. And, researching with an electronic encyclopedia is often easier for kids than searching using the tools available from an online service or the Internet. Built especially for kids, these CD-ROMs feature search and browsing commands that can be called with just a click of the mouse.

If You Get One Encyclopedia, Get Microsoft Encarta 96

Of all the electronic encyclopedias on store shelves, we recommend Microsoft Encarta 96 (the most current version, as this book went to press). Sporting a sophisticated link to online resources, enhanced content, and a refined interface, Encarta remains at the top of its class. In *FamilyPC*'s family-based testing in early 1996, Encarta received the coveted FamilyTested Top Rated seal.

GET SMART: *If you have access to the Web, take a peek at the Teacher's Guide to Encarta 96. You can find the Teacher's Guide at the following address:*

http://www.microsoft.com/k-12/resources/tags /encarta96/default.htm

In addition to Encarta's online connection — which updates the encyclopedia monthly — 300 of the 26,500 articles are brand new, and 3,000 have been updated. Encarta 96 also contains 300 new photos and illustrations, 205 updated and new general maps, nine new urban maps, nine new videos, and two new InterActivities (interactive treatments of such subjects as world languages and nutrition).

Another new feature in Encarta 96 is the Home Screen, which lets you jump to any of the encyclopedia's eight components with a single click. InterActivities now have their own home screen, too. From this screen, you can access the InterActivities as well as two interactive population and climate charts that make their debut in this edition of Encarta.

The new Guided Tours provide an introduction to Encarta's abundance of material by taking you on a journey through 80 subject areas in the encyclopedia, including mysterious monuments, great books, and games from around the world. For example, the Famous Movies tour has

---

Each month, you can update Microsoft Encarta 96 with new material by downloading Yearbook files from The Microsoft Network or the Web. This is the best method we've seen for keeping an electronic encyclopedia current.

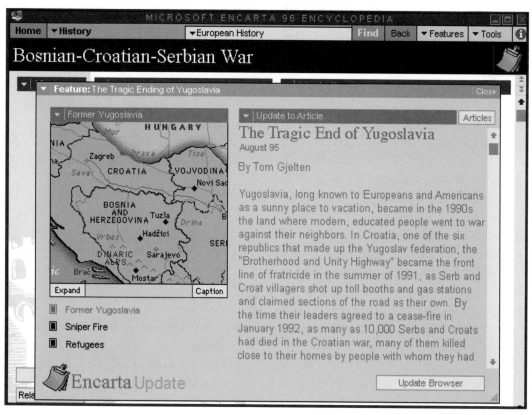

The Pinpointer is the starting place for all your searches of the Encarta 96 encyclopedia.

11 stops, including *The Wizard of Oz*, *Casablanca*, and *Snow White*. You can hop off the tour to explore any avenue that interests you and then hop back on when you want to continue.

The Teacher's Guide includes 40 different learning lessons in subjects ranging from creative writing to architecture. Although the lessons are designed for teachers and the classroom, many can be easily adapted for at-home projects.

In other enhancements, Encarta's improved copying and printing capabilities let you copy or print a whole article or just a section you specify. Footnotes are inserted automatically into reports you create with most Windows-based word-processing programs. And, for quick access to articles you frequently use, you can now create shortcuts and place them on your desktop.

But Encarta's unique Pinpointer, the encyclopedia's nifty search system, is what

Research Can Be Fun

Want to help your kids get familiar with Encarta's Pinpointer? Have them take a crack at this find-the-fact game using the encyclopedia.

Separated at birth

What do these people have in common? Use Encarta 96 (we turned to the online version on The Microsoft Network) to find out.

1. Richard Henry Lee and Thomas Jefferson
2. Amelia Earhart and Wiley Post
3. Shaka and Cetewayo
4. Yury A. Gagarin and Valentina Tereshkova
5. Ty Cobb and Honus Wagner

Answers

1. Both signed the Declaration of Independence.
2. Both were famous aviators who died in plane crashes.
3. Both were famous chiefs of the Zulu people in Africa.
4. The first man and woman, respectively, to orbit the earth.
5. Both were famous baseball players elected to the Baseball Hall of Fame in 1936.

makes this CD-ROM such a super research tool for schoolwork. Kids can search by word, category, media, time, and place.

Search and Ye Shall Find

To use Encarta 96 for at-home research, kids take charge of the encyclopedia's Pinpointer. Using keywords and then branching off with the encyclopedia's hypertext links (those two basic facts of digital research life, again), even early-elementary-school-aged children can easily master the Pinpointer.

To call up the Pinpointer, click on the Find button at the top of the Encarta 96 window (you can also access it from the CD-ROM's Home Screen). At the left, you see a list of found articles. A row of buttons on the right lets you conduct different kinds of searches.

Want the simplest type of search? Click on Word Search, enter your keyword in the topmost blank (below the phrase *Find all the articles that contain the word*), and click on the Search button. The list at the left changes to show all the articles in Encarta with that word. For example, using Pinpointer's single-word search tool with the keyword *Mars*,

To find exactly what you're looking for, filter the list of articles by using any or all of the search buttons.

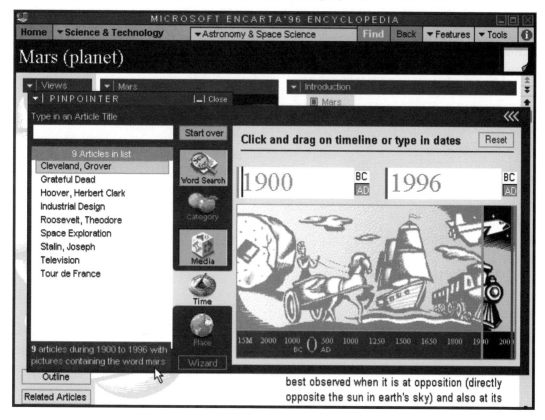

best observed when it is at opposition (directly opposite the sun in earth's sky) and also at its

we found more than 100 articles.

To narrow the search, use the search tool labeled *Find all the articles that include the words.* Although Encarta 96 doesn't call this search a Boolean AND, that's what it is. You usually see a much shorter hit list of articles on the left when you use this tool; we found only four articles when we used *Mars* and *NASA* in our sample search.

Pinpointer's most sophisticated search method combines the Word Search with the other buttons: Category, Media, Time, and Place. You can select different content categories in Encarta 96, pick a medium such as Pictures, define a range of years, and narrow it all down to a geographic area. Each button adds to the search, further filtering the list of articles. And Encarta 96 even reminds you which filters you've used (For example, "9 articles during 1900 to 1996 with pictures containing the word mars").

Then Leap with Hypertext

Encarta 96 uses hypertext to cross-reference information. Hypertext words are shaded in light brown; a click on one takes you straight to that article.

Encarta also offers a wealth of other research-friendly tools. For example, kids can explore the encyclopedia using the Inter-Activities, they can review world events on a graphical time line, or they can just browse through different subject categories.

Spend a few minutes with the researchers in the house to show them Encarta's Notemark tool, a handy way for them to take notes as they look through the encyclopedia. When they're done researching, have them click on the List button when a Notemark is on the screen. A complete list of all Notemarks appears. Kids can then call up each in turn, copy the text, and paste it into their report.

Chapter 8

Science Is Fact, Not Fiction

WHAT MAKES STARS CLUMP INTO GALAX-ies? How does your body fight the flu? And why does the Earth sometimes shake, rattle, and roll like a cement mixer?

Those questions, and millions more, are all part of science.

But in times of tight budgets, science often gets short shrift in school. You can reverse this trend — and help your children explore the wonders of science and the scientific process — by transforming the family's computer into a learning station that can take your kids into the 21st century.

To help you get started, we show you where to find enticing kitchen science experiments that you and your children can try. Then, we cover a wealth of homework ideas and resources for everything from anatomy and astronomy to Earth science

and dinosaurs. For even more science-related homework help, check out Chapter 9, which concentrates on environmental issues such as weather and the ecology.

Cool Science Experiments and Projects

One of the best places to introduce science to kids is in the kitchen. With a clear counter-top and some around-the-house ingredients, you can transform your kitchen into an elementary science laboratory. One moment, you and your children are investigating static electricity by rubbing a balloon against various objects; the next, you're building a seltzer-tablet-fired rocket that demonstrates propulsion.

Such simple demonstrations not only *show* kids some science, they also make ter-

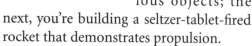

rific science projects for satisfying elementary- and middle-school homework requirements. These projects might not win blue ribbons at the science fair, but with minimal effort, your kids can transport them to the classroom for some Wow!-generating grades.

But where do you find kitchen science projects? You can look in made-to-order science books, on a handful of CD-ROMs (where they're often peripheral to the program itself), and on the vast information resource called the Internet.

We prefer the Internet — the World Wide Web, to be specific — as a resource for this kind of stuff. The online world contains a slew of such projects, and they're all free for the taking.

Science doesn't have to be complicated — or costly.

Start Here

Using the World Wide Web is all about using *hotlinks*, the connections that take you from one Web page to another, with just a click of your mouse. (For more information about hotlinks and hypertext on the Web and other online services, check out Chapter 7, "Wading into the Information Pool.") GNN and Yahoo are two of the best starting points for finding science addresses on the Web. Both list scads of science-related sites you can visit.

To access the GNN page that lists science-related hotlinks, enter this address in your Web browser:

http://gnn.com/wic/wics/sci.new.html

Here's the address that you can use for accessing Yahoo's listing of science sites:

http://www.yahoo.com/Science/

GET SMART: *Many of the sites accessible from GNN and Yahoo deal with subjects beyond the scope of elementary- and middle-school classes, and are more appropriate for high-school students. It's smart to surf with your kids to find — and then bookmark — the science sites best suited for their ages and interests. (We've never seen naked science, but when a Web page tries to explain quantum physics,* even *our eyes glaze over.)*

You Can with Beakman & Jax
Ages 5–9

Based on the popular TV show "Beakman's World" (which is based on the *Beakman & Jax* book series), the You Can with Beakman & Jax Web site presents several how-things-work projects and other science information. Here's the address for this colorful Web site:

http://www.nbn.com/youcan/

Kids can click on characters to read about how glasses work and what the nose does for those in the know. The best part of this site, however, is its "50 Questions" page, which you find at this address:

http://www.nbn.com/youcan/questionlist.html

Although we found only 35 questions (and answers) when we last looked, they

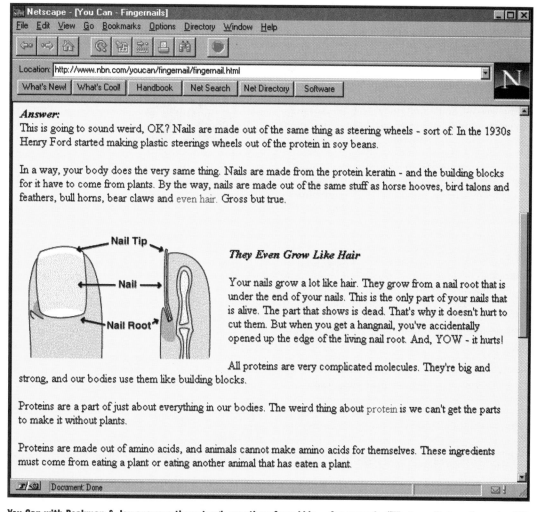

You Can with Beakman & Jax answers those tough questions from kids — for example, "What are fingernails made of?."

cover a mind-boggling range, from "What are fingernails made out of?" to "Why is poop brown?."

This part of the You Can with Beakman & Jax Web site provides kids with lots of excellent ammunition for an at-home episode of "How Things Work." (For even more ideas, see "How Things Work," later in this chapter.)

Bill Nye, the Science Guy
Ages 5–9

"Bill Nye, the Science Guy," another PBS science show for kids, uses its Web page (http://nyelabs.kcts.org/) to post an episode-by-episode guide, with one home how-it-works experiment per episode. To go directly to that part of the site, enter the following address in your Web browser:

http://nyelabs.kcts.org/
nyeverse/shows/shows.html

Most of the projects are easy — they're perfect for preschoolers and kids in the early elementary school grades — and can be done with stuff you have around the house. This page also provides links to lots of other science-for-kids sites.

Newton Science Try Its
Ages 5–9
The Newton Science Try Its Web page offers a half-dozen kitchen science experiments, courtesy of "Newton's Apple," a PBS science show for kids. To access this page, enter the following address in your Web browser:

http://ericir.syr.edu/Projects/Newton/

Although the directions aren't the step-by-step kind, the projects are so simple that you won't need to do anything more than print out the page and then assemble the ingredients. The scientists in your family can try a variety of projects, such as a pop bottle barometer, a listening device made from rubber bands and a spoon, and a magical paper fish that swims under its own power. The projects are suited for both preschoolers and young elementary -school-aged kids.

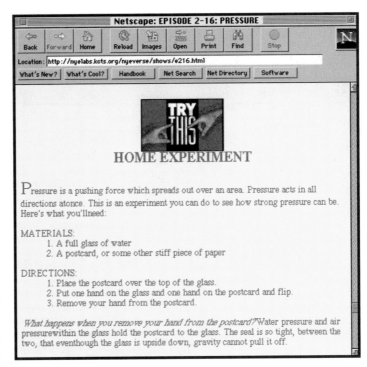

Each episode of "Bill Nye, the Science Guy" includes a you-do-it project or home experiment.

Helping Your Child Learn Science
Ages 5–9
An online collection of 16 at-home science projects, the Helping Your Child Learn Science Web site describes simple experiments kids and parents can do together. To access this page, enter the following address in your Web browser:

http://www.ed.gov/pubs/parents/Science/index.html

The projects include rubbing balloons to produce static electricity, growing plants to demonstrate photosynthesis, and grabbing Jell-O in an experiment about lubricants. Short explanations accompany each project so that everyone understands how things work. This page — which is almost all text, with hardly a pretty picture to break up the monotony — also includes information about a dozen different community-based science activities, ranging from zoo trips to science summer camps.

Beakman's Electric Motor

Ages 10–14

"Beakman's World," the fast-paced science show on Saturday mornings (check your local listings) has its own Web page (http://www.spe.sony. com/Pictures/tv/beakman/beakman.html), but it's limited to promotional stuff. Go to Beakman's Electric Motor, instead. The address for this Web page is

http://fly.hiwaay. net:80/~palmer/ motor.html

An engineer who put together one of the show's projects — an electric motor made from, of all things, the cardboard tube inside a roll of toilet paper — has posted simple instructions and several illustrations to help you and your kids make this gizmo.

★ TRY THIS! ★

Write a Science Project Paper

Doing science at home can be fun, but to turn a kitchen experiment into a real-life project that meets homework requirements, your children may need to provide supporting material — perhaps a short paper — to augment the hands-on work.

If your child's teacher doesn't set the ground rules for writing a paper to accompany the project, you can do so. Because science experiments generally have four parts — observing, predicting, testing, and explaining — you can help your child set up a word-processing document that includes four big, bold headings with titles like these:

✓ **What I think:**

My observation about something — for example, "Static electricity comes from rubbing your shoes across carpet."

✓ **What I predicted:**

What I thought would happen *before* I did the experiment or research.

✓ **How I tested:**

The detailed steps I took to find out whether my prediction was correct.

✓ **What I found out:**

What I actually found out from my test or experiment, and how well I predicted what would happen before I tested.

Choose layout options that make these headings stand out from the rest of the text. For example, you can center them horizontally on the page or print them in color.

Science at Home

Ages 10–14

Although *Science at Home* — a hands-on science activity book for grades 4–8 — was funded by the U.S. Department of Energy and developed at the Los Alamos National Laboratory, it wasn't available on the Web when we looked — something about pending negotiations for its commercial publishing debut (your tax dollars at work). Fortunately, you can find one cool sample experiment from this book at the following Web site:

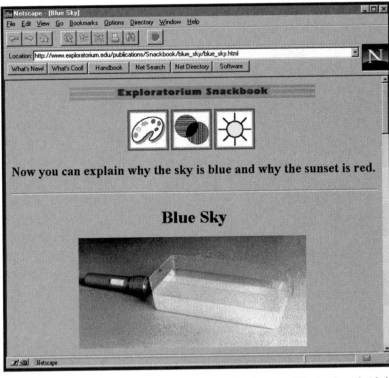

The Exploratorium's Science Snackbook samples include photos and illustrations that help you and your children visualize the experiment or project.

http://education.lanl.gov/RESOURCES/Science_ at_Home/SAH. rocket.html

Head to this page for step-by-step instructions on making a seltzer tablet rocket and to learn a bit about how propulsion works.

Hands-On Science

Ages 10–14

San Francisco's Exploratorium is famous for its kid-appropriate, hands-on science exhibits. It also publishes *The Exploratori-um Science Snackbook*, a collection of 107 experiments and demonstrations that are essentially scaled-down versions of the types of interactive exhibits that you can see in the museum itself. Before you spend $30 for the book, though, check out the eight sample projects at the Exploratorium's Web site. Just enter the following address in your Web browser:

http://www.exploratorium.edu/publications/ Hands-On_Science/Hands-On_Science.html

With experiments ranging from a fog generator to a "Why is the sky blue?" demo, you and your young scientists can find projects aimed at elementary-, middle-, *and* high-school-aged children. The projects at this site are more complicated than simple kitchen experiments; in fact, some of these may be just what your kids need when they're casting about for last-minute science fair project ideas.

Science Fair Research Directory
Ages 15 and Up
If your kids are gathering information for science fair projects, they can find lots of links to science-related Web sites at the following address:

http://spacelink.msfc.nasa.gov/
html/scifairt.html

When we checked out the Earth and Space Science section (this site lists scores of references in subjects ranging from biology to zoology), we found a Mars atlas that uses images collected by the Viking lander.

Science Fair Forum
Ages 15 and Up
On The Microsoft Network (go word: **ScienceFair**), dedicated science fair participants can find a slew of helpful information, including bulletin boards where kids share ideas, describe their projects, and chat about problems. The information in the Science Fair Forum won't transform your children into Westinghouse finalists, but if you already use MSN, make sure they know about this resource.

MSN's Science Fair Forum includes links to Internet science sites and bulletin boards where kids can trade ideas.

For our recommendations of more science and experimentation software, check out Chapter 14, "Homework Software."

Dinosaurs Deliver

When it comes to dinosaur data, many kids have even bigger appetites than that of a Tyrannosaurus rex. Although dinosaurs no longer rule the Earth, they do rule many kids' minds.

You can take advantage of this interest by steering your children toward dinosaur-related homework projects when the teacher leaves the specific subject up for grabs. This is a smart move for two reasons. First, their natural fascination with the reptiles will keep your kids digging for information long after they would have given up on another topic. Second, you can choose from a well-stocked library of available dinosaur reference software. Put the two together and you've got the recipe for some instant science homework.

Like all good multimedia reference CD-ROMs, Microsoft Dinosaurs uses hypertext to take users to other, associated information. Click on the "Meat-eating dinosaurs" line, for example, and the program displays text and pictures related to that subject.

Go Online!

When kids look at pictures of dinosaurs on the home PC's puny screen, it's hard for them to understand how *big* dinosaurs really were. A trip to a real museum — one with real dinosaur fossils — can put things in perspective. Unfortunately, you probably don't live next door to a world-class natural history museum.

Instead, your kids can surf the Web and crawl through virtual representations of some of the continent's best dino exhibits. The bones still look tiny on the PC's screen, but who's complaining when admission is free?

Most browsers let you save any image you see on a Web page, providing a slick way to collect pictures of dinosaurs, their fossils, or real-life museum exhibits. Check your browser's Help file for details.

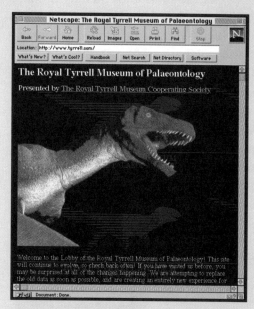

By going to the Tyrrell Museum's Web page, you can walk through this Canadian museum without stretching your legs.

Dinosaur Hall

http://ucmp1.berkeley.edu/exhibittext/dinosaur.html

Cruise through a virtual version of the University of California Museum of Paleontology, where you'll read about dinosaur diversity and myths, view skeletons, and dig up information such as how fast dinosaurs moved.

Dinos to DNA

http://www.bvis.uic.edu/museum/Dna_To_Dinosaurs.html

Take an interactive walk through the premier exhibit at the Field Museum of Natural History in Chicago, one of the country's best museums for dinosaur exhibits. This is one of the best dino sites on the Web, chock-full of information about the world in which dinosaurs lived.

The Royal Tyrrell Museum of Paleontology

http://www.tyrrell.com/

For most of us, it's a long drive to Alberta, Canada, so this Web site is as close as we'll probably get to the Tyrrell Museum, one of the world's leading paleontology museums. The Tyrrell's Web site is easily understandable to younger viewers, but these pages are still packed with enough stuff about dinosaurs to keep mom and dad at the screen.

Microsoft Dinosaurs

Of the numerous dino CD-ROM databases on store shelves, we recommend Microsoft Dinosaurs, the undisputed champ in a *FamilyPC* FamilyTested head-to-head comparison with several other multimedia dinosaur titles. Aimed at children ages six and up, Dinosaurs is rich in content and graphics, and early elementary-school homeworkers can easily operate the user interface on their own. Dinosaurs is a helpful homework tool and a fun program for at-home learning and playtime.

Microsoft Dinosaurs provides four main avenues for unaided inquiry: an atlas, which lets you locate dinosaurs throughout the earth; a time line, which locates the reptiles through the ages; an index; and a list of dinosaurs by family. In addition, dinosaur expert Don Lessem takes kids on 14 guided tours to explore such issues as what makes a dinosaur a dinosaur and how to recognize theropods (easy — they all had sharp teeth, menacing claws, and a taste for meat).

GET SMART: *Looking for a specific dinosaur to study? The program's Find command — which you access by clicking first on the Index button and then on the Find button — isn't as much help as it should be. Instead, go to the Index, click on the first letter of the dinosaur's name (on R for Rhoetosaurus, for example), and then click on the dinosaur's name.*

If you want to use material from Microsoft Dinosaurs for a project or just for fun, you can print pictures and text from any part of the encyclopedia. You can also personalize the family's PC by creating screen savers and wallpaper of dinosaur pictures.

Inside the Body

Them bones, them bones… And the heart, the lungs, the arteries, and the veins. All that stuff inside the human body might be invisible to us, but it's still in there, and it's still good fodder for science-related homework that can get a boost from the family's PC

★ TRY THIS! ★

Build a Paper Skeleton

A skeleton in the closet may be scary, but one out in the open is merely educational. How about building a skeleton as a science project? It's simple.

Start with one of the paper or cardboard skeletons that stores sell around Halloween — the kind you might hang in a window or tack to the front door to spook trick-or-treaters.

Using an anatomical reference work — A.D.A.M.: The Inside Story is perfect for the task — note the names for the major bones in the skeleton. Enter the names into a word-processing document, leaving several blank lines between names. Use a large font size for these labels — say, 24- or 36-point type.

Cut out the labels, and with A.D.A.M. on the screen for reference, glue the labels onto the appropriate bones.

★ TRY THIS! ★

Do-It-Yourself Dino Projects

Whether your kids have to complete a homework assignment, prepare a report, or just want to have some fun, dinosaurs make a great subject. In the following sections, we present four fun dino-project ideas.

Make a Dinosaur Diorama

Dioramas make great projects for elementary school students, letting them meld *regular* homework with arts and crafts. The combination is usually a big hit with kids in this age group.

Your children can use Microsoft Dinosaurs to help them build a snappy diorama. After researching a specific aspect of dinosaurs — perhaps the habits of plant-eating dinosaurs of the Jurassic period — they can either print pictures of the appropriate dinosaurs straight from any screen (just click on the Options button at the bottom and then click on Print) or copy the dino pictures from the Picture Gallery (click on Options and then on Picture Gallery). If they copy pictures from the Picture Gallery, they have to paste the pictures into an art program of their choice. However, using an art program, kids can resize the pictures so that the dio-

PICTURE GALLERY

Copy Picture | Make Wallpaper | Gallery List

Microsoft Dinosaurs includes some of the sharpest looking dinos since *Jurassic Park* hit the theaters.

rama's dinosaurs are approximately to scale. Microsoft Dinosaurs also includes several scenes your kids can print to make good diorama backgrounds.

After printing the images — preferably on a color printer, but your children can always color the dinosaurs and scenery with pencils or markers — the kids can mount the pictures on thin cardboard or tagboard. Slot another piece of cardboard at right angles to the dinosaur model, and it should stand up in the diorama. Finally, paste the background scenes to the rear of the diorama.

Create a Deck of Dinosaur Cards

Every dinosaur screen in Microsoft Dinosaurs includes a Fact Box that lists the time period in which the dinosaur lived, where it lived, what family it belongs to, and other interesting information. To display the Fact Box, click on the Facts button in the upper-left corner of a dino's screen.

Your child can create a deck of dinosaur trading cards by printing these Fact Boxes and then mounting them on thin cardboard or tagboard. They make

Continued on page 160

excellent flash cards for kids who want to learn as many dinosaur names as possible (*lots* of kids want to do this). Cover the bottom half of the card — including the name of the dinosaur — and see if your child can name the creature.

Make Some Toy Dinos

(Okay, this isn't a homework project, but we think it's too cool to pass up.)

Your kids can make paper dinosaur toys by using Microsoft Dinosaurs. Here's how.

Copy an image from the Picture Gallery, paste it into an art program that offers a Flip command (most do), and then print the picture. Next, select the image of the dinosaur with the art program's selection tool, choose Flip (your drawing package might call it something else, such as Flip Horizontal), and print the image a second time. You now have mirror images of the dinosaur. Finally, glue the two pictures, back to back, onto a piece of cardboard. Cut out your toy dino, and play!

Chart Dinosaur Sizes for Your Report

Microsoft Dinosaurs makes a super reference CD-ROM for reptile research. If your child is writing a report on dinosaurs, pitch this idea: Use information from the program's Fact Boxes to chart the relative sizes or weights of several dinosaurs.

It's easy with an integrated program such as Microsoft Works or ClarisWorks. First, gather data from Microsoft Dinosaurs on the reptiles you're studying. If you're writing a report about theropods

— the flesh-eating dinosaurs — look at the Fact Box for each therapod and then jot down the dinosaur's name and weight.

Enter the name and weight (in tons) of each dinosaur in the integrated program's spreadsheet. It should look something like this:

	A	B	C	D
Meat Eater Weights				
1		Weight (in tons)		
2	Allosaurus	1.5		
3	Tyannosaurus rex	7		
4	Albertosaurus	2		
5	Megalosaurus	1		
6				
7				

Select all the data in the spreadsheet by clicking on the upper-leftmost cell and dragging the mouse to the lower-rightmost cell. Then choose the command for creating a chart. In Microsoft Works for Windows 95, for example, choose Create New Chart from the Tools menu. Finally, click on the chart, pick Copy from the Edit menu, and then use the Paste command to add the chart to your report.

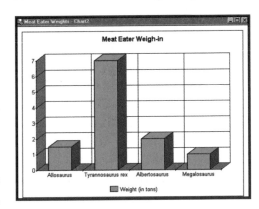

A chart like this comparison of dinosaur weights adds a lot to any dinosaur report.

or Macintosh.

Middle-schoolers may have specific anatomical assignments from health class, and the study of the human body is fascinating enough that younger kids can justify using it as the foundation for general science reports and projects. But unlike some other science subjects — such as astronomy and Earth science — anatomy gets skimpy treatment within the pages of paper-based *and* electronic encyclopedias. To *really* explore this part of science, you need specialized resources on CD-ROM or from the vast libraries of the online world.

We think we've found just what the virtual doctor ordered.

3-D Body Adventure
Ages 8 and Up

The 3-D Body Adventure takes kids on a three-dimensional ride through the inner workings of the human body. *FamilyPC*'s Family Testers enjoyed the trip so much that they gave this program the coveted *FamilyPC* Recommended seal of approval.

The program has four parts. The 3-D Body Theater offers 16 3-D movies that show how the various parts of the body work (3-D glasses are included). In the movies, you can perform such feats as flying through the middle of the brain or taking a roller coaster ride down the spine.

Like A.D.A.M.: The Inside Story (which

With 3-D Body Adventure, your kids get an inside view of human anatomy, including a trip through the brain.

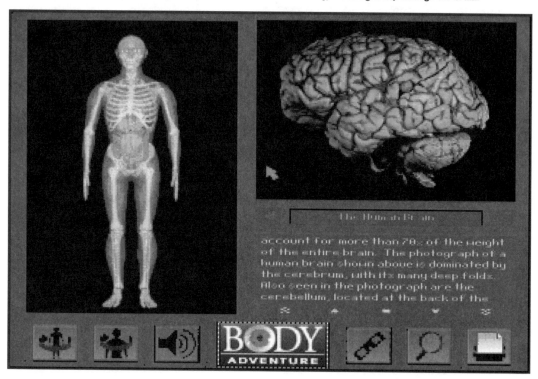

we describe next), this CD-ROM's strength is its Reference section. You can rotate a body or a torso and then click on body structures or organs to learn more. The program presents this information in the form of a scrolling block of text that kids can read or have narrated. In a separate window, kids can view the selected body structure or organ. They can also click one or more times to examine additional details about the subject. For example, clicking on the liver calls up a screen that discusses the many chemical processes the liver performs. From there, kids can click again to see a liver cell.

Although kids can print text from the Reference area, they can't save the text or any of the program's graphics to disk, something that would be extremely useful in preparing school reports and projects.

A.D.A.M.: The Inside Story
Ages 10 and Up

A.D.A.M.: The Inside Story provides children ages 10 and older with a spectacular-

Go Online!

Search the Web using a keyword such as *anatomy*, and you'll find lots of sites. Too bad most of them are better suited for medical professionals (or at least med students) than for school-aged children.

Exceptions *do* exist, such as this pair of pages tailor-made for kids.

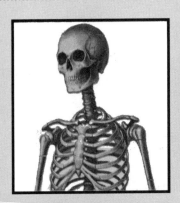

This skull is really a super teaching tool. Click on any bone, and you'll hear its name pronounced.

Click the Bones You Wanna See
http://www.cs.brown.edu/people/art035/Bin/skeleton.html

In anatomy, it ain't "the head bone connected to the neck bone." Each bone has its own name, and the tongue sometimes trips over the Latin roots of these names. Send your children to Click the Bones You Wanna See, a click-and-hear Web page, where they can point to any bone in the skeleton and hear the bone's name pronounced. (You may have to configure your Web browser so that it plays the sound files it downloads; refer to the Web browser's Help file for more details.)

The Heart: A Virtual Exploration
http://sln.fi.edu/biosci/heart.html

Part of the Franklin Institute Science Museum, this journey through the human heart lets kids watch QuickTime movies of the heart, listen to heartbeats of various speeds, look at X-rays, and see animations of blood pumping and the heart working. This extensive exploration of the pump that keeps us going is most appropriate for children aged 10 and older.

ly detailed portrait of the inner workings of the human body. *FamilyPC* testers who recently tried this CD-ROM found it especially effective as a reference tool.

A.D.A.M., which stands for Animated Dissection of Anatomy for Medicine, uses detailed medical illustrations based on sophisticated software used by medical schools. A.D.A.M.: The Inside Story contains 3,500 pieces of original color art, assembled into a complete human body.

You can explore either a male or a female body, in front or back views. (To avoid questions by the youngest children, parents can choose to cover the male or female genitalia with a fig leaf.) By clicking on a scroll bar, you strip away successive layers of the body's workings. You can then click on any body part to identify individual components. From a menu, you can also quickly examine any of the body's 12 anatomical systems.

A section called the Family Scrapbook discusses issues related to all 12 anatomical systems, including such subjects as how a cut heals, conception, and pregnancy. In this section, anatomical inquiry puts on a human face as contemporary adult characters Adam and Eve narrate more than four hours of slide shows, animation, and video with a mix of intelligence and humor.

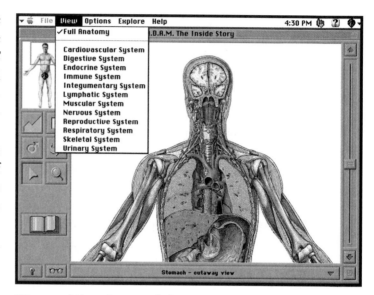

Kids can quickly explore any of the body's anatomical systems by selecting options from a menu. Then they can learn about related issues such as healing, conception, and pregnancy.

Unfortunately, you can't copy or print any of the elements in the program, such as the images or the medical definitions. That means kids cannot grab images from the program and insert them into their own reports, a failing shared by 3-D Body Adventure.

This shortcoming notwithstanding, our family testers rated A.D.A.M.: The Inside Story not only a superb reference tool, but a great learning program, too.

Space Science and Astronomy

When the shuttle astronauts repaired the myopic Hubble space telescope several years ago, they upgraded one of its microprocessors, replacing an older model with, of all

Research Ideas

When the teacher assigns research projects related to human anatomy, tell your kids to grab the family's electronic encyclopedia and start searching! Within a few minutes, kids will discover all kinds of interesting anatomy-related ideas and facts for reports and research papers. To help your kids get started, here are some possible research ideas:

What They Knew and When They Knew It
Search words to use:
medicine and *history*
We may not know how *everything* in the body works, but compared to people of only a hundred years ago, we're medical geniuses. The history of medicine — and our understanding of how the body works, how it becomes ill, and what makes it heal — makes for an intriguing report for upper-elementary-school- and middle-school-aged students. For example, did you know that people once believed they had to bleed to recover from an illness? Yuck!

Leonardo, the Doctor
Search words to use:
Leonardo da Vinci and *anatomy*
Leonardo da Vinci — painter, inventor, all-around genius — also dabbled in medicine. In fact, his anatomical drawings were among the first realistic portrayals of the human body.

things, a 386-based CPU. Imagine! That's at least one, and probably two, processor generations older than the CPU in your home PC. In fact, your home PC has more computing horsepower than the Apollo spacecraft that went to the moon and back.

You can put that horsepower to work exploring a virtual version of outer space. Your home PC or Macintosh can mutate into a planetarium, a cute guide to the solar system, or a pipeline to the most up-to-date information (and pictures, don't forget the pictures) from NASA and its far-flung fleet of spacecraft and robot explorers.

When you gotta go, you gotta go — into space, that is.

The Magic School Bus Explores the Solar System
Ages 6–10
Based on the popular book series of the same name, the Magic School Bus Explores the Solar System takes kids ages six to 10 on an interplanetary voyage that's both educational and entertaining. *FamilyPC*'s Family Testers thought it was out of this world, and it's our must-get pick for introducing space science and astronomy to elementary-school-aged children.

In the Magic School Bus Explores the Solar System, animated teacher Ms. Frizzle gets lost in space. Your child's job is to explore our solar system aboard the Magic School Bus, collect clues, and find the Friz. By winning Whatsit games during his travels, your child earns tokens that he can place in the Friz Finder to elicit clues about the Friz's location.

GET SMART: *The Magic School Bus Explores the Solar System isn't really set up as an encyclopedia, but kids can glean basic facts about the planets by clicking on their pictures in the classroom and then clicking on Cool facts about....*

While the kids search for Ms. Frizzle, they also learn about our solar system. They can read reports and get facts about the planets and watch videos from NASA and the world-famous Jet Propulsion Laboratory (which manages all of NASA's interplanetary probe missions).

The software also offers nine science experiments kids can perform. In Design O' Ring, for example, kids create their own rings while learning that Saturn's rings consist of a combination of rock, ice, and dust.

Magic School Bus Explores the Solar System does more than simply show astronauts traveling into space; it presents information about the planets in a fashion that attracts kids' attention. If your kids dig the sciences, enroll them in Ms. Frizzle's class.

RedShift 2
Ages 12 and Up

Older kids who want to explore the solar system — and beyond — don't need a telescope to see the stars. Instead, they can put a personal planetarium in the home computer by using any of several astronomy programs. For children ages 12 and older, we recommend RedShift 2. RedShift 2 includes hundreds of stellar photos, as well as satellite-style maps of Mars, the Earth, and the Moon. It lets you look at a virtual sky from any place on the globe, and throughout thousands of years. It's like looking through the telescope of a major observatory, only better, because RedShift 2 can also create three-dimensional fly-bys of planets and their moons, as though you were on a deep-space probe zooming through the solar system. Even more impressive, you can save the fly-by missions you create and then replay them like movies, on the computer screen.

The colorful command center of Magic School Bus Explores the Solar System takes kids to any of the planets.

GET SMART: *The best place to begin your deep-space exploration is in RedShift 2's tours of the solar system. After starting the CD-ROM, click on Guided Tours instead of Main Program. After a couple of guided tours, you'll be ready to plan your own missions.*

The Earth Moves

The Earth is a mysterious place, and kids love mysteries. That's why it's worth your time — and money — to point your children toward some of the Earth science resources that appear on the family's computer when you load a CD-ROM or dial the modem. But where should you begin?

Although the subject ranges from geology to plate tectonics, kids — younger children, in particular — seem most drawn to two pieces of the Earth science puzzle: volcanoes and earthquakes. When the Earth moves this dramatically, it's bound to hold their attention.

In the following sections, we outline several resources (both online and CD-ROM) and homework projects that will open up the Earth and let it swallow — figuratively, of course — your kids.

RedShift 2's interface may look confusing, but with some patience, navigating through the universe is a snap.

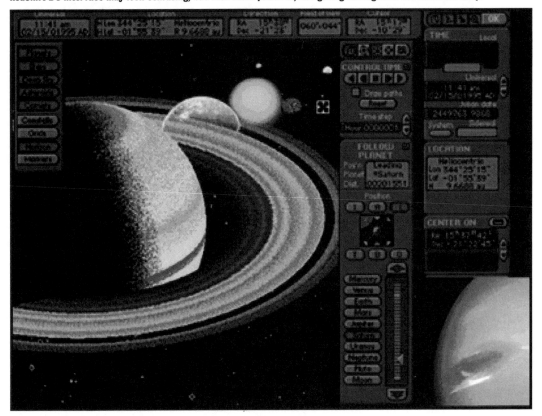

★ **TRY THIS!** ★

Draw the Planets to Scale

Specialized astronomical CD-ROMs are useful additions to your learning library. Even without such programs, however, your children can still do research and produce elementary projects and reports on the subject by using tools you probably already have: an electronic encyclopedia and a drawing program.

It's hard to grasp the relative sizes of the planets, but with a bit of artwork, the vast differences become crystal clear.

Use the encyclopedia to find the diameter of each planet. Next, calculate the *relative* diameter of each planet by dividing *its* diameter by that of the Earth. (The computerized calculator included with Windows or the Mac helps out here.) Finally, translate the relative sizes to drawing sizes by using 1 inch for the Earth. You end up with something like our "Size Matters" table.

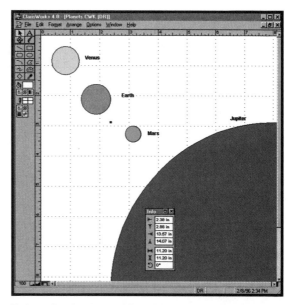

To draw the planets to scale, you have to manually resize the circles representing the planets. For example, if the Earth is 1 inch wide, Jupiter's diameter must be 11.2 inches.

Open your draw program. (It must be a *draw* program, not a *paint* program, because only a draw program shows you the size of each object you create. For details about the difference between draw and paint programs, see Chapter 10). The draw module in ClarisWorks is a good pick.

Draw a circle representing the Earth. Click on the circle to select it and then choose Object Info from the Options menu. Change the size of the circle to exactly 1 inch. Create a circle for each of the planets and adjust the size of each circle to match the diameter-to-draw size you calculated for that planet.

Size Matters

Planet	Diameter	Relative Size	Diameter to Draw
Earth	12,756 km	100 %	1 inch
Venus	12,103 km	95 %	.95 inch
Mars	6,794 km	53 %	.53 inch
Jupiter	142,984 km	1,121 %	11.2 inches

Go Online!

It only *seems* like nothing happens in space. But space science and astronomy often change faster than the shuttle rises above the Florida beaches. Your kids can stay on top of the subject — and do some incredible research — by using the Web to connect to a rocket-full of sites that NASA operates.

Here's our list of don't-miss outer space sites.

Welcome to the Planets

http://stardust.jpl.nasa.gov/planets/

Welcome to the Planets is a superb guided tour of the solar system, complete with full-color pictures of the planets (taken from space probes) and vital statistics about each. Other parts of this site take kids to detailed information about planetary missions such as Voyager, Magellan, Galileo, Viking, and the Hubble. This is an excellent starting place for children 10 and older who want to do research on the solar system.

NASA Educational Sites

http://quest.arc.nasa.gov/
nasa-resources.html

For a full list of all the NASA-sponsored education-oriented Web sites, check out the NASA Educational Sites listing. From here, you can launch to virtually every part of NASA.

Online Interactive Projects

http://quest.arc.nasa.gov/interactive.html

Although the "Sharing NASA" projects are meant to bring together schoolchildren in collaborative explorations, kids at home can use them, too. Each multimedia-rich project lasts one to three months, letting kids share in the thrill of real-life space missions. Recent projects include "Online from Jupiter," which highlighted the Galileo probe's approach to the system's biggest planet; "Live from the Hubble Telescope," in which several orbits of the famous telescope were dedicated to student observations; and "Women of NASA," in which kids got to meet and chat with female scientists and astronauts.

NASA's educational project area is waiting to take kids on interactive journeys with real scientists.

University of Bradford

http://www.eia.brad.ac.uk/
eia.html

Cool! Head to the University of Bradford site if you want to control a real robotic telescope. After you register, you can ask the telescope to look anywhere in the northern sky. Because the telescope is in England, try this site in the afternoon and early evening from here in the U.S. This site also lists other automated telescopes that you can operate over the Internet.

Boil and Bubble: The Lava Story

Talk about fireworks at homework time! Volcanoes, among the most awesome of the Earth's natural phenomena, can't help but grab your child's attention. With massive explosions, huge plumes of ash, and rivers of lava, an active volcano is a lot like a dinosaur — big, mean, and (usually) at a safe enough distance to be fascinating, not frightening.

One CD-ROM worth exploring is Vol-cano: Life on the Edge, a slick, coffee-table-book-style exploration of the subject. Multimedia from top to bottom, Volcano offers a wealth of voice narration, video clips, sharp photographs, and maps that serve as navigational aids to recent major eruptions. Self-contained narratives explore such topics as the people who live in the shadows of volcanoes, the destructive power of the earth, and volcanologists, the scientists who study

---

★ TRY THIS! ★

Real-Life Astronomy for Everyone

Nothing's more impressive than the spread of the Milky Way across the sky. Everyone — kids included — is awed by the stars, but few of us know the names of those bright points of light, how to spot more than the most elementary constellations, and where the planets appear in the heavens.

For some firsthand observation of the sky — and an excellent foundation for a cool science project or report — you can combine information from the home computer's planetarium package with observations from an outdoor session.

1. Run the astronomy program — RedShift 2 is a good choice — and display the night sky. Set the location and the time to match your position and the current date. (A parent might have to do this for younger children, because navigating an astronomy program is often a complex task.)

2. Set the program so that it shows only those stars and planets visible to the naked eye (stars are rated by magnitude, with fainter stars having a higher value; magnitudes between -1.6 and 6.2 can be seen without a telescope).

3. Print a star chart from this display.

4. Find a convenient spot to view the sky, away from light pollution. In all but the smallest towns, you probably need to drive into the country.

GET SMART: If you plan to use a flashlight, tape red cellophane over the flashlight's lens. The dim, red light should be enough to read by, but it won't disturb your night vision once you're out in the field.

5. Orient yourself with the star chart (which usually shows the sky from a specific direction). Use the flashlight to peek at the chart, select a prominent star, and then try to spot it in the sky. If you have a telescope, you can see the fainter stars and determine a star's color.

volcanoes. A bit like a series of short TV documentaries, Volcano rarely does more than scratch the surface, but it works well as an introduction. Its reference section is actually quite good, with entries that clearly explain everything from ash to volcanic gases.

GET SMART: *Give your children a head start on researching by suggesting these keywords they can use to search the family's electronic encyclopedia: volcano, lava, magma, Mount Saint Helens, and geology.*

If you have an electronic encyclopedia such as Microsoft Encarta 96, you don't need to spend money on specialized Earth science software for homework help. Like other CD-ROM encyclopedias, Encarta has a wealth of information about volcanoes and earthquakes. Elementary- and middle-school students can find more than enough information for their Earth science reports and projects.

For more Earth science software, see Chapter 14, "Homework Software."

Volcano: Life on the Edge is just one of the multimedia Earth science titles. It explores the inner workings of our planet, including topics such as the destructive power of the earth and scientists who study volcanoes.

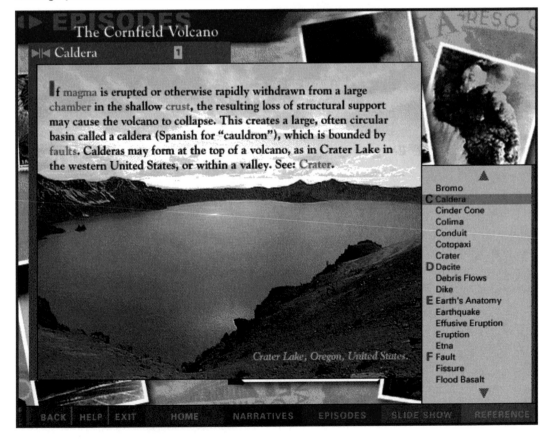

★ TRY THIS! ★

Take a Fiery Trip Around the World

Your kids can take a trip around the world to see volcanoes, and they don't have to leave the house (at least, not until they want to show the results to their class). To start this trip, just point them to Volcano-World:

http://volcano.und. nodak.edu/vw.html

This Web site, manned by professional volcanologists and educators, is an everything-you-want-to-know place that offers lesson plans (perfect for parents home-schooling their children), tons of photographs, and a library full of facts. This site even has an Ask a Volcanologist area, where kids can pose questions and get answers from the experts.

You can quickly show your kids how to create a visual tour of the world's active volcanoes using your Web browser. The best place to start is Exploring Earth's Volcanoes:

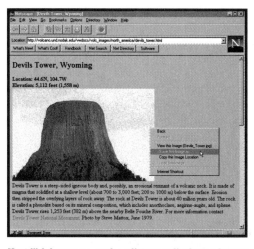

Most Web browsers, such as Netscape Navigator, let you save images from the screen so you can use them in your own reports and projects.

http://volcano.und.nodak.edu/vw docs/volc_images/volc_images. html

Pick a region and peek at several images. (Many shots were taken by orbiting astronauts, giving a view rarely seen in textbooks and paper encyclopedias.) Save the desired images with your Web browser. (In Netscape Navigator 2.0, for example, you simply right-click on the image and then pick Save this image as... from the menu that appears.)

If you and you kids use an encyclopedia for this virtual volcano road trip — Encarta 96 works well — browse through the encyclopedia's images, copy the images you want to use one at a time to empty pages in your paint or draw program, and then save each image as a separate file.

Finally, use these images to create a presentation — it can be either a printed presentation or an electronic presentation to be shown at school on a computer — with software such as ClarisWorks or Kid Pix Studio.

If necessary, copy and paste the images from the art program files to the program you're using to build the digital presentation of the world's volcanoes.

For more information on building a dazzling presentation, check out the how-to suggestions we provide in Chapter 13's "Projects Go Digital."

★ TRY THIS! ★

Shake, Rattle, and Roll with Earthquakes

One big advantage online resources have over CD-ROMs is that online information is always changing, while material on CD-ROMs remains static (updateable CD-ROM-based software is very rare). This is important for researchers who want to track earthquakes over a recent period.

This cool project requires Internet access, an electronic encyclopedia, and an art program.

First, point your Web browser

(those included with online services such as America Online, Prodigy, CompuServe, or The Microsoft Network are fine) to Earthquake Information:

http://www.civeng.carleton.ca/ cgi-bin/quakes

This puts you on the Web page of the National Earthquake Information Service (NEIS), which lists information about the latest

quakes, including their location, their magnitude, and the date they occurred. Use the map at this site to spot some quakes, such as all those in North America. Over a period of several days, weeks, or months, note the locations and magnitudes of earthquakes in your selected area on a map.

GET SMART: Create a bull's-eye on a blank page in your art program, select the bull's-eye, and then choose Copy from the Edit menu. Open the document containing your map, choose Paste from the Edit menu, and move the bull's-eye to the approximate location of the quake.

You can use a paper map or find one in the family's electronic encyclopedia; most of these include maps you can print or copy to an art program.

After pasting the map into an art program, you can draw bull's-eyes at the spots where earthquakes happened. Using the art program's text tool, you can label the location of each quake, its magnitude, and its date.

Plot recent quakes using Internet-available maps and an art program.

How Things Work

The expression E = MC^2 has *something* to do with science. And there *is* something called the Law of Thermodynamics. Too bad neither fact — nor much else from our science classes of yore — can help us answer the questions kids ask, such as "Why is the sky blue?" or "How do they know how much the earth weighs?"

Fortunately, at its most basic level, science focuses on understanding how things work — for example, how sound travels, how a boat floats or an airplane wing lifts, and how three atoms of explosive gas manage to make water. How things work: That's something kids can understand.

Kids, especially young children, can get a grip on science if you skip the theory and the formulas in favor of simply explaining how things work and letting the kids try lots of hands-on experiments. Great science software does just that, and *FamilyPC* has sniffed out the best how-it-works software through its family-testing evaluations.

Our favorite programs do a terrific job of

Go Online!

Ask-A-Geologist

http://walrus.wr.usgs.gov:80/docs/ask-a-ge.html

Teachers can't know everything. That's why the Ask-A-Geologist Web site is so neat. Anyone can quiz real scientists from the United States Geological Survey about geology. If you're wondering whether your part of the country ever had a quake, or you're curious about why Texas is flush with oil while West Virginia has coal deposits, you can ask the experts.

Kids transmit their questions by using e-mail (if you don't want to bother looking at this page, the e-mail address is Ask-A-Geologist@usgs.gov). Unfortunately, this site doesn't catalogue previous questions and answers.

Earth Science
HyperStudio Stacks

http://volcano.und.nodak.edu/downloads/stack.html

If you have a Macintosh, head to the Earth Sci-

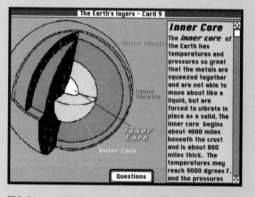

Kids learn at their own pace with self-contained Earth science lessons in HyperStudio, on the Mac.

ence HyperStudio Stacks, where you can download a slew of excellent Earth science adventures. (You also have to download a copy of HyperStudio Player, which is available from this page.)

The HyperStudio stacks cover such topics as

Continued on page 174

plate tectonics, the various levels of the Earth (from the mantle to the inner core), and volcanoes. Each stack is a self-guided tour through a specific part of Earth science and even includes questions you can urge your children to answer when they're finished. Other files on this page include complete lesson plans, hands-on experiments (we like the one in which you demonstrate the effects of an earthquake by tapping a table that holds a pile of sand), and vocabulary lists. They may be aimed at teachers, but you can easily adapt them for home learning or home-schooling.

We highly recommend this Web site for Mac families.

U.S. Geological Survey Earthquake Maps
http://quake.wr.usgs. gov/QUAKES/CURRENT/
You can check out recent earthquake locations in California and Hawaii by heading to the U.S. Geological Survey Earthquake Maps Web site. When you arrive, click on one of the files with the extension HTML or GIF. You can find tremor maps for Los Angeles, San Francisco, the Mojave, Monterey, the island of Hawaii, and other locations.

giving your kids a jump on the kind of science they'll explore in school. Just as important, these CD-ROMs include activities and experiments that your children can adapt for homework projects. And, we describe some things you can do with (and in some cases, without) these CD-ROMs to start your small scientists thinking.

Which makes more sense to kids, reading the phrase "Newton's third law of motion" or watching a Fourth of July rocket shoot into the sky because gas rushes out of its engine? We thought so.

What's the Secret? and What's the Secret? 2
What's the Secret? and What's the Secret? 2, a pair of spin-off CDs from the PBS television show "Newton's Apple," are deceptively deep programs that take elementary-school-aged kids on an multimedia junket into everyday science. Starting with ques-

tions such as "What keeps a roller coaster going?" or "How does my brain think?," these programs whip up a recipe of interactive experiments, video clips, and crystal-clear information.

GET SMART: *If your kids take to the What's the Secret? CD-ROMs, use your Web browser to send them to the Web site sponsored by the PBS television series, "Newton's Apple." To visit this site, enter the following address in your browser:*

http://ericir.syr.edu/Projects/Newton/

Activities based on each episode are available for reading and printing, and make super science experiments and miniature projects.

Each What's the Secret? disc covers four broad areas. The first edition addresses bees, sound, amusement parks, and the circulatory system; the second volume covers flight, brains, glue, and the Arctic. Unfortunately, these topics aren't well connected; each is a self-contained exploration involving activities both on and away from the computer. In What's the Secret?'s roller-coaster section, for example, you roll a ball down the track to discover the relationship between friction, kinetic energy, and potential energy. Away from the computer, a simple project has you using string, a rubber band, books, and pencils to demonstrate the theory of friction. First, you drag the books over a surface. Then you use the pencils as

rollers underneath the books (similar to the manner in which many archaeologists believe the ancient Egyptians used rollers to move the pyramid's stone blocks).

Other areas of the original program investigate sound (including how it travels and a bit about the Doppler effect), examine the inner workings of the heart, and illustrate bee behavior. Tough terms are clearly explained, video clips add to the lessons, and, if you like, you can print the off-computer experiments and use them for reference.

The best thing about these CDs is their hands-off approach to hands-on science.

What's the Secret? sends you away from the computer to conduct experiments, such as this demonstration of friction.

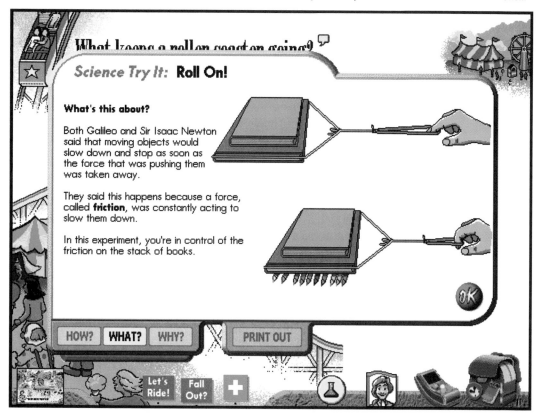

What's the Secret? and What's the Secret? 2 let kids discover for themselves how (and why) things are as they are, with just a bit of coaching.

Widget Workshop and The Incredible Machine 2

With Widget Workshop or The Incredible Machine 2, you can choose either the direct approach or slide in under kids' radar. Both programs use the home computer to show children the inner workings of gadgets and gizmos by literally letting kids make it on their own.

Widget Workshop lets kids put down parts to solve one of the 25 ready-to-go scientific puzzles. Kids build electrical circuits, see how colors combine, calculate calories, decode secret messages, and even run experiments that turn gravity on its ear.

Widget is firmly grounded in science, and its Erector-set style opens things up for creative kids who want to compose their own projects. However, everyone can get a good start with the included booklet, which outlines a slew of science activities, complete with step-by-step directions. Although the program — which doesn't demand a CD-ROM drive — may be tough for younger kids, it's nevertheless a smooth blend of fun

---

★ TRY THIS! ★

Sound Off

Sound may be all around us, but how it gets from point A to ear B is a mystery to most of us. Audio is one of What's the Secret?'s areas of expertise; two of its hands-on experiments illustrate how sound travels and demonstrate the Doppler effect (in which a sound seems higher as it approaches you and lower as it moves away from you). Here are two demonstrations to try:

• Sound transmission requires vibration, a medium through which the sound can travel (such as air or water), and your ear (to receive the sound waves and transmit the signals to your brain). To hear this transmission in action, try the old tin-can-on-a-string toy. Punch a small hole in the bottom of two tin cans, string them together (tie a knot at each end of the string to secure it to the tin can), and talk into the open end of your can while the string is stretched taut. The person on the other end listens by putting the open end of the can to her ear. The cans vibrate when you speak into them, the medium is the string, and the ear... well, the ear is yours.

• Rather than assemble the twirling noisemaker described by What's the Secret?, just take the kids to a busy street corner. Tell the kids to listen as cars approach, come alongside you, and then go by. The sound is higher as the car nears, and it's lower as the car drives away. (You might also want to mention that modern weather radar uses the Doppler effect for more precise monitoring of wind speeds.)

Shoot off all the fireworks.

The Incredible Machine 2 doesn't teach science per se, but it's an entertaining way to show kids cause and effect.

and learning.

The Incredible Machine 2 (TIM2) focuses on fun, but it's such an engaging game — and got such raves from our *FamilyPC* Family Testers — that you should add it to your software collection. Like Widget Workshop, TIM2 features puzzles you solve by creating gadgets from bins of parts. However, science takes a backseat to entertainment in TIM2, because the puzzles have you shooting off fireworks or making a mouse run around the screen. If you really want to stretch the point, TIM2 works as a cause-and-effect tutorial: Drop a ball on a match, and it lights; light that match, and it ignites a rocket. Just don't expect TIM2 to do much teaching.

Science Sleuths

Real-life scientists are detectives who wear white lab coats. To uncover the mysteries of the universe — or just find out how something works — they have to follow clues, come up with a theory, and prove the case. With the Science Sleuths series of CD-

★ TRY THIS! ★

Slip and Slide

You probably don't have a mass spectrometer around the house (we *did*, but we sold it at a yard sale this summer), but you can create an experiment without one. One of the cases in Volume 2 involves an automobile accident. Of course, friction plays a big part in a car's capability to stop quickly. Here's how to conduct an at-home friction experiment:

● You need a piece of stiff cardboard about six inches wide and at least 2 or 3 feet long, a rubber-soled shoe to represent the car's tire, a protractor (to measure angles), sandpaper, aluminum foil, plastic wrap, some cooking oil, and a cup or so of ice chips.

● Put the shoe at one end of the cardboard, with the protractor at the other end. Raise the shoe's end of the cardboard until the shoe just starts to slide. Note the angle of the cardboard. (This angle is simply a relative measurement of friction.)

● Wrap or tape other materials — for example, the plastic, the foil, or the sandpaper — to the bottom of the shoe, and test again. Record the angles you see on the protractor.

● Smear some oil on the cardboard to simulate an oily road, or pour the ice chips to represent snow. Try the tests again, and record the results.

ROMs, kids can follow this process — it's called the *scientific method* — on their own.

Science Sleuths puts an investigator's cap on kids and asks them to solve some mysterious cases. These two titles (Volume 1 and Volume 2 are currently available) may lack away-from-the-computer activities, but both are strong in the how-things-work department. To solve a mystery, children have to use tools to examine the "scene," pore through documents to uncover clues, and form theories by collecting and collating data. An excellent choice for middle-school-aged kids, Science Sleuths is the best package on our list for illustrating the power of the scientific method.

Because the two cases in Volume 1 both have six levels of difficulty — each with a different conclusion — your kids can play Science Sleuths numerous times before exhausting its content. Each case offers video clips, documents and databases, investigative tools, and a notebook for jotting down your results.

★ TRY THIS! ★

What's Gravity?

For serious science students, Widget Workshop is the best pick of this pair. You can jump-start your child's interest with this creation:

1. Want to build an experiment that compares the time it takes a baseball to fall a mile on Jupiter and Earth? Assemble the parts and connect them as shown here. You can use a four-way splitter piece to start the balls and the stopwatches simultaneously.

2. You have to customize both gravity well pieces. In the first gravity well piece, select *baseball* and *Jupiter* from the lists and then enter *5280* (the number of feet in a mile) in the box. In the second, pick *baseball* and *Earth* and then enter *5280*.

3. Flick the switch, and the balls drop. You can see that the ball falling on Jupiter is already ahead of the one falling on Earth.

4. The stopwatch results show that objects fall faster on Jupiter than on Earth. That's because Jupiter has more mass, and so has a stronger gravitational field, than Earth.

Chapter 9

Our Planet
The Environment and Ecology

YOU CAN TELL A LOT ABOUT PEOPLE BY how they care for their possessions. People who carefully maintain their car, regularly paint their house, and repair rather than toss know the value of managing their resources.

The same holds true with the planet. How we care for the world — its resources, its diverse ecosystems, the boundless life in those ecosystems — tells a lot about us. Unfortunately, it's not always a pretty story.

Global warming, endangered species, pollution: we all should be thinking about those things. Many teachers do, and they use these environmental topics (among others) as the basis for science classroom study and for homework assignments.

When your children work on homework assignments that involve the environment, the creatures that live on the land and in the

ocean, and some of the natural world's wildest weather, use this chapter to give them ideas and sources of information. (For more science-related software, ideas, and activities, check out Chapter 8, "Science Is Fact, Not Fiction.")

Animals and Their Worlds

It's not tough coaching kids to take an interest in animals; children have a natural affinity with the natural world (much more so, sad to say, than most adults). Smart teachers understand the connection, and they use it to their advantage by emphasizing animals and their environments during science studies.

With this in mind, you should not be surprised when your kids bring home research and report assign-

ments related to animals. Armed with *The FamilyPC Guide to Homework,* you and your home computer can help place animals in their habitats, focus your children's attention on the most important facts, and take them on exciting electronic field trips and virtual wildlife safaris.

The only problem with using the family's PC or Mac is the vast number of software programs that spotlight the subject. In the following sections, we send you to the best, provide a project idea, and shine the lights on animals online.

Animals 101: Start General

Your kids can complete many animal- and wildlife-related homework assignments without your spending another dime on software. If you have an electronic encyclopedia such as Microsoft Encarta 96 (the en-

---

★ TRY THIS! ★

An Illustrated Food Chain

It's a fact of life: Big animals usually eat small animals. That's how big animals get bigger and *stay* bigger. This characteristic of animal life is called the *food chain.* That term may not sound scientific, but it's sure descriptive. With some help from the home computer, kids can easily create an illustrated food chain, which makes a unique report or project.

To start, select the animal at the top of the food chain. Using your digital encyclopedia or other animal reference resource (a CD-ROM or the Internet), work down the food chain. Which animal is the main diet of the creature at the top of the chain? And what does that animal eat? Although some reference works may use hypertext in their articles to take you

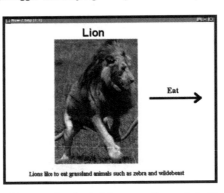

Lions like to eat grassland animals such as zebra and wildebeast

Unless you download pictures small enough to fit several on one page, your food chain will stretch across several printed pages.

and your child on part of this journey, you'll probably have to look up each animal separately. By playing detective, you can usually piece together the chain.

As you uncover each creature in the food chain, digitally copy a picture of it from the CD-ROM or the Web page, and paste the picture into a blank document in your paint or draw program. (If the pictures are small, you can paste them all into one document. Just make sure you leave room between the pictures so that later you can easily select and move them around.) Draw arrows from one animal to another to show who eats who, and leave room at the bottom of the page for any explanatory text your child may want to add.

cyclopedia we recommend in *The FamilyPC Guide to Homework*), you have a top-notch animal reference resource already on the computer. An encyclopedia such as Encarta is especially useful as a starting point for research. Kids can delve into the encyclopedia for general information about an animal before they move on to other resources that offer information to them in greater depth.

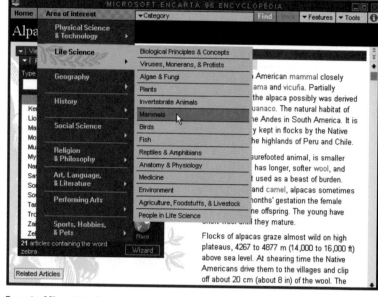

Encarta 96's categories narrow the article choices to a specific subject and subtopic. Use them to browse the encyclopedia when you're not sure what you want.

Encarta offers several ways to locate information about animals. To research a specific animal, kids should use the Word Search tool in Encarta's Pinpointer. Click on the Find button at the top of the Encarta window, then click on Word Search in the box that appears on the left side of the screen. Enter a keyword — *zebra*, for example — in the topmost blank, and click on the Search button. The list at the left now shows all the articles that include the word *zebra*.

Your kids can also search for information by using Encarta's categories. Click on the Area of Interest button at the top of the screen, highlight *Life Science*, then select one of the available choices. For example, *Mammals* is a good pick for most land-roving creatures. Using Encarta's categories — rather than searching for a specific keyword

— is a smart move for kids who want to browse the available articles in the encyclopedia (perhaps because they're not sure *which* animal they want to research).

GET SMART: *Encarta summarizes the results of a search at the bottom of the Pinpointer window. For example, if you enter* zebra *in Word Search and click on the Sound icon, Encarta displays the phrase "X articles with sounds containing the word zebra" (where X represents the number of articles Encarta found).*

To see which animal articles in the encyclopedia are accompanied by multimedia components — that is, sounds, pictures, and even video clips — click on the Media cube in the Pinpointer and then click on the

Only the most dangerous animals have a home in Dangerous Creatures, an excellent reference CD about animals, their habitats, and the food chain.

Dangerous Creatures
Ages 8 and Up

If your kids get thrills from thinking about animals with fangs, claws, and horns, send them to the Dangerous Creatures CD-ROM from Microsoft. Packed with hundreds of animals, from alligators to warthogs, Dangerous Creatures lets kids explore creatures native to the Amazon, North America, Africa, and Australia.

Narrated video clips show many of the animals in action. By heading to Animal Audio, children can click on any animal to hear it roar, buzz, snarl, or hiss. Children can also look at animals by habitat or weapons, or

appropriate icon at the right (the Sound icon, for example, for sounds). The list that the Pinpointer displays at the left now shows only those articles that include the multimedia element you chose.

Animals 201: Get Specific

If your kids want to know more about animals than your family's electronic encyclopedia can tell them, they can explore any of several creature-specific CD-ROMs. Many of these programs are strictly for reference and research, but the best — including the three programs that we recommend here — present their information using hundreds of pictures, provide real-life video clips of the various animals in action, and put the different creatures in the context of their respective habitats.

Wide World of Animals includes audio, video, and text information on more than 700 species.

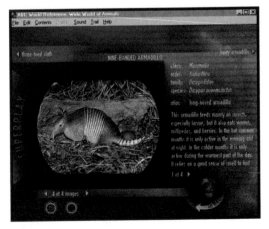

check out Dumb Things People Do, which includes practical safety tips such as staying away from a mother bear and her cubs.

GET SMART: *The information in Dangerous Creatures' Dumb Things People Do section can serve as a solid foundation for a report or a research project. To put a personal touch on the report, your kids can interview friends and family about their experiences with animals.*

Wide World of Animals
Ages 8 and Up

For an even more dramatic digital reference work, try the Wide World of Animals CD-ROM (for both Windows and Macintosh). With data on more than 700 species, lots of video and audio, and several pictures of each creature, Wide World is a good pick for kids who want to research beyond the encyclopedia.

Wide World extensively uses maps of biomes and species habitats to give children a better idea how animals fit into the big picture. A taxonomy tree lets kids click through phyla and genera to see how creatures are related, and more than a dozen 3-D environments provide you-are-there views of ecologies ranging from the poles to the tropics. Unfortunately, you can't copy any of the images from Wide World to drop into school reports or projects.

The Animals 2
Ages 7 and Up

The San Diego Zoo, one of the country's most renowned animal parks, was among

---

Go Online!

The Internet is crawlin' with creatures! If your kids are looking for detailed information about animals — almost anything that walks, crawls, slithers, hops, flies, or swims — send them on a trip through the Internet's vast resources. It's not as exciting as a trip to a real zoo or a wildlife park, but it doesn't demand an airline ticket or an admission fee and it's open 24 hours a day, 7 days a week.

This short list is just a sampling of the animal sites on the Web. For a longer list, we recommend you use the Internet's search tools (check out Chapter 7 for details on how to use these tools). Another good starting point is Ya-hooligans!, the kid-style Web directory, and in particular its Animals category:

> http://www.yahooligans.com/Science_and_Oddities/Animals/

The Electronic Zoo
http://netvet.wustl.edu/e-zoo.htm

The Electronic Zoo is a great leaping-off point for homework help with anything to do with animals. The first thing to do is click on the Animals icon (a paw print); from here, your child

Continued on page 184

can get information about domesticated creatures and wildlife of all kinds. And the Zoo's Animal Image Collection is packed with hundreds of pictures of animals. To go directly to this collection, use this address:

http://netvet.wustl.edu/pix.htm

The Bear Den

http://www2.portage.net/
~dmiddlet/bears/

The Bear Den offers facts and more facts about the bears of the world, with lots of pictures and an amazing amount of background information. Kids can read in-depth reports on each of the world's eight species of bears (Brown, American Black, Polar, and more), including their physical characteristics, the number world-

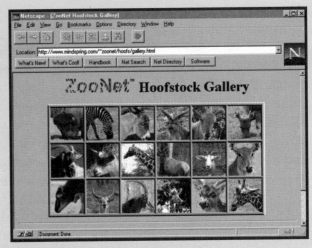

ZooNet is a super spot for kids who need images to spice up their reports.

wide, bear habitats, and why they hibernate. If your child is into bears, or needs to do some research on bears, this is the place to go.

ZooNet Image Archives

http://www.mindspring.com/~zoonet/gallery.html

With links to an almost overwhelming number of animal images, the ZooNet Image Archives should be on your Web browser's bookmark list if your kids need to download pictures for research projects or reports.

Virtual Safari

http://www.period.com/safari/safari.shtml

Although the Virtual Safari Web site covers only a small number of animals, the content is well organized and suitable for young children. They'll find maps showing the animal's habitat, some fun and interesting facts, huge pictures, and lots more.

Bearish on bears? Then head to The Bear Den, which includes information on all the world's bears.

the first to use a CD-ROM to open its virtual gates to children. Although this second edition of The San Diego Zoo Presents the Animals improves on previous versions by offering more video, photographs, and narration about the zoo's exhibits, the best enhancements are the new features that take you beyond the zoo itself. The most striking addition is The Waterhole, which gives kids an up-close look at animals in their natural habitats. Other parts of the disc target prereaders. For example, The A to Z Gallery has photos of 26 animals, one for each letter of the alphabet.

Of course, children can also visit this virtual zoo's exhibits, including the nursery and more than 200 mammals, birds, and reptiles. All together, your admission ticket to this CD zoo gets you more than 1,300 photos, thousands of pages of text (including habitat descriptions), and more than 100 video clips.

For other top-quality programs that cover animals and their habitats, see Chapter 14, "Homework Software."

How's the Weather?

Sunny to partly cloudy, with a chance of rain. Thunderstorms possible in the afternoon, tornado watch tonight, and a hurricane warning tomorrow.

The weather is always changing. And to keep up with the weather, your kids must keep up with technology. For homework assignments related to weather, that means using the resources found on online services and the World Wide Web.

Although kids can study weather patterns and learn what makes weather work by cracking a textbook, they can have much more fun by exploring weather from the interactive display of a home computer. Weather reports created on the family computer change almost as rapidly as real weather changes outdoors.

Weather is a common subject of study in almost every grade. In elementary school, children chart the week's

The Animals 2 mixes an exploration of habitats with colorful graphics, fun sounds, and enough information to keep the most curious creature-watcher busy for hours.

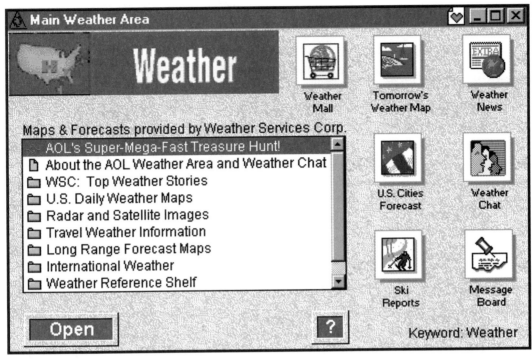

America Online's Weather area provides five-day forecasts, weather news, and lots of colorful weather maps.

weather. Middle-school-aged kids explore weather forecasting. And in high school, students investigate the causes of weather. No matter how old your kids are, the home computer can help them with weather-related homework.

In the following sections, we walk you and your kids through several projects and point our weather radar to some of the best online sources for weather information.

How Accurate *Is* a Weather Prediction?

It's happened to all of us: sunny weather is forecast for tomorrow, so we plan a picnic or a camping trip. And what happens? It rains. And rains. And rains.

In the newspaper, on the radio, and on television, weather reports forecast — some might say *guess* — tomorrow's weather. But how accurate are these forecasts? By comparing the forecast weather with the real thing, kids can produce an interesting report. Here's how.

GET SMART: *Most online services also provide weather forecasts for your city or area. In America Online, for example, you can find these reports in the Weather area (keyword* **Weather***) by clicking on the U.S. Cities Forecast button.*

Start on Sunday by watching a local television station's five-day weather forecast or by looking in the local newspaper for this week's forecast. Such forecasts usually predict the high and low temperatures for each day, the chance of precipitation (rain or snow), and how cloudy the sky will be. Have your child make notes of the forecast.

GET SMART: *To check your city's weather, point your Web browser to The National Weather Service — Interactive Weather Information Network (**http://iwin.nws.noaa. gov/iwin/graphicsversion/main.html**). Click on the Local Weather button, then on your home state when the map of the U.S. appears.*

Every day, you and your child should check the weather. You need to know the high and low temperatures for the day and the amount of precipitation; you can find all this in your local paper or by watching the local evening news on TV. Your child can make the call on whether the day was sunny, partly cloudy, or cloudy.

Your child can organize and present this information by creating a spreadsheet (see Chapter 4 for details about how to use a spreadsheet). Enter labels for each part of the weather forecast for each day,

with a column for *Forecast*, and another for *Real Weather*. (The accompanying figure shows one way to organize this data). Create a column titled *How Accurate*, and have your child enter his opinion there; he can use phrases like *Right On*, *Good*, and *Fair*, or whatever rating he chooses.

For some advanced spreadsheet work — and an even slicker report — your child can create a graph comparing the forecast high and low temperatures with the actual highs and lows.

Build a Weather Station

The National Weather Service spends millions each year tracking and reporting the

---

This is just one way you and your child can organize the data you collect to compare weather forecasts with actual weather.

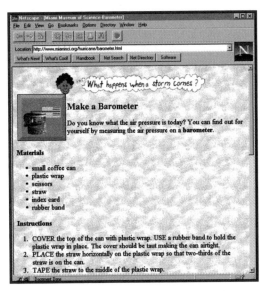

A barometer measures air pressure and is useful for predicting storms. This Web site shows you how to make one with common household materials.

weather. Fortunately, your kids can build their own weather station for a lot less.

GET SMART: *Use the Web browser's Print command (found in the File menu) to print copies of the instructions so you don't waste connect time (and connect fees) while you build.*

A kid-created weather station — complete with a barometer, a thermometer, a rain gauge, and other instruments — makes an excellent weather-related science project, either for a project fair or as a long-term homework assignment in elementary or middle school.

One of the best how-tos we've seen for building a weather station is available on the Internet at the Miami Museum of Science's

Web site. To check it out, point your Web browser to this address:

http://www.miamisci.org/hurricane/ weatherstation.html

Then click on each of the main menu's four components — wind, moisture, temperature, air pressure — to read the construction instructions. The directions are clear and the materials inexpensive. (In fact, you may have many of them already in the house).

This site also includes instructions — and the necessary forms — for recording and graphing rainfall and the temperature, as well as detailed descriptions of several weather-related experiments.

When you want a bit of virtual weather excitement, check out the Storm Chaser Home Page, which includes information and images involving tornadoes and other types of severe storms.

Welcome To The Storm Chaser Homepage!

Nasty Weather

Your child decides to write a report on tornadoes, but she's stumped. She needs some super images of nasty weather to illustrate the research she has culled from books and the family's electronic encyclopedia.

GET SMART: *WeatherNet (**http://cirrus. sprl.umich.edu/wxnet/**) is simply the best place to be on the Web when weather gets in your (or your kids') blood. Check it out.*

Send her to The Storm Chaser Home Page, where she can find too-close-for-comfort images of twisters:

http://taiga.geog.niu.edu/chaser/chaser.html

The dramatic images on The Storm Chaser Home Page were snapped by brave photographers and storm enthusiasts. Other links on this page take her to eyewitness accounts of severe storms, a glossary of storm terminology, and an excellent Frequently Asked Questions (*FAQ*, in Net-speak) document, which spells out everything about chasing storms. She can go directly to this FAQ page by pointing the family's Web browser to the following address:

http://taiga.geog.niu.edu/chaser/chasfaq.html

Weather Software

Want more weather than the online services and the Internet provide? Why not turn your PC or Mac into a 24-hour weather station? It's easy when you download, then run, some weather-related programs. Many are *shareware,* which means you can try them out without paying; if you decide to keep the program, you then pay a *registration fee* to the software maker

The best place to go

Blue-Skies, a shareware weather program for the Mac, lets kids view interactive weather maps, see animations of satellite weather photos, and more.

for weather software you can download is WeatherNet's archive:

http://cirrus.sprl.umich. edu/wxnet/software.html

When we last looked, the archive listed 13 PC programs and two for the Mac, including hurricane trackers, map makers, and programs that automatically download National Weather Service data and display it in graphical form.

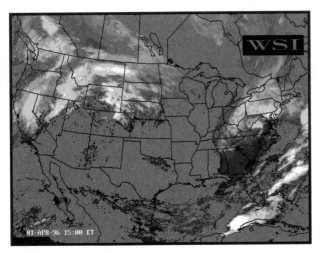

Kids can use weather maps — for example, this satellite image that was downloaded from America Online — for a meteorology presentation at school.

H is for High, L is for Low

The weather maps you can download from online services or the Internet look nearly as sharp as the graphics typically used on local television news broadcasts. Your kids can take advantage of this by retrieving online maps, printing them, and using them as the basis for an oral presentation in which *they* play meteorologist.

GET SMART: If storm chasing fascinates your child, and she wants to do even more research, encourage her to ask questions of the experts. Many of the storm chasers who post material linked to the Storm Chaser Home Page include their e-mail addresses. Your kid could conduct an e-mail interview with one or more chasers.

After downloading maps, import or copy them into your paint or draw program and then print them out. Although many maps show the entire country, you can focus on your region or state by cropping the image or manually erasing everything but the part of the map you want to show.

Types of weather maps that make good ammunition for a meteorology presentation include

- Tomorrow's conditions
- Satellite images
- Radar images
- Rainfall forecasts

GET SMART: Several of the weather maps found on America Online use the same scale and perspective. That characteristic allows you to overlay one map transparency with another to show, for example, a satellite image (which displays cloud cover) and a radar image (which shows current rainfall) at the same time.

Print the weather maps on transparencies. Most office-supply stores stock transparencies for ink-jet and laser printers. By printing the maps on transparencies, your child can easily show them to the entire class by using an overhead projector (a piece of presentation hardware most schools have on hand). Color transparencies work best for this type of presentation; they more closely resemble the weather maps familiar from TV.

Water, Water, Everywhere

In 1492, Columbus sailed the ocean blue. If he set sail today, he wouldn't find the waters to be quite so colorful. Pollution and intensive fishing have significantly degraded the quality of the world's oceans, a situation that alarms not only environmentalists and government leaders, but millions of children as well.

Studying the 70 percent of the Earth that's covered with water, exploring the ecosystems and the life-forms they contain, learning how the oceans are endangered and how they can be resuscitated ... all of this fascinates kids. When they see the ocean, they see a wonderful place full of exotic creatures and exciting natural science. The resources and projects that we describe here can augment your child's in-school studies of this important subject. (It's a great topic for family study, too.)

You can help your kids become amateur oceanographers, marine biologists, and undersea explorers by using the family's PC or

In the Magic School Bus Explores the Ocean, kids take a trip with Ms. Frizzle and explore seven different eco-zones of the undersea world.

★ TRY THIS! ★

Make a Miniature Deep-Sea Vent

Nearly 20 years ago, researchers in the deep-diving submarine Alvin (the same vessel that was later used to explore the wreck of the Titanic) made an amazing discovery. Miles below the surface, where the temperature is barely above freezing and the pressure is almost 300 times that at sea level, a series of rocky vents were spewing huge clouds of dark — and very hot — water.

Volcanic activity heats the water spurting from these vents to temperatures exceeding 500 degrees. That warms the nearby ocean enough to sustain life. And what life! Weird sea creatures — the strangest look like long, red tubes — thrive in the utter darkness.

To demonstrate how a deep-sea vent works, your elementary-school-aged children can make a miniature version with common household items, take it to school, and present it as a project or in lieu of a report. Here's what they need:

- A large glass container or jar — for example, an empty, economy-sized mayonnaise jar or a glass pitcher

- A much smaller bottle with a narrow neck, such as an empty Tabasco (hot sauce) bottle

- Food coloring (red works great)

- Hot water and ice-cold water

To see your miniature deep-sea vent in action, fill the large glass container with cold water — the colder the water, the better. Next, fill the small bottle with very hot water and then add a couple of drops of food coloring.

If the large container's mouth is wide enough to get a hand in, put a finger over the top of the small bottle and then set the small bottle upright in the large container. (If the mouth of the jar isn't wide enough, you can tie string around the neck of the small bottle and then lower it in.)

When you remove your finger from the mouth of the small bottle, the red-colored water starts spewing out. Your deep-sea vent works!

Do you know why? (Hint: Warm water rises; cold water sinks.)

Put cold water in one jar and hot water in another; you just made a miniature deep-sea vent!

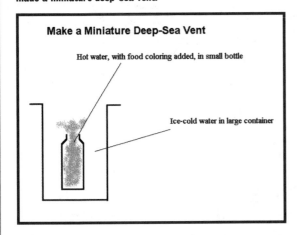

Make a Miniature Deep-Sea Vent

Hot water, with food coloring added, in small bottle

Ice-cold water in large container

Mac. In the following sections, we highlight two waterlogged (but *not* watered-down) CD-ROM reference and learning programs, hoist the signal flags to mark some of the best aquatic online resources, and send kids to the computer for a pair of nautical homework projects.

Raise the anchor!

The Magic School Bus Explores the Ocean

Ages 6–10

Filled with facts and lots of fun activities, and based on the popular PBS children's television show, The Magic School Bus Explores the Ocean stars a gang of cartoon kids and Ms. Frizzle, the leader of the band (and the driver of the Bus). This program offers a nice blend of science fact and learning fun.

The Magic School Bus Explores the Ocean drops kids into seven different water-related zones — from the beach and tidal pools to the deep sea and a coral reef. Each zone features an interactive science experiment that shows kids things like how waves work and how fish adapt to their environment. A dozen games and numerous clickable animated objects entice younger children to take a dip in the undersea world.

Several show-and-tell multimedia reports might nudge your children into research ideas of their own, but don't expect this CD-ROM to serve as an insightful reference work. (Your electronic encyclopedia can do that.) Instead, point your kids toward Ms. Frizzle when you want to get them excited about science in general, and the ocean in particular.

Microsoft Oceans

Ages 8 and Up

Part of Microsoft's Exploration series, Microsoft Oceans treats the oceans of the world as an integral part of Earth's ecology. In addition to looking at all kinds of sea life, the CD-ROM explores volcanoes, earthquakes, and weather systems, as well as human interactions with the sea, such as fishing, canal building, oil drilling, and pollution. You get a very complete picture.

You can browse the program through the five main pathways: Marine Life, A World of Water, People and the Sea, Index, and a guided tour with one of six animated characters. These guides host occupation-specific tours (oceanographer, scuba diver, solo sailor, eighteenth-century seaman, or alien visitor) that cross liberally into other pathways. As you browse, you discover fascinating sea trivia everywhere. For example, did you know that most life-forms at the ocean's greatest depths are transparent because not enough sunlight reaches those depths for pigmentation to occur?

GET SMART: *Microsoft Oceans makes a great reference work for older kids creating custom maps to illustrate their reports on ocean conditions or marine life. For more information about how to create such maps by using an electronic atlas and an art program, check out Chapter 5, "People and Places."*

Animation and other multimedia effects both entertain and instruct. For example, traveling arrows map the migration patterns of whales and the patterns of ocean

Microsoft Oceans explores interconnections between marine ecosystems and the rest of the Earth's ecology.

currents. And the program rewards correct answers to the many short quizzes by playing amusing nautical animations.

Microsoft Oceans delivers a working knowledge of the oceans and the interconnections of their ecosystems in an easily navigated environment.

Want to explore other CD-ROM oceans? Take a look at Chapter 14, "Homework Software," for more scientific and environmental software.

Shipwrecked!

The oceans may be filled with life and fit for scientific studies of all sorts, but they've also served as humanity's highways for centuries. And where ships sail on the seas, you can find shipwrecks.

One of the most famous disasters at sea

is the sinking of the Titanic in 1912. Steaming through the North Atlantic late on the night of April 14, it struck an iceberg. In less than three hours, the Titanic was gone, taking more than 1,500 passengers and crew to a watery grave.

The tale of the Titanic captivates kids. The disaster was truly a life-and-death story; it had heroes and villains and featured the technological marvel of its day. Suggest tackling the Titanic as the subject of a report, and it's likely that your kids will bite.

Resources for researching the Titanic are close at hand when you have a Web browser and a modem. For starters, try the page titled In Memoriam: RMS Titanic. Enter this address in your browser:

http://www.xnet.com/~cmd/titanic/

This Web page offers plenty of information about the ship, its passengers, and its sinking.

On the Titanic Home Page, you can take a virtual tour of the ship, hosted by its builder, Thomas Andrew (who perished when the liner went down). Complete with photographs, plans of the ship, and fascinating facts, this Web page gives younger children an excellent introduction to the disaster. To visit the Titanic Home Page, enter the following address in your Web browser:

http://iccu6.ipswich.gil.com.au/~dalgarry/

But the best Web resource for this homework assignment is RMS Titanic: 83 Years Later. Using newspapers of the period to document the event — including scores of digital images of actual newspaper clippings, headlines, and stories — the site gives kids a chance to read the same news as the people who lived during those times. To get to RMS Titanic, enter this address in your browser:

http://www.lib.virginia.edu/cataloging/vnp/titpref.html

Although the Titanic sank more than 80 years ago, you can still tour its decks by using your Web browser to visit the Titanic Home Page.

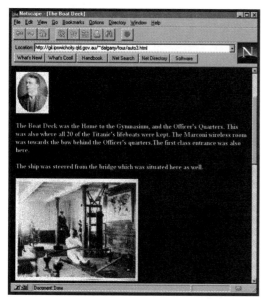

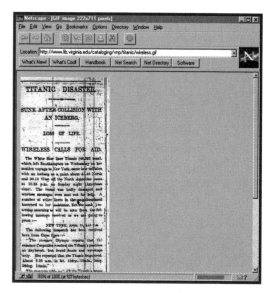

Researching real accounts of the disaster is easy when you use the scanned images of newspapers of the period at the RMS Titanic: 83 Years Later Web page.

After doing the research, your child can start the report or project. Taking a cue from the RMS Titanic: 83 Years Later Web site, your child can create a newspaper front page that includes all of the information that he gathered.

GET SMART: *This approach — writing a report in a newspaper front page format — works for all kinds of history reports and projects. For more ideas on how to use newspapers to complete homework assignments, check out Chapter 6, "The Past Is a Blast."*

With the right tool, your child can easily create a newspaper. A desktop publishing program such as Microsoft Publisher (which is the package that we recommend in *The FamilyPC Guide to Homework*) works well for this task.

Although Publisher lets you pick from several predesigned templates — including a newsletter format — the program is so easy to use that you can quickly build your own design. That's what we did.

Press Ctrl-N to open a new document and then click on the Blank Page tab. Select the Full Page icon and click on OK. Next, use the text tool (it looks like an uppercase *A*) to create a banner by clicking at

An unusual way to present historical information is by creating a pretend newspaper with a desktop publishing program such as Microsoft Publisher (ClarisWorks or Microsoft Works can do in a pinch).

the upper-left corner of the document and dragging to the far right. Enter a headline (we used *All My News*) in a large type size, such as 72 points.

GET SMART: *Many images on Web pages are GIF files; Publisher doesn't support this format. You have to load these files into an art program that supports GIF and then use the program's Save As command to translate them into a format Publisher recognizes, such as PCX.*

Create other text frames for your report by using the same click-and-drag operation. We made one for the headline of our Titanic story and another for the story itself. To add an illustration, use the Picture

tool to click-and-drag a picture frame into place. Use your browser to download one or more images from the Titanic Web sites and then place them on the page by using the Picture File command in the Insert menu.

After writing the newspaper-style report, your child can print it on a color printer (assuming you found color illustrations on the Web) and then sit back and wait for the good grade.

How Green Is My Planet?

Kids recycle with a vengeance and get angry whenever they see a factory belching smoke. Kids spend more time thinking about the environment and how to protect it than do most adults. Maybe they realize the world has to last a lot longer for *them* than for grown-ups.

Whatever the origin of kids' fascination with the environment and their attempts to make the world around them a bit greener, smart teachers use that fascination to foster an interest in science. That leads to homework assignments. And as in every other subject, that means your kids will probably ask you to lend an ear or offer an idea.

In the following sections, we point out a top-flight program for cultivating an interest in the environment among the younger set and then aim our Web browser to some terrific environmental information resources for older kids. Get them interested; help them get the information they need. That one-two punch works with almost any subject covered in *The FamilyPC Guide to Homework.*

Ozzie's World

Ages 3–8

Ozzie's World uses games, stories, and other activities to help kids ages three to eight learn about science and ecology. Based on the results of *FamilyPC*'s tests with real-world families (who gave the program an 87 out of 100, more than enough to collect the *FamilyPC* Recommended seal), we think Ozzie is the otter to buy if you want to nurture your kids' interest in environmental matters.

In Ozzie's World, hoses talk, lettuce leaves shiver, and other magical things occur. The program contains instructions for 40 hands-on science activities kids can conduct away from the computer. In one, kids learn how rainbows form and how to use a garden hose to make their own rainbow in the backyard. A coloring book contains 40 pictures kids can paint and print. The program also includes a half-dozen stories with Earth-

Go Online!

If your kids want to sail even larger oceans of information about oceans, put their digital ship on the Internet, where scores of sites highlight oceanographic, biologic, and historic pictures, text, and movies.

Most of all, we like to cruise the virtual waves of the Web, because it offers content on al-most any ocean-related topic. And lots of the information is fit for kids. Here are some sites we recommend for dropping your browser's anchor.

Hypercard Stack of Great Whales

http://unite.ukans.edu/
UNITEResource/
783750390-447DED81.rsrc

If you have a Macintosh and your kids are fascinated by monsters of the Deep, you should download the Hyper-card Stack of Great Whales. This cool hypercard stack in-cludes plenty of illustrations and other information about all the whales of the world.

Continued on page 198

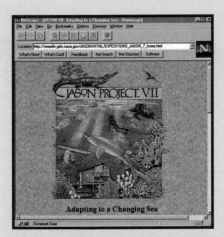

For kids interested in joining oceanographic expeditions, the Jason Project is one of the best sites on the Web.

The Jason Project

http://seawifs.gsfc.nasa.gov/JASON/HTML/JASON.html

Founded by Dr. Robert Ballard, the oceanographer and discoverer of the Titanic, The Jason Project is a series of electronic field trips. Although it's designed primarily to allow classrooms to connect to actual expeditions via live video links, kids at home can follow along by reading the expedition journals, trying their hand at some of the activities, and viewing images of the project in progress. The most recent expedition let kids track research done in the coastal waters off Florida, where Ballard and his team explored reefs, the Everglades, and other habitats. Kids can also review all the previous expeditions by visiting this Web site.

Ocean Planet

http://seawifs.gsfc.nasa.gov/ocean_planet.html

Based on an actual all-ocean Smithsonian exhibit that covers topics ranging from environmental issues to the creatures that live in the world's waters, Ocean Planet lets kids walk through a virtual museum, search for objects to view and text to read, take a digital tour created by the curator, and print fact sheets and family activities to try at home.

Keiko the Killer Whale

http://www.presys.com/ohwy/k/keiko.htm

The star of the movie *Free Willy* found a happy home in a huge facility on the scenic Oregon coast. By accessing this page, kids smitten with the orca can follow the aquarium's attempt to ready him for eventual release into the wild.

WhaleNet

http://whale.simmons.edu/

Although the WhaleNet Web page is most appropriate for older students, kids of all ages will be fascinated by the accounts of tagging whales with electronic monitoring devices and then tracking their migration.

El Niño is an ocean current that periodically disturbs the planet's weather patterns. This map from the Smithsonian's Ocean Planet exhibit shows some of El Niño's effects.

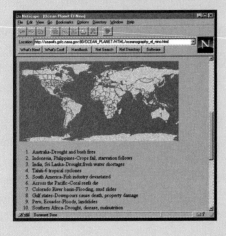

Kids learn about their environment through experiments and games in Ozzie's World, a science program that earned the *FamilyPC* Recommended seal of approval.

friendly themes that you can read to your kids.

For additional programs that stress ecology and the environment, including a terrific simulation that puts kids in charge of an endangered tropical island, head to Chapter 14, "Homework Software."

Older Kids Get Green on the Web

General science software aimed at older kids — grades 3 and up — often makes use of environmental themes. (For example, Science Sleuths includes a digital investigation of an oil spill; for more details about this science software series, see the section "How Things Work," in Chapter 8.) However, few programs for kids in this age range give the environment their full attention.

For environmental information, you *could* point your children toward an electronic encyclopedia, but a better solution is to fire up the family's Web browser (the browsers available through online services such as America Online, The Microsoft Network, Prodigy, and CompuServe work fine). On the Internet, you can find reams of infor-

★ TRY THIS! ★

Recycle Paper

Making paper means cutting down trees, grinding up the wood, and then mixing the mess with nasty (and smelly) chemicals. Or does it?

Making recycled paper — paper made from paper — saves trees and energy and produces fewer pollutants than making paper from scratch. That's why we stack old newspapers at the curb for the recycling truck.

You can make recycled paper in your kitchen and turn out some unique paper products at the same time. Here's what you need:

- Newspaper (two full sheets) torn into two- or three-inch squares
- Water (two to three cups)
- White glue (two tablespoons)
- Coat hangers (several)
- Old panty hose (several pair)
- Tape
- Scissors
- Food processor
- Clothes iron

Here's how you do it:

1. Untwist the coat hangers and form the wire into 6-inch-square frames. You need one frame for each sheet of paper you want to make. Tape any sharp edges of the wire.

2. Cut off the legs of the panty hose. Stretch one leg over each of the wire frames and tie a knot in each end of the panty hose.

3. Dump a handful of paper scraps and some water into the food processor. Close its lid and turn it on the highest speed. Add more paper and water until all the paper and water are in the food processor. Leave the food processor running for 2 to 3 minutes. You should have a gray glob of paper pulp in the food processor (the gray comes from the ink used to print the newspaper).

4. Fill the kitchen sink with about 5 inches of water and then add the glue. Dump in the paper pulp and mix it all up with your hands or a large wooden spoon.

5. Place one of the wire frames in the bottom of the sink. Slowly lift the frame out of the water. Let the water drip out of the mixture for at least a minute or two. Stir the paper/water mixture in the sink before inserting another wire frame.

6. Lay the wire frames in the sun to dry. Let the paper dry completely and then gently peel off the paper.

7. Use the iron — at its hottest setting — to steam the paper flat, removing most of the wrinkles and making it smooth enough to write or draw on.

Your child can turn this fun activity into a homework project for science class by writing a short report explaining the process and outlining the steps involved.

mation, activities, and virtual field trips to environmentally interesting areas.

GET SMART: *Naturalists and environmentalists find the Galapagos Islands especially interesting because of the diversity of life there. In fact, Charles Darwin spent considerable time examining the flora and fauna there before writing his groundbreaking book,* The Origin of Species. *You can read the complete text of this book, as well as Darwin's* Voyage of the Beagle, *by pointing your Web browser to* ***http://www.literature.org/ Works/Charles-Darwin/.***

One of the best places to visit is TerraQuest. Enter this address in your browser:

http://www.terraquest.com/

TerraQuest takes kids on virtual scientific expeditions to exotic parts of the world, including Antarctica and, most recently, Equador and the Galapagos Islands. You follow this cyberspace adventure by reading daily journals written by members of the expedition, viewing images posted on these Web pages and exploring the wildlife and cultures. Although TerraQuest doesn't focus exclusively on environmental issues, it offers plenty of in-

formation on ecology, ecosystems, and endangered species.

Another good Web spot to visit is Environmental Education (also called E-E Link). Enter the following address in your Web browser:

http://www.nceet.snre.umich.edu/index.html

Maintained by the National Consortium for Environmental Education and Training, E-E Link features a huge amount of educational material focusing on the environmental sciences. Don't let its classroom orientation scare you off; E-E Link's activities, documents, fact files, and links to other

TerraQuest's virtual field trips explore environmentally active and important parts of the world, such as Antarctica and the Galapagos Islands.

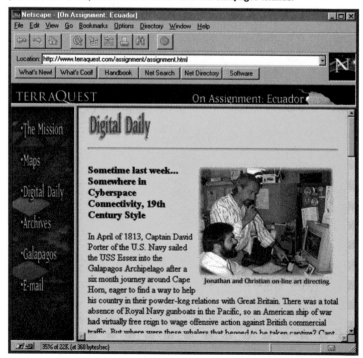

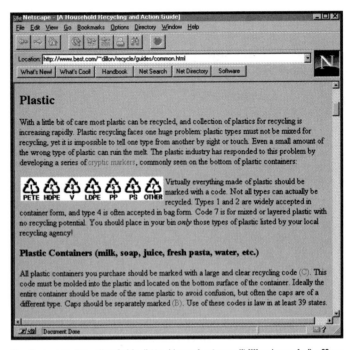

The Consumer Recycling Guide (http://www.best.com/~dillon/recycle/) offers tips and advice on how to recycle household items.

Web sites are excellent resources for kids studying the subject. One of its best areas deals with endangered species. To visit this part of E-E Link, head straight to this address with your Web browser:

http://www.nceet.snre.umich.edu/EndSpp/Endangered.html

On this page, kids can find lists, maps, fact sheets, and images of extinct and endangered species, as well as connections to a variety of different programs and projects that are trying to save endangered species and foster conservation of our natural resources.

Chapter 10

Artistic License
Art on the Family Computer

ART COMES EASY TO KIDS. AND ALTHOUGH it's not the same as paint on canvas or crayons on newsprint, art also comes easy to the family computer. But art can be — and should be — more than just for fun.

Art plays an integral part in the classroom, and it should be an important element of homework. Whether kids are illustrating reports or science projects, creating banners as backdrops to oral presentations, or designing covers for short stories and poetry collections, art skills come in handy at homework time.

No homework-capable computer is complete without at least one art program. (For our recommendations, see Chapter 2, "The Bare Necessities.") With the right art software and the tips and projects we present in this chapter, you can point your preschoolers toward some time-worthy art activities, turn el-

ementary-school kids loose on several how-to lessons, and send your middle- and high-school-aged students on a globe-trotting exploration of art masterpieces.

Now, *that's* art the easy way.

Early on in Art

Even the youngest children want to stay on the computer when they're playing with art software. And even the most computer-phobic kids usually take to painting and drawing on the screen, though they may flat out refuse to look at anything else.

We have a simple explanation for why this is so. Art on the computer is art without mistakes, and it's art with an unlimited range of colors and tools. Want to erase that house on the hill? It's gone in moments. Need another color? No need to worry about dried-out markers or missing crayons.

★ TRY THIS! ★

Connect the Dots

Puzzle books are great fun, but they have one shortcoming: You're limited to playing only those games that appear in their pages. With your computer and a drawing program, your kids have an unlimited source of puzzles.

You can quickly and easily create your own connect-the-dots puzzle. Using one continuous line in a color *other than* black, create a line drawing. Make sure you use the same color for the entire drawing, and avoid using any color fills or textures.

Use the pencil tool to place black dots at various points along the line and at the intersections of lines. (In the Windows 3.1 Paintbrush program or Windows 95's Paint, double-click on the brush and select the dot shape.) Number the dots (or use letters if you have fewer than 27 dots).

Select the color you used for the drawing, and choose the paint-can tool. Click on the inside and then the outside of the drawing, and the lines blend into the background. Then choose white from the color palette and click anywhere on the

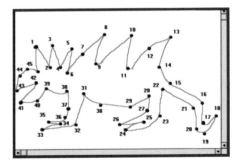

You and your child can create and play with an endless supply of connect–the–dots puzzles you can produce on the family computer.

Use Kid Pix's Edit Stamp option to erase the middle of any stamp.

screen. You now have numbered black dots on a white background.

To make a connect-the-dots puzzle by using Kid Pix stamps, select a stamp and then choose the Edit Stamp option. With the color white selected, use the pencil tool to erase the middle of the stamp and all but a few points along its edges. Now place your stamp on the screen, enlarging it as you stamp it (in Windows, hold down the Shift and Control keys; on the Mac, hold down the Shift and Option keys). Using the dot-to-dot paintbrush tool, place numbered dots at each point on your stamp. To return the stamp to its original condition, choose Edit Stamp and click on Restore Original.

In Flying Colors, choose the paintbrush tool's dot option and slide the setting bar to the right. As you draw the outline of your picture, the dots are spaced far apart, so you can go back and number or letter them. Save the file, and your kids can connect the dots and color the picture.

Enticing kids into creating computerized art is so easy that your biggest problem may be keeping the color printer stocked with paper and ink. Or you might have a tough time deciding which artistic software you should buy. (With oodles of paint and draw programs on the market, that's not an easy decision.)

Although preschoolers, kindergarteners, and kids in the lower elementary grades may not have many homework drawing assignments, they can turn to art for both at-home fun and for enhancing homework in other subjects. You just need to encourage their creativity by providing the right software and some at-home projects.

Get the Picture?

Although the terms *paint* and *draw* are often used interchangeably to describe computer art programs, they actually divide the artistic process into two camps. The difference between *paint* programs and *draw* programs originates from the way each type creates the objects you see on screen (which in turn determines the kinds of actions you can perform with those objects).

When you create a rectangle (or a line, or a curve, or any other object) in a *paint* program, that graphic is actually made up of numerous dots, or *pixels*, arranged in the *shape* of a rectangle. The paint program lets you do things such as erase only a corner of the rectangle, or select and move part of the rectangle to a new position in your painting. In a *draw program*, on the other hand, your rectangle is a single, discrete object. You can move the entire rectangle, stretch it, copy it, or delete it, but you can't manipulate isolated pieces of it.

Art, but Which Art?

Picking the best art program for your young children is a daunting task. You just have too many choices.

For first-time computer artists, we think Broderbund's Kid Pix Studio should be at the top of your list. In fact, we like Kid Pix Studio (and its less expensive sibling, Kid Pix 2) so much that it's the only art program we list in Chapter 2, "The Bare Necessities." Head there for a complete rundown on what this excellent paint program can do.

Another package we can't say enough about is Crayola Amazing Art Adventure, a paint program aimed at kids ages three to six (*FamilyPC*'s Family Testers also applauded loudly for this program, as they did for Kid Pix Studio). A colorful smorgasbord of painting fun, Crayola includes a wacky painting module and plenty of activities. (Amazing Art Adventure is now part of the Crayola Art Studio 2 CD-ROM; this package also includes Crayola Art Studio, an art program aimed at kids ages six to 12. If you're looking for Crayola Amazing Art Adventure in a software store, ask for Art Studio 2, instead.)

The paint module includes a fill tool with 50 designs, such as rainbows and checker patterns; a watercolor tool that lets young artists mix colors; and a tool that lets them easily create circles, squares, cubes, and other

Go Online!

For art ideas and other programs, check out the Blackberry Creek area on AOL (keyword **Black-berry**). When we last looked, Blackberry Creek included a dot-to-dot program (in versions for both the Mac and Windows), sports trading card templates, ink-blot pictures (a really cool way to get kids' imaginations going), frame templates (to frame your artwork), and a Kids' Art Gallery for sharing the stuff your children create.

A Web site called Carlos's Coloring Book Home contains a half-dozen coloring pages kids can complete while

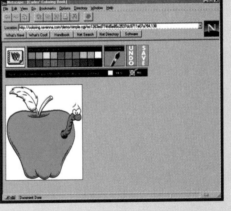

Carlos's Coloring Book is cute — it lets kids color online — but it can't match an art program on your own computer.

they're online. The process is slow — even slower than coloring with an art program on your PC or Mac — but it's a neat trick. Of course, you can simply print the pages with your Web browser and then hand them over to the kids for traditional coloring. You can visit Carlos's Coloring Book Home by pointing your Web browser to this address:

http://www.ravenna.com/coloring/

Aunt Annie's Craft Page is another good arts and crafts pit stop on the World Wide Web. She describes how to use common household materials to make projects such as homemade stamps (the kind on paper, not the type found in art programs such as Kid Pix Studio), homemade paper, and cool appliqués. You can even download a shareware program called Aunt Annie's Crafts from this site. You can find Aunt Annie's Craft Page at the following Web address:

http://www.coax. net/annie/

Your child's artistic masterpiece may end up on the family's refrigerator, but the audience for that is small compared to The Refrigerator, a Web-page-based contest in which kids' artwork can be seen by anyone connected to the World Wide Web:

http://www.seeusa.com/refrigerator.html

Each week, this Web page posts five pictures. The art doesn't have to be computer generated; in fact, it must be submitted on paper ... talk about low-tech!.

Viewers vote, and the winner goes to the Hall of Fame. Cool!

shapes. The program also has 150 stickers of people, animals, dinosaurs, and other images, as well as 60 animated stickers. A keyboard speaks the letters as kids type them. Kids can apply visual effects to their pictures, including wind-blown and splattered effects.

If your child makes a mistake, she can erase parts of her work or explode the whole thing in 20 different ways. In addition to all the painting fun, Amazing Art Adventure contains 12 activities, such as coloring books, mazes, and hidden pictures. In the Jungle Adventure Coloring Book, for example, your child can color jungle pictures and then watch them animate.

For other great drawing and painting programs, see Chapter 14, "Homework Software."

Art Lessons

When it comes to art, a funny thing happens to kids between preschool and grade school. Art goes from being an activity they enjoy without inhibition to something they think they "can't do" or "aren't good at." Blame it on adults who tell them to color inside the lines, or on kids' own emerging sense of what looks

Kids launch into art activities or freehand painting from Amazing Art Adventure's colorful opening screen.

right, but suddenly, art just isn't as much fun anymore.

Fortunately, the family computer rides to the rescue. With a top-flight multimedia art program installed and at the ready, the machine gives kids an amazing array of drawing and painting tools, from wacky paintbrushes to spray paint and stamps. However, more experienced artists want more powerful art tools to handle art class assignments (before discarding chalk, paint, and pencils, check with the art teacher to

★ TRY THIS! ★

Create Custom Coloring Books

Coloring books are another nifty way to get the youngest members of your family interested in art, but some kids can whip through a coloring book faster than a modern artist throws paint on a canvas. And why is it that most coloring books hype characters from movies or Saturday morning cartoons?

You can create custom coloring books for your kids, which they can then tint either at the computer, using their art program, or away from the machine, using low-tech crayons and markers.

If you're the artistic type and can draw simple shapes, try your hand at creating coloring book pages by using your art software. A digitizing tablet comes in handy here. (A digitizing tablet makes a much more natural input device for art; kids use a pencil-like stylus rather than the difficult-to-control mouse. We recommend the $190 Wacom ArtPad II. For more details, see Chapter 2.) Use relatively wide brushstrokes or lines for the outlines of the coloring book shapes.

However, most of us couldn't draw a horse if one appeared in the living room. If you're artistically challenged, point your Web browser to Barry's Clip Art Server:

http://www4.clever.net/graphics/clip_art/ clipart.html

This Web site has hundreds of black-and-white images that make good coloring book material. Most are in the GIF format, so your art program must be able to import this type of file. Otherwise, you need a utility program that can convert this format into one suitable for your kids' paint or draw program. If you need this type of utility program, we recommend Paint Shop Pro, a shareware program you can obtain on CompuServe (**GO JASC**), from most other online services, and on the Web:

http://www.jasc.com/index.html

Because it's shareware, you can try out Paint Shop Pro before paying for it; if you like it and use it, you should register, or pay for, the program.

After downloading an image (and perhaps converting it to a format your art program recognizes), open it with your art program. Save each image as a separate file so that your children can color the picture using their art program or print each page for away-from-the-computer coloring.

make sure your children can use the PC or the Mac), as well as artistic additions to other homework projects and reports.

Unfortunately, schools sometimes skip the artistic basics (budget cuts often slash art first), which leaves your kids out in the cold. As we've said before, artistic ability is a boon to kids working on homework assignments and projects in subjects ranging from science (charts and diagrams) to social studies (maps and illustrations).

Art Explorer Deluxe for the Mac includes more tools than most real artists use, including stamps, brushes, and dye tints.

To help you cover these sometimes-ignored basics, we've assembled four easy art lessons on perspective, drawing, colors, and pointillism. Your children can complete these lessons at home, with virtually any paint or draw program.

Painting, but Not by Numbers

One top-notch Macintosh paint program fit for kids ages eight and up — actually, a good pick for the entire family — is Art Explorer Deluxe. This program contains all the basic tools you expect in a family paint program: several brush styles and sizes, basic shapes, even the obligatory exploding eraser. It goes beyond the expected, though, to include several features other family paint programs lack, including blends and textures, as well as glaze, dye, and tint capabilities. Other features include invert, darken, and lighten effects, and charcoal, marker, calligraphy, spatter, texture, and smudge tools.

In the Fun menu, kids find tools for creating bubble patterns, kaleidoscopes, oozing lines, and a half-dozen other neat effects. The Geometry menu contains tools for creating kinetic shapes (one looks like a Slinky, for example), 3-D boxes, stars, and spirals. Art Explorer offers numerous activities, including Stamp Itz, which features hundreds of stamps; Color Itz, which provides outline images kids can color; and Build Itz, which encourages kids to mix and match pieces to make wild and weird characters.

Dabbler 2 is another good pick for older children — especially if you're looking for a program that teaches art techniques and provides a full set of tools. This program works on the Mac *and* under both Windows 3.1 and Windows 95. Although Dabbler 2 didn't score well with *FamilyPC*'s Family Testers in the magazine's most recent roundup of paint programs, we think it's worth your while, especially if you have in-the-home artists who want to go beyond the basics.

Dabbler 2's most intriguing artistic feature is its capability to mimic traditional materials, allowing your kids to produce computer art that doesn't *look* like computer art. Use the crayon tool, for example, and colors build up as you lay each one down in turn. Kids can select from a library of paper textures, apply stencils, and, best of all, view and use the online multimedia tutors, which show them how to draw cartoons and create animated flipbooks.

For other great drawing and painting programs, see Chapter 14, "Homework Software."

Art Lesson 1: Get into Perspective

Drawings and paintings don't have to look realistic to be beautiful. But when you want your work to look as if you could reach out and touch it, you need to give it *perspective*. Perspective is the illusion of depth on a flat surface; it comes from the way you arrange lines, colors, and objects — three easy-to-manipulate features of any good drawing or paint program. Because your family PC or Mac lets you easily manipulate, duplicate, and arrange objects of different sizes, shapes, and colors, you have a great platform that you can use for experimenting with perspective.

To get started with perspective drawing, try creating a landscape. Pick a point in the center of the screen, about two-thirds of the way up from the bottom of the page. This point is called the *vanishing point*, because it's where all the lines of the drawing meet and seem to

Artwork created with Dabbler 2 doesn't look computerized. Use its chalk tool, for example, and the result looks as if you rubbed real chalk on real textured paper.

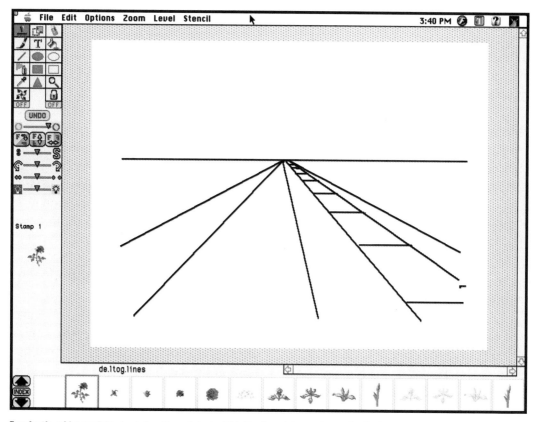

For depth, add a vanishing point — the point at which the lines intersect — and a horizon line to the first stage of your perspective drawing.

disappear. Now, with the straight-line tool, draw six randomly spaced lines from the vanishing point to the sides and bottom of the page. These lines will form the roads, rivers, and fields that add depth to your landscape.

Try turning two of the lines into a set of railroad tracks by drawing horizontal lines between them. (Hint: The lines should start out far apart and get closer together as you approach the vanishing point.) You can draw lines up and out from the vanishing point to indicate mountains in the distance (make these lumpy, if you like). Finally, draw one hori-

zontal line, parallel to the bottom of the page, running through the vanishing point. This is your horizon line. Already, even without colors or objects in the scene, your picture should have depth.

Increase the picture's depth by adding color. In general, colors fade in the distance. With this rule in mind, make the colors of your roads, rivers, and fields change from strong and bright at the bottom or the edges of the page to soft and muted toward the top. To keep the color changes subtle, choose shades fairly close to each other, and blend the edges together by using the program's spray-paint tool or by scribbling with the thinnest line of your pencil tool. With colors added, you should be able to see perspective and depth developing even more.

Now create even greater depth by adding objects to the scene (if your paint or draw program offers stamps, use these for instant objects). Keep in mind two more rules of perspective:

● Objects in the distance look smaller than objects in the foreground.

● Objects in the foreground partially obscure objects in the background.

If you're using Kid Pix Studio, for example, you can create a line of crabs marching down the road by using the Rubber Stamp tool. Start with the smallest crab stamp and

place your crawly critter close to the vanishing point. Then stamp on successively bigger crabs, as you move toward the edge of the page. If you want the crabs to appear close together, overlap them.

Add other stamps along the other roads, rivers, and fields. The stamps don't have to be straight, as long as you make them smaller as they get closer to the vanishing point. And don't forget to add tiny stamps to your horizon line. Before you know it, you have a picture that looks like you could jump right in.

Art Lesson 2: Take Note and Shape Up

Look around while squinting your eyes, and you can see that all objects — even complex ones — are nothing more than combinations of simple shapes: squares, rectangles, triangles, circles, and ovals. Now look at the placement of those shapes. How are they related to each other? Where does one begin and the other end? At what angle do they sit?

Once you learn to see the world as a series of simple shapes and realize that the relationships among them is what gives them character, you have the basic framework for drawing nearly anything.

Try This: Draw someone's face by using the basic shapes in your computer's art program. Choose a per-

Muted colors in the distance add to the illusion of perspective.

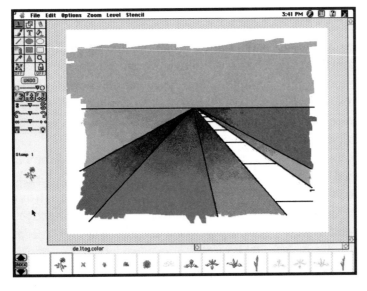

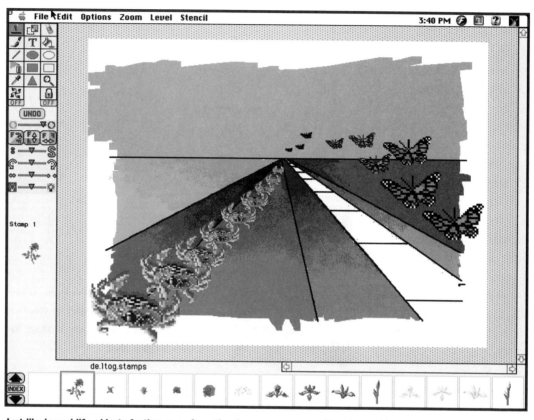

Just like in real life, objects farther away from the observer appear smaller; closer objects seem larger.

son with distinctive or unusual features or use a well-lit, close-up photograph of a face. If you want to start out really simply, try drawing a baby's face or your favorite cartoon character from the newspaper.

Start with the shape of the head. Decide whether it's long or short, wide or narrow, squared off like a rectangle or pointy like a triangle. Then draw it with the appropriate shape-making tool. Experiment with overlapping shapes — for example, you might need to combine an oval (for the top of the head) with a square (for the jaw). After you get the basic shape in place, erase all of the interior lines.

Next, look at the eyes. Are they more like ovals or oddly shaped triangles? Perhaps they're set close together, or maybe they tilt down or up at the corners. Again, you might have to draw the shapes yourself or alter an existing shape to get it just right. Note where the eyes are located in the head: about halfway down — not higher up, as many inexperienced artists seem to think. How about those eyebrows? Are they bushy enough to be braided or almost too sparse to be seen? Do they go straight across or arch like bridges?

Continue with the nose and the mouth, again paying close attention to the relationships between the shapes, as well as the shapes themselves. For example, the eyes and the mouth may be separated by a long, triangular nose or a short, roundish one. As for the hair, have fun — you can even give your model a different hairstyle.

When you're done, stand back and compare your drawing to the real thing. If it's pretty far off the mark, don't despair. Look at each shape and its placement and try to figure out what went wrong.

A baby's face makes a good subject for your first drawing lesson; most are simple in shape but distinctive in appearance.

Art Lesson 3: Mix 'em Up

Choosing colors is an art in itself. A color wheel helps you learn about mixing colors and contrasting colors; even the most experienced artist uses a version of the color wheel when picking paints.

A simple color wheel consists of the primary colors — red, blue, and yellow — and the secondary colors — purple, green, and orange. To make a color wheel by using your paint or draw program, draw a circle, divide it into six pieces (like pieces of a pie), and number them 1 through 6. Next, use the program's paint-can tool to put the *primary colors* red, blue, and yellow in spaces 1, 3, and 5, respectively.

Then fill in the spaces for the *secondary colors*. Purple goes in space 2, because blue and red, which border that space, make purple. Green goes in space 4, because blue and yellow make green. Orange goes in space 6, because yellow and red make orange. (Although this color wheel stops here, if you mix any of the secondary colors, you get a tertiary color, such as brown.)

You can save your color wheel or, if you have access to a color printer, print it and keep it around as a reminder of the art of choosing colors.

Art Lesson 4: Get the Point

Did you know that your eyes can mix colors? In the 1880s, French artist Georges Seurat developed a painting technique called *pointillism*. In pointillism, artists paint colored dots very close together; when you view the dots from a distance, they seem to mix to form a new, vibrant color. By using your computer, you can easily create a pointillist painting — you just need an art program and your handy color wheel.

GET SMART: *You can check out some original Seurat paintings on the World Wide Web by pointing (no pun intended) your browser to*

`http://www.pride.net/~dbirnbau/seurat/index.html`

First, draw a simple scene — perhaps the outline of a house and a tree — by using the program's pencil tool. Now check your color wheel. If you want the tree to have orange, autumnal leaves, color it with tiny red and yellow dots, which will look orange from a distance. A spray-paint tool (most programs have one) is ideal for this job. The pencil tool will do in a pinch (though this requires lots of mouse clicks). The closer and denser you make the dots, the better the colors mix.

Do the same with red and blue dots to make a purple house and with yellow and blue dots to make green grass. To make a brown tree trunk, mix any

two secondary colors — all make shades of brown. Finish your painting with a light blue sky made of blue and white dots.

GET SMART: *For faster pointillist painting, draw a small area of different-colored dots (for example, red and yellow, to make orange) and then copy and paste the group of dots several times, to create an even larger area. With your art program's Copy and Paste commands, you can use this larger color blob to paint in whole sections of your illustration.*

Because pointillism is a very soft, blurry style, you should leave the edges of objects a bit ragged, so they bleed into each other

Use your paint or draw program to create a color wheel like this one.

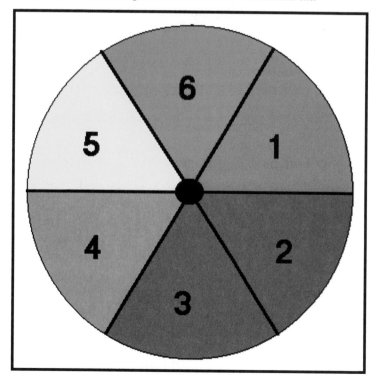

Dots and more dots: With any art program, kids can create pointillist paintings — and learn how colors mix.

and look more natural. When you finish your pointillist painting, stand back and let your eyes work their color magic.

Appreciating Art

Kids should know more about art than how to hold a paintbrush or fire up their computer's paint program. They should know something about the history of art and have a chance to see museum-quality art in person. Art is, after all, an integral part of our culture and our civilization.

But even the most extravagantly funded school district doesn't have enough money to send students on globe-trotting field trips to famous museums in faraway cities. To appreciate the art of the masters — da Vinci, Rembrandt, Picasso, and others throughout history — kids can only stare at coffee-table-sized art books, right? Wrong. Thanks to several CD-ROM packages and countless sites on the World Wide Web, older students can get a grasp of art through the home computer. Both the CD-ROMs and the Web pages serve as virtual museums, guiding viewers through galleries and showing paintings on the computer screen. They are not the same as really being there, of course (there's nothing like standing inches away from a painting, close enough to see the brush strokes), but they are a lot less expensive than an airline ticket!

Of course, these disc-based and online art explorations can serve as reference works for middle- and high-school-aged kids working on homework assignments for art, history, or social studies classes.

Museums on Disc

Numerous art museum tours on CD-ROM have been released during the past year or so. Ranging from the relatively obscure to the world famous, these electronic museums take you through their halls and let you get up close and personal with the artwork. The best provide lots of additional information, ranging from artists' biographies to time lines showing the often overlapping impact of the masters.

One such CD-ROM is Le Louvre, an extraordinary self-guided tour through one of the world's most famous museums, the Louvre in Paris. You can use the index, explore each of the Louvre's buildings, or use the time line to head straight to a favorite pe-

Le Louvre offers audio commentary about almost all of its paintings.

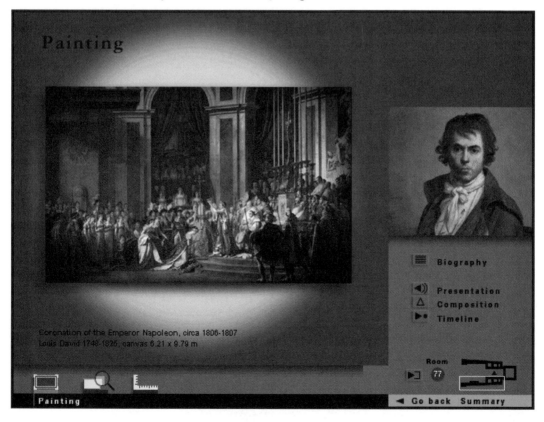

riod — for example, 17th century French paintings.

Once in the museum, you can view each room, expand any painting to full-screen size, and listen to more than two hours of commentary (just like a personal guide!). Animations and narration accompany many of the most famous paintings, pointing out composition and highlighting details that only a curator would know. With more than 300 images and 200 pages of text — the biographies of the artists are especially valuable for research — Le Louvre is one whale of a field trip.

GET SMART: *Le Louvre makes it a snap to research painters from a specific period. Choose a period from the Timeline and then click on each of the paintings in turn. For notes on each painter, click on Biography. You can't copy text from the program, so take notes the old-fashioned way.*

Masterpiece Mansion takes a completely different tack. Aimed at kids 12 and older, it combines art appreciation with some clever game-like elements. Using more than 150 famous works of art — these range from ancient Grecian statues to 20th cen-

Masterpiece Mansion isn't just for kicks. Its reference section meets the research needs of younger kids.

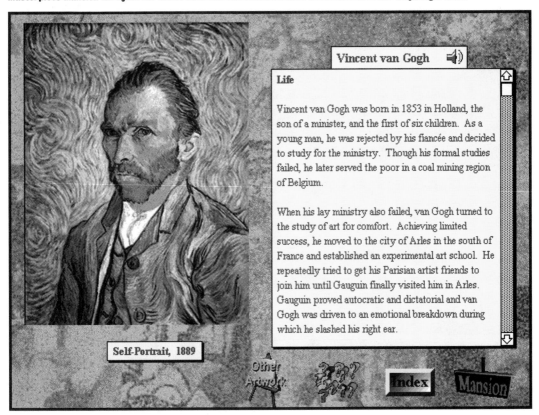

tury paintings — Masterpiece Mansion presents puzzles and games that children must solve and play in order to escape the mansion. It's also a decent reference work for elementary- and middle-school students — its Art Explorer and Biographer Explorer modules present information about major periods in art history and biographies of 45 famous artists.

For additional museum tours on CD-ROM, check out Chapter 14, "Homework Software."

Museums on the Fly

If you were to buy a CD-ROM for each museum you want to show your kids, the *ticket price* would soon match that of airfare to Paris. For that reason, you should also rely on the Internet's World Wide Web for your kids' art-related research needs.

You can find hundreds of art-related sites on the Web. Some are appropriate for kids; some are not. Fortunately, you can preview any museum before you open the doors for your children.

We put together a three-city, three-stop museum tour for you to explore, but you can easily assemble one yourself. Just use one of the Internet's search tools to scope out other museums, bookmark each intriguing place, and take your kids on a digital field trip of your own design.

For tips on finding information on the Internet, see Chapter 7.

First Stop: Paris and the WebMuseum

The ultimate Internet art museum isn't really a museum at all — not a real one, any-

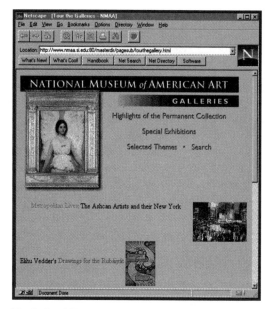

The National Museum of American Art includes a search tool to speed up research.

way. Instead, the WebMuseum's virtual galleries take you to hundreds of outstanding images of paintings. To visit the WebMuseum, enter the following address in your Web browser

http://sunsite.unc.edu/wm/

The Paul Cezanne exhibit is superb, but you should probably start your kids at Famous Paintings:

http://sunsite.unc.edu/wm/paint/

This massive collection of the world's most recognizable art on canvas also includes short biographies of scores of painters, which your kids can use for elementary research.

One of Michelangelo's gifts to the ages, the Sistine Chapel is accessible online. The close-ups are awesome.

Second Stop: Washington, D.C. and the National Museum of American Art

Even if you can't get to our nation's capital, your home computer can take you to the National Museum of American Art, part of the Smithsonian Institute:

http://www.nmaa.si.edu:80

The paintings at this site are truly stunning, and the multimedia presentation is among the best we've seen in Internet art. You can view more than 1,000 works of art, and you can take any of several self-guided tours that highlight special exhibitions and usually include video clips and audio you can play through your Web browser. This out-standing site also offers hotlinks to educational information.

Last Stop: Rome and the Sistine Chapel

Just one of several separate sites that highlight art at the Vatican (you can reach them all through this page, however), the Sistine Chapel is famous for the awe-inspiring artwork of Michelangelo. You may not get a crick in your neck from staring at the ceiling, but you can pick from a dozen or more different views of each section of the chapel. If your child needs to research Renaissance art, this is a must-see stop on the tour:

http://www.christusrex.org/www1/sistine/0-Tour.html

Chapter 11

In Song and On Stage

Music and Drama

S OMETIMES, IT SEEMS THE FAMILY COM-
puter can help with almost any subject. Want to sing songs or write your
own music? Can do. Like to play make-
believe on stage and off?
Ditto.

Music and drama, two
fine-arts subjects that
often don't get the attention they deserve in
school, can come alive on
the home computer.
Equip the machine with
a software program or
two, and it becomes a
credible music tutor and
a hands-on drama
maker.

Teachers don't assign
homework in these sub-
jects as often as they do
in the core areas of study — such as math,
writing, history, or science — but the tools
we highlight and the projects we outline
can be used by almost any child, for a wide

variety of classes. Rather than write yet
another history paper about someone from
the political world, why not tackle a famous
figure in music? Looking for a way to make
a report *really* sparkle?
Add some sounds or
some music clips to the
document. We show you
how in this chapter.

Make Some Music!

Preschoolers love to
make sounds by beating
on pots and pans (music
to *their* ears, if not to
their parents'). But at
some point in their
school careers, many kids
lose interest in music.
Maybe it's because the subject gets short
shrift in too many schools today (in this
cost-conscious era, schools may drop band
from middle-school offerings or dispose of

music teachers in elementary schools). Or maybe music becomes less an entertaining activity and more like work.

Whatever the reason for the falloff in interest, you can do something to reverse this trend. With the family's PC or Mac, you can foster an appreciation for music in your youngest children and provide some terrific musical creativity tools for older kids. We have several software packages in mind that do that, and more.

GET SMART: *If you want to use a PC for any music-making activity, the machine must be equipped with an audio board and speakers. (All Macs are audio-capable right out of the box.) For top-quality audio, you want a 16-bit sound card with an FM synthesizer. Most PCs come with such a card. If your machine lacks such sound capability, consider the SoundBlaster 16, which typically sells for less than $100.*

Unless your children play musical instruments (and therefore practice at home), they rarely have music homework. Don't let that stop you from trying to build their interest in music. With an idea here and another there, you may be able to prod your child into considering a music-related report or enhancing an existing report or project with tunes. In the following sections, we show you how to demonstrate the possibilities to your kids by using the programs you already have in the house.

And to beat the music drum even louder, we point our baton to a pair of kid-appropriate places on the World Wide Web

where your children can learn how to make their own music.

Strike up the band!

Music Software for Your Young Musicians

Your family PC or Mac is more than a writing tool or a number cruncher. Thanks to its multimedia hardware — a CD-ROM drive, audio capabilities, and speakers — it's also a toe-tappin' jukebox. When equipped with one of the many software programs that use sound as a teaching tool, the computer can encourage even the youngest child to explore music.

We think three programs in particular have what it takes to get young kids — preschoolers and children in grades 1 through 3 — in front of the virtual keyboard and keep them there.

Lamb Chop Loves Music
Ages 3–7

Although some folks may categorize Lamb Chop Loves Music as an interactive storybook (*FamilyPC* did when its Family Testers reviewed the program), this entertaining CD-ROM also offers a delightful introduction to music.

A cute mixture of a storybook, games, and a junior encyclopedia, this tale within a tale begins with Lamb Chop saying that she wants to learn to play the piano. Shari Lewis, who always has a hand in Lamb Chop's exploits, suggests that the lively lamb might first consider all the other instruments that she might play. In order to acquaint Lamb Chop with these, she recounts the classic tale of the

Lamb Chop Loves Music is first and foremost a first-rate interactive storybook, but its emphasis on music also makes it a good pick for introducing preschoolers to the subject.

Making Music
Ages 5 and Up

Slightly older children — or anyone who would rather paint notes than figure out a tune from sheet music — should head instead to Making Music. You don't have to know how to read or write notes to have fun with this Windows and Mac CD-ROM. To compose music, kids just draw a picture. (Think of Making Music as a musical version of finger-painting or a tune-happy KidPix–style program.)

In the composition area, each stroke of the paintbrush creates a note. The longer the line, the longer the note. The higher you draw it on the screen, the higher the pitch of the note. Change color and the instrument changes. After creating a tune, you can listen to the *painting* as it plays. Other areas of the program let kids play with pitch and rhythm and

Musicians of Bremen.

In addition to the story, kids will find lots to explore in Lamb Chop Loves Music. In the Game Room, for example, preschoolers can play five activities designed to enhance their understanding of music. In the Song Jumble game, kids rearrange pieces of a song — represented by illustrated musical blocks — into the correct musical and visual order.

The Music Store introduces young ears to the world of orchestral musical instruments. By visiting four different rooms, children learn the shapes and sounds of string, woodwind, brass, and percussion instruments (and how each instrument is played). In the String room, for example, Horse plays the instruments while Shari narrates a brief introduction to each instrument's capabilities. Your child will enjoy playing with this CD-ROM.

With Making Music, creating a tune is as easy as painting a picture. To explore rhythm and melody, for example, kids just put birds on a wire and place eggs along the bottom.

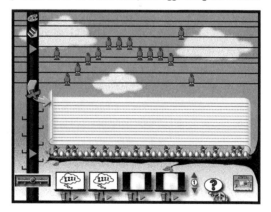

★ TRY THIS! ★

Make Homegrown Music with Kid Pix Studio

As we already said, your child probably won't have music homework. But that doesn't mean music — or any other kind of sound — has to take a leave of absence from your kid's reports and projects. Like art, sound and music can be effective additions to all kinds of homework.

We think Kid Pix Studio is the best program for elementary-school-aged kids who want to add sound or music to their assignments. Kid Pix Studio gives kids fun-to-use painting tools, lets them enter text, and provides a slick slide-show module for assembling a presentation. More important, your kids can save a slide show as a file that they can run on another computer, even if that computer doesn't have a copy of Kid Pix Studio. Of course, Kid Pix Studio lets you add sound.

If you equip your computer with a microphone, adding sound to a picture is a snap in Kid Pix Studio.

GET SMART: To record sound, you need a microphone connected to your PC or Mac. Most Macs come with a microphone, but you probably need to buy one for your PC and then jack it into the mic connector on the computer's sound card. Look for a hands-off model — one that either stands on a base or has a clip that lets you attach it to clothing — so that kids can continue to use the keyboard and mouse while recording.

You can add one sound to each Kid Pix Studio document. Just select Record Sound from the Goodies menu and, when your child is ready to record, click on the Record button (the one with the large circle on it). Click the Stop button to stop the recording and then click the Save button to save the recorded sound (which the program automatically attaches to your Kid Pix Studio document.) Possible uses of sound include snippets of songs your child has written, narration (perhaps for a digital, illustrated oral report), or sound effects to punch up a short story.

To make a slide show for a presentation, click on the SlideShow button in the Kid Pix Studio main menu. Import the sound-enhanced documents one at a time; the sound button at the bottom of each slide window should turn on (green means *on*).

When your child's slide show is all set, save it by selecting the Save A StandAlone command from the File menu. This saves the slide show as an executable file (as an EXE file on the PC). Copy that file to a floppy disk, and your child can take it to school and run it on a computer there. (Of course, that computer must have sound capability and speakers, or the teacher won't hear the sounds you recorded.)

introduce them to the various elements of song structure.

KidRiffs
Ages 5–11

Looking for a program that teaches music in a more traditional fashion? If so, check out KidRiffs, a fun, hands-on musical program designed to teach children the different ways in which songs and tunes are assembled. With a variety of simple, recognizable melodies to manipulate (including "London Bridge" and "Old MacDonald"), kids explore five rooms, each dedicated to a different aspect of musical composition, including rhythm, timbre, and scales.

Each room features approximately 10 aspects of sound that kids can control, ranging from the simple (choosing an instrument) to the more sophisticated (investigating ways of notating and accenting notes). Although each room covers all the elements of musical composition, there's no right or wrong way to go; kids set the pace themselves.

At the Instrument Inn, for example, kids hear the riffs played by any one of more than 100 instruments, or they can record their own tunes. And at the Scale Shack, kids can transpose these melodies into various keys and modes, so they can hear the same riff played in any scale.

Kids can make their own melodies by using either a keyboard on the screen or the computer's keyboard. By trial and error, even kids with little or no musical background can figure out the melodies to favorite songs.

Check out Chapter 14, "Homework Software," for more music programs suitable for young children.

Making Music for Older Kids

Older children with an interest in music probably play an instrument. They know how to read music and how to play it, but now they want to write their own. Can the family's computer help them, too?

You bet.

Kids learn about scales, tempo, and rhythm with KidRiffs, a hands-on exploration of musical concepts disguised in a colorful interface.

★ TRY THIS! ★

Add Sound to a Report

Sound-enhanced reports aren't just for young children. Middle-school and high-school students can also add sound, narration, and music to their reports. And you probably won't have to buy another piece of software to make that possible.

Kids using integrated programs such as Microsoft Works or ClarisWorks, or a full-blown word processor such as Microsoft Word, can easily add sounds, voice narration, and musical clips to their homework assignments. Like the Kid Pix slide shows, these sound-enhanced assignments must be turned in to the teacher in the form of a file on disk.

Launch your integrated program or word processor. All three of our recommended writing tools for this age group — Microsoft Works, ClarisWorks, and Microsoft Word — let you add sounds to a document. We show you how to add sound to a Microsoft Works for Windows 95 document, but you use a similar process to create sound enhanced documents in the other programs.

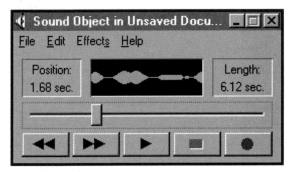

When you insert an audio object in a Works document in Windows 95, this Sound Recorder window appears.

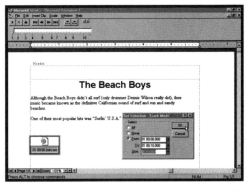

This dialog box lets you set the length of the audio clip you're recording from a CD.

Record original sound or narration

Open the Works document in which you plan to add audio. Move the cursor to the spot in the document at which you want to place the sound. Select Object from the Insert menu, and in the dialog box that appears, pick Wave Sound. Windows 95's Sound Recorder applet pops up on the screen.

To begin recording, click on the red Record button at the far right of the Sound Recorder window. Sing, make noises, or speak into the microphone. Click on the square Stop button (second from the right) to stop recording. Choose the Exit and Return... command from the File menu. Works now displays a sound icon in the document.

To play this sound, just right-click on the

Continued on page 227

object (that is, position the mouse pointer on the object and click the right mouse button) and then pick Play from the Wave Sound Object menu.

Record music clips from a CD

Put a CD in the PC's CD-ROM drive, open the Works document in which you plan to add the clip, and place the cursor in the location at which you want the audio added. Select Object from the Insert menu and then pick Media Clip from the dialog box that Works displays. The menu at the top of the Works screen changes to show Media Player's controls. Select CD Audio from the Insert Clip menu at the top of the screen. Using the Media Player controls, select the portion of the CD you want to record. (You can use the Set Selection window to designate the starting time, the ending time, and the length of the audio selection; choose Selection from the Edit menu to do this.) Now pick Copy Object from the Media Player's Edit menu. The recording appears in the Works document as an object labeled CD Audio. You can move this object anywhere in the document.

GET SMART: To read this report — and listen to the sounds embedded within it — the teacher must have a computer equipped with the same application your child used for creating the report.

To play this sound within the document, right-click on the CD Audio object and then select Play Media Clip from the pop-up menu that appears.

Music Mentor 2.0
Ages 12 and Up

For beginning composers, we recommend Music Mentor 2.0, a full-featured musical package that lets kids (and musically inclined adults) create, record, edit, and print original compositions.

GET SMART: *Eenie, meenie, MIDI. MIDI (which stands for Musical Instrument Digital Interface) is the recognized standard for translating musical notes into the numbers a computer understands. (And, of course, back the other way, from numbers to notes, and thus sounds.)*

To enable your budding musicians to use Music Mentor's complete suite of tools, you need to invest in a MIDI-capable instrument. (A keyboard is usually the best pick for an at-home MIDI instrument. Look for a MIDI instrument in a home electronics store that carries both computers and keyboards.) You also need a MIDI interface (an add-on card that you must install inside the computer) and cables that connect the keyboard to the computer.

Once you have all that gear plugged in, your kids can compose at the keyboard. Music Mentor captures every note played and puts it on the screen in the proper musical notation. Alternatively, your kids can create a tune by selecting notes from the Note Palette and dropping them onto a scale. Other features let your kids mix multiple tracks, change instrument sounds, and adjust the tempo. To edit a tune, your children simply cut and paste notes or move

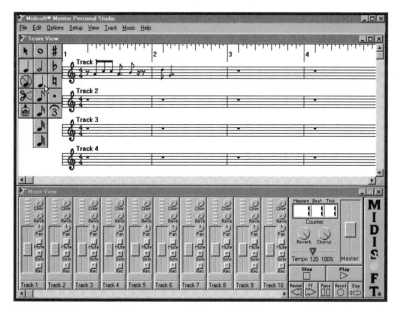

Music Mentor's composition screen may look overwhelming to young children, but making music is actually quite simple: Just play a MIDI instrument, or as we've done here, drag notes from the palette at the upper left onto the staff.

Roll Over, Beethoven

No matter *what* some teachers think, music doesn't begin with Bach and end with Beethoven.

You improve your chances of getting your kids excited about music history, composers, and songwriting when you give them choices, rather than lock them into a litany of long-gone, long-haired musicians. And helping you get your kids excited about music is exactly what we aim to do here, as we present a variety of music information resources on CD-ROM and from the online world.

them around on the screen.

When your kids wrap up their composition, Music Mentor prints out the score. That's perfect for advanced music students taking composition classes in high school; just compose, print, and hand in the sheet music.

Music Mentor also does a good job of teaching music and demonstrating musical concepts such as timbre and harmony. Self-guided tours take kids through the fundamentals, and the program's prerecorded MIDI files can be modified by young composers eager to write music, but hesitant to start from scratch.

Chapter 14, "Homework Software," lists our recommendations for other first-rate music programs for older children.

GET SMART: *Music mutates faster than you can spin the dial on the radio. Keeping up with musical changes, especially in popular music, requires a fast-on-its-feet resource such as the World Wide Web. Our recommended starting point for all things musical is Yahoo's Entertainment:Music section:*

http://www.yahoo.com/Entertainment/Music/

Kids can use these resources to complete homework assignments, reports, and projects for subjects other than music. Does your child need an idea for a biographical report in English? Steer him toward an out-of-the-ordinary figure (in other words, someone other than George Washington or Abraham Lincoln) such as Aaron Copland, one of the most recognized American composers of this century (but still virtually unknown to most people). Is he looking for a fresh idea for a history project? Aim him at a pair of music-in-American-history CDs.

When you want to move music past the Bachs and Beethovens, check out the CDs and World Wide Web sites we describe in the following sections.

From classical to rock and roll, your kids are sure to find what they're looking for.

Go Online!

Whether your kids are musical prodigies or they are just interested in playing around with tunes, you should steer them toward these two intriguing music sites that we found on the World Wide Web.

Mozart's Musikalisches Wurfelspiel
http://mendel.berkeley.edu/~jchuang/Music/Mozart/mozart.cgi
Anyone can make a minuet or trio by heading to Mozart's Musikalisches Wurfelspiel. This Web page uses a musical composition game that Mozart invented in 1787 to generate minuets from random numbers.

You can compose a minuet in moments by letting the computer pick the numbers, or you can enter your own numbers from your Web browser. If you use the Microsoft Internet Explorer as your browser, the music automatically plays in the background. Are you using another browser? Then you need a MIDI player program to hear the tune. (This site also offers directions for adding MIDI capabilities to Netscape Navigator, another popular browser.)

Click on the Compose a Minuet link at the Mozart's Musikalisches Wurfelspiel Web page. In less than a minute, you'll be listening to a Mozart-style composition created from random numbers.

Jack's Harp Page
http://www.volcano. net/~jackmearl/index.html
You don't need to spend hundreds of dollars on a musical instrument. Not when you put an inexpensive harmonica in your kid's hands. After doing so, point your child to Jack's Harp Page. Jack Earl — who taught himself to play the harmonica — will send your child 10 free lessons via e-mail. What a deal! And who knows? You might discover the next blues legend.

Music of Yesterday

You can't ignore composers such as Bach and Beethoven, but other people have made music over the centuries, too. We found two excellent sources of information about classical composers that kids can use to research music of the past.

Microsoft Composer Collection
Ages 12 and Up

One of the most economical musical CD-ROMs around, Microsoft Composer Collection costs only about $50, but delivers more than 15 hours of multimedia music and information. On a bang-for-the-buck scale, this three-composer collection (Mozart, Bach, and Schubert) is a steal (assuming your kids want in-depth information about any of these three composers, of course).

Each of the three CDs treats its composer of choice in much the same way. Encyclopedic articles provide biographical information, an audio guide lets kids listen to the music, and the Close Reading section digs deep into the compositions by sending

---

Biographical information is only part of the Microsoft Composer Collection. Kids also learn about the instruments of the time.

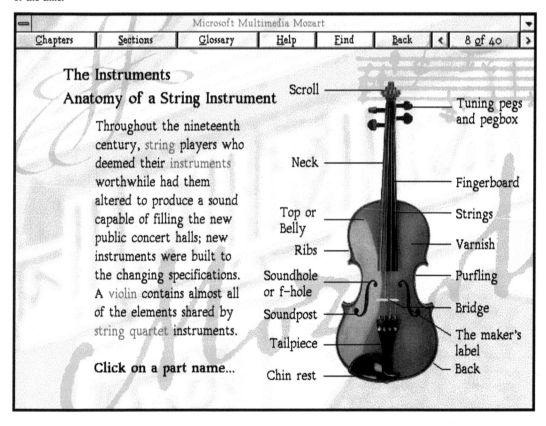

Rather than go to Cleveland, you can tour the Rock and Roll Hall of Fame, read biographies of famous performers and bands, and even listen to some of their music, all from the comfort of your home.

the score to the PC's speakers while presenting detailed commentary on the screen.

Kids learn fascinating facts about the composers' lives and, just as important, a bit about the world in which they lived. Other areas describe the instruments of the period, and the program includes several games and quizzes (great for parents home-schooling their kids).

GET SMART: *One of the best ways to learn about music is by listening to it. Don't forget that your Windows 95 PC or your Macintosh can play audio CDs without any additional software. To play an audio CD in Windows 95, just insert the disc into the drive. On the Mac, you must first open the AppleCD Audio Player, which you find in the Apple menu.*

ClassicalNet

For a one-stop information shop catering to classical music interests, you can't beat ClassicalNet. It includes extensive informational files, links to other classical music Web pages, and where-to-buy advice for anyone searching for the best audio CDs on the subject. Although this site — like many other music pages on the World Wide Web — is primarily a resource for listeners, it does have some information useful to young researchers digging up facts about composers of the past. The search tools here let kids use keywords to cull the site's information. To reach ClassicalNet, enter this address in your Web browser:

http://www.classical.net/music/

Music of Today

Do your kids thirst for more modern music? Among the hundreds of music-related sites on the World Wide Web, we pick three that demonstrate the wide variety of information available to you and your children via the computer and its modem.

Rock and Roll Hall of Fame

You can musically move your kids closer to today by sending them to the virtual version of the Rock and Roll Hall of Fame (the non-

Music In American History

Music doesn't exist in a vacuum. It lives and breathes as part of the culture that makes it, plays it, and sings it. You can teach your kids that lesson *and* give them a new angle they can use when researching and writing reports for history or music class, by handing them a pair of music-in-history CD-ROMs.

Sing an American Story

(MediAlive; 408-752-8500; Windows and Mac CD-ROM, $29). A decidedly kid-oriented collection, Sing an American Story looks at 15 folk songs, their origins, and their place in American history. Kids ages five to 12 can learn more about the building of railroads across the country by listening to tunes such as "John Henry" and "I've Been Working on the Railroad," or get an idea of slavery and civil rights when they hear

"Down by the Riverside." Animated drawings accompany each song, along with the lyrics and historical background about the song and its era.

History of American Music

(Queue; 800-232-2224 or 203-335-0908; Windows and Mac CD-ROM, $75). This collection of more than 400 songs opens a window on several facets of American history — including slavery, coal mining,

and colonization — for kids ages 10 and up. The CD-ROM includes the sounds of spirituals, cowboy ballads, and Native American songs, along with lyrics, historical details, and tips on where to look for more information about each era. If Native American life interests your kids, they can cue up the Kiowa Love Song and listen to the haunting flute while they read about the role music played in tribal life.

Songs your child will love — such as "The Erie Canal" — make Sing an American Song a fun tool for simultaneously teaching history and music.

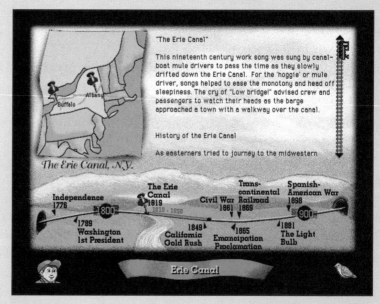

virtual version is in Cleveland, Ohio), where they can view the list of the "500 Songs That Shaped Rock and Roll," read short bios of many of the bands and performers, and even download and listen to snippets of many of the songs. (Okay, to your kids, even *this* music may be ancient history.) You can visit the Rock and Roll Hall of Fame by entering the following address in your Web browser:

http://www.rockhall.com/

GET SMART: *Many Web sites play sound, music, and even recordings of radio broadcasts. One popular sound-playing technology (the Rock and Roll Hall of Fame site uses it) is Real-Audio. To hear these sounds, you must first equip your Web browser with the RealAudio Player. Go to the RealAudio Web page for more information and to download the for-free RealAudio Player:*

http://www.realaudio.com

TV Bytes: The WWW TV Themes Home Page

Music is everywhere, even on television. The TV Bytes Web site is pure fun, but it could serve as an excellent resource for kids writing reports and papers on popular culture. Due to overwhelming interest, you must register to download the TV theme songs from this site (they're still free, though). And the site limits you to downloading only five theme songs each day and eight more each night. You can find scores of TV theme songs from shows past and present, including kids' shows, comedies, dramas, and westerns. To explore the world of TV theme songs, enter this address in your browser:

http://themes.parkhere.com/themes/ tvthemes.html

Mozart Among Us

Christopher Rouse, Steve Reich, Lee Hoiby, George Crumb. Who *are* these people?

Twentieth-century composers, that's who. If your kids need to cast their research net for the next Mozart, point them in the direction of the Mozart Among Us Web site. This site includes biographies of notable composers, lists of their works, and the record labels that publish their compositions on audio CD:

http://www.io.com/~glenford/Mozart_ Among_Us_TOP.html

The Play's the Thing

Putting on a play isn't a typical homework assignment. If drama interests your children, however, you can put tools into their hands that let them produce plays. Kids with a flair for the dramatic can uncover a unique way to fulfill creative-writing assignments.

Although a word processor is the computerized tool of choice among professional playwrights, kids can turn to something better: play-making software that lets kids present animated dramas on the screen of their PC or Mac. With any of the three programs we recommend, kids can choose actors, pick scenery and props, write or record dialogue, and then direct the action. These programs make it seem as though you have put a tiny drama company inside the computer.

Making the transition from creating these plays at home to staging them at school may be more difficult than handing in a paper-based report, but we have some suggestions for handling that, too. Check out "Try This! Present the Play at School," later in this chapter. And for drama-happy kids, we also include some tips on how they can use their home computer to produce some of the support materials for at-school plays, such as playbills, tickets, and advertising banners.

Turn down the lights, raise the curtain. It's show time!

Microsoft 3D Movie Maker

Ages 8 and Up

Microsoft 3D Movie Maker turns your children into directors, letting them breathe life into their ideas, which take shape on your computer screen as animated 3-D movies. The *FamilyPC* readers gave this program a *FamilyPC* Recommended rating. In fact, 3D Movie Maker scored higher than any of the other digital dramas we endorse.

Although tricky to use, this sophisticated program's 3-D effects will astound you. To successfully create a movie with the 3D Movie Maker software, kids must master more concepts than in the other programs we recommend. For that reason, we think this program is best suited for upper-

elementary-school- and middle-school-aged kids.

GET SMART: *Before creating an animated movie with 3D Movie Maker (or any of the other play- or movie-making programs we recommend), your children should have a rough idea of the play or movie's plot and the types of characters they plan to cast. That won't stifle their creativity, but it will make the creative process go more smoothly. (Movie directors do the same thing before they shoot a single frame of film.)*

3D Movie Maker comes with a dozen movie sets in which your kids can create scenes from several camera angles. On these empty scenes, they place actors (they can use a total of 40) and record their movements by dragging them with the mouse. Your kids can rotate the actors in full circles and use commands to make them run, fall, jump, and perform other actions. 3D Movie Maker comes with a plentiful supply of props to decorate scenes.

Your kids can add dialogue by selecting prerecorded phrases or by recording their own words (they need a microphone for this). They can also add text, sound effects, and music to any scene. And if your young directors get stuck for ideas, they can consult the nifty Splot Machine. Each time they pull the machine's handles, they change the scenario, adding different scenery, protagonists, props, and background music. When they find a combination they like, your kids simply click and, right away, they're off movie-making.

Budding directors learn the ropes, from camera angles to character types, in 3D Movie Maker. The mini-movies you create look sharp, thanks to the 3-D images, but the program takes patience to master.

Hollywood

Ages 9 and Up

Hollywood is a mini animation machine that lets your children write, direct, and play in their own animated "talkie." *FamilyPC*'s testers gave this program a big thumbs up and awarded it a *FamilyPC* Recommended seal. We think Hollywood's simple operation (it's much easier to use than either 3D Movie Maker or Opening Night) makes it the best pick for young, elementary-school playwrights.

To create a movie in Hollywood, you choose a setting and then select from a cast of 10 cartoon animal characters. You control characters' actions by placing them on

a background and choosing their roles, moods, hobbies, and voices from pop-up menus. As you add scenery and music and move the characters, the program automatically documents these actions and writes a script. You can view the script at any time, edit the automatically entered stage directions, and, most important, add dialogue. When you complete your script, Hollywood shows the movie and computer-like voices recite the dialogue. (It sounds like robots are reading your script.)

Despite all the fun this program provides and the intriguing plays it produces, the quality of the computer-generated voices is disappointing. (We really can't fault Holly-

★ TRY THIS! ★

Present the Play at School

Your child can't easily stage a virtual play or an animated movie at school. Unlike a report written with a word processor or artwork created with a painting program, a digital play can't be printed and turned over to a teacher. And because the school probably doesn't have a copy of

PKZIP for Windows comes in handy when you need to squeeze files to fit on a floppy disk.

the program your child used to create her play or movie, she can't just toss a floppy disk into her book bag and load her production on a computer in the classroom. When your children produce a play or a movie on the home computer, how can they get it to school?

GET SMART: Before you take the software to school, make sure the classroom computer can run the program. You do this by checking the software's operating requirements and comparing them to the hardware — the amount of memory, the speed of the microprocessor, the video capabilities, and so on — inside the school's PC or Mac.

You *could* drag your computer to the classroom, set it up, and then run the play. But that means carting a car full of hardware. Instead, bring the play-making software to school and load it on one of the

school's PCs or Macs. (All three of our recommended programs come on CD-ROM; only 3D Movie Maker comes in a PC-only version.)

Install the program on the school's computer and then copy the file you created at home (the one that contains your child's play) from a floppy disk to the computer's hard disk. If the file is larger than 1.44MB — the capacity of a floppy disk — you need to compress the file to make it fit on a floppy.

One method for compressing files on the PC relies on a shareware program called PKZIP for Windows 2.0, which you can find in the software libraries of every online service and on the Internet at this address:

http://www.pkware.com/

PKZIP for Windows compresses a file and then later expands it to its normal size.

GET SMART: When your child finishes the in-school demonstration of his or her drama, delete any files you copied from the CD-ROM onto the school computer's hard disk.

wood for this; the current state of text-to-speech technology limits what the program can do.) If you can put up with the unrealistic (but humorous) voices, Hollywood is an excellent choice as a computerized drama maker.

Opening Night

Ages 8 and Up

In Opening Night, kids create and direct their own multimedia plays set in Victorian England. Of our three recommended play-making programs, Opening Night most closely resembles the real directing process and produces a digital drama most like a real-world play. Although Opening Night wasn't awarded a *FamilyPC* Recommended seal (it missed the mark by a narrow margin, however), we still believe this program should be your first choice if you want a realistic play-making experience on the PC.

Opening Night contains hundreds of props, over 100 scenes, and more than 40 costumed actors. These actors are all *photorealistic images* — tiny, digitized video versions of real actors — that you can manip-

The cartoon characters in Hollywood look like animals, but they talk like robots. To change characters and settings, you simply click on the pictures at the bottom of this main screen.

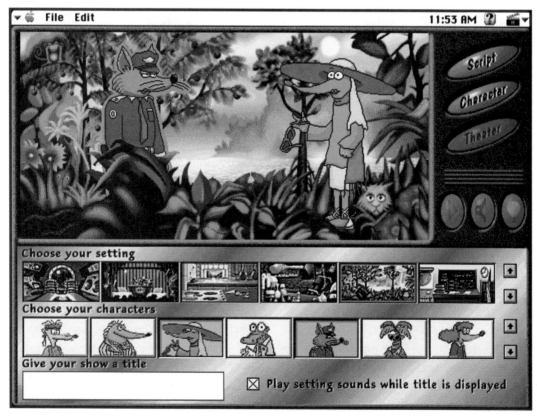

★ TRY THIS! ★

Support Your School Play

Homework comes in many guises. Sometimes it's not even required or given a grade.

When your child's class or school puts on a play, you can help out by producing many of the materials needed for a successful run on the stage. And you probably already have the program we think is tops for this kind of paper production.

Using the Print Shop Deluxe Ensemble II, you can easily assemble great-looking banners, signs, and posters to advertise the play, and customized tickets to sell for the performance.

It took us only 5 minutes to design this custom ticket.

The Print Shop Deluxe Ensemble II includes a wide variety of ready-made projects that you can print as is (or modify as much as you want), and it makes designing custom paper products almost as simple. To prove our point, we show you how to create a ticket for the school play by using Print Shop:

1. Press Ctrl-N, to create a new document.

2. Click on the Stationery button and then on the Start from Scratch button in the next dialog box.

3. Click on the Business Cards button in the next window and then on the button marked Wide in the following box.

4. Make sure Blank Page is selected in the list labeled Graphics and then click on OK.

5. Choose a layout for the ticket from the Select a Layout list in the window that appears. We used Business Card 12, here. Click on OK.

6. Double-click on the graphics object and choose a piece of clip art that you think works for the ticket (we used the one called Drama).

7. Double-click on each text object and type the text you want. We used the top text object for the name of the play and the bottom object for the place/date/time details. You can easily change the color of the text, the font, or the size of the font.

Your ticket is finished! Option: Create another text object to add the words *Admit One* to the ticket. To do this, select Add from the Object menu and then pick Text from the submenu that appears. Type *Admit One* and place this text in an empty space on the ticket. We made two copies of the text box containing the words *Admit One*, rotated them (pick Rotate from the Object menu after selecting the text object) and then placed one at either end of the ticket.

ulate to create your own drama. To make an actor move, for example, you just click and drag her about the stage. Among the characters, you can find burglars, aristocrats, commoners, and children. You can add sound effects and music and write a script that the computer reads in digitized voices (the same robotic voices used in Hollywood) while your actors play their parts. Your kids can also print their script and use it as the foundation of a real play (the program also prints playbills) or to hand over to a teacher as a finished project.

However, the program is sometimes difficult to use. Editing a work in progress is awkward, time-consuming, and may be beyond the abilities of young children. And the actors' costumes, the backgrounds, and the props lock you into the narrow time frame of the Victorian period. Still, we think Opening Night is the most realistic play maker on the market.

The Digital Bard

Who's the biggest name in drama and the playwright most studied in America's schools? William Shakespeare, of course. If a dramatic work ends up on your child's classroom desk, the odds are high that it carries the Bard's byline.

Some middle-school classes read Shakespeare's plays, but these titles usually appear in high-school English classes. It's not so much the subject matter as it is the Elizabethan language that demands older students.

Kids studying Shakespeare in school can use some help: they need help understanding the meaning of his dialogue; they need help untwisting the plot twists of his plays; they also need help simply following the action from Act I, Scene I to the final curtain call. You can provide this help by equipping the family computer with a play-specific CD-ROM or by showing your kids how to dial up a Shakespearean page on the World Wide Web.

Opening Night, the most realistic among our trio of play makers, lets kids create Victorian-era productions by clicking and dragging actors across the stage, and by typing in text as dialogue.

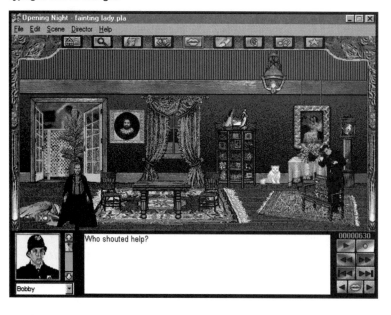

Go Online!

If your kids can't get to Broadway, maybe Broadway can come to your kids. Stage-struck middle-school and high-school students looking for more information about a career in drama — or maybe just seeking advice about the roles they play or the plays they produce at school — can slake their thirst for knowledge by surfing the World Wide Web's theater resources.

Playbill On-Line's colorful interface sends kids to several areas of dramatic interest.

Theatre Central
http://www.theatre-central.com/
The acknowledged one-stop drama shop on the World Wide Web, Theatre Central may be more useful to professionals, but kids who are involved in producing plays in middle or high school can use these links, too. The listings here take you to playwriting resources; pages highlighting renowned actors, composers, and directors; drama training programs; publications dedicated to the craft; and more. However, Theatre Central is so popular that this site is often inaccessible (try it on the weekend and late at night if you have trouble connecting during business hours).

Playbill On-Line
http://wheat.symgrp.com/
playbill/html/home.html
Another information-packed page on the World Wide Web, Playbill On-Line sports a colorful interface that makes this site attractive to kids. Several sections of this site are of particular interest to middle- and high-school-aged children looking for research resources for theater-related homework. Its quiz and contest area contains tough trivia questions:

http://wheat.symgrp.
com/cgi-bin/plb/quiz?
cmd=list

The Celebrities On-line spot posts online interviews with real theater people (perfect when kids are looking for biographical information about living actors, directors, and playwrights):

http://wheat.symgrp.com/
cgi-bin/plb/celeb?cmd=list

And the art collection offers images of real-world playbills and billboards, and actor photos you can download or capture by using your Web browser:

http://wheat.symgrp.com/cgi-
bin/plb/art?cmd=search

Romeo and Juliet

It's not surprising that *Romeo and Juliet*, with its tragic depiction of young love gone wrong, is one of the first Shakespeare plays presented on CD-ROM (and one of the most-read plays in the Bard's repertoire). But it *is* a great relief to find that this was done so well. Supported by a BBC production of the Royal Shakespeare Company, this title exudes Elizabethan ambiance through its period design and supporting elements.

The play itself is the core of the program. The program displays the text on one side of the screen against screen backdrops, while photos of the scene's characters appear on the right. Videos are available at certain points in the presentation, and audio is always available. A time line along the bottom of the screen highlights the current act and scene and lets you move instantly to any point in the play.

This disc also explores Shakespeare's life. Examples from the play illustrate the plot, the performance, the characters, the themes,

Kids can examine Macbeth in detail through videos, text, even talk-along karaoke.

and the language; you can experience these through audio or video clips or by directly accessing the text.

Macbeth

Visually gratifying at every turn, Voyager's Macbeth is presented in a sleek, modern interface of gray lattice accented with red (for the blood that Lady Macbeth can't clean from her hands). You can access the text of the play by clicking on a box in a matrix that lists each act and scene in the play. Instant annotation boxes explain words and phrases, and the disc offers extensive commentaries, summaries, and critical essays.

The CD emphasizes different approaches to interpreting the play. This accounts for the fairly lengthy video clips from film productions by directors such as Roman Polanski, Orson Wells, and Akira Kurosawa. The program also stresses the spoken word. At any time, you can listen to actors from The Royal Shakespeare Company reading the parts.

In-depth character analysis is just one facet of the Romeo and Juliet CD-ROM.

Go Online!

The Bard lives on... on the World Wide Web, that is. If your children study Shakespeare in school — most high-school students read *Romeo and Juliet*, *Macbeth*, and *Hamlet* — remind them that Shakespeare is now part of the information age.

Of the numerous Shakespeare sites on the Web, we think these are the two worth bookmarking.

The Complete Works of William Shakespeare
http://the-tech.mit.edu/Shakespeare/works.html

With the World Wide Web and a modem close at hand, who needs a thick book containing the collected works of the Bard? This super site — maintained by the Massachusetts Institute of Technology (MIT) — not only contains all of Shakespeare's plays, but within each, lets you leap via hypertext links to an extensive glossary of Elizabethan language. You can also search through all the text of all the plays (did you know that the

word *sword* appears in all but two of Shakespeare's plays?).

Macbeth
http://www.webcom. com/falcon/Macbeth.html

Among the many nifty resources on the Web site maintained by Roger Burnich, a high-school teacher in Stamford, Connecticut, is this eminently readable, scene-by-scene

summary of *Macbeth*. (You *have* to like a teacher who starts his study guide with the line "*Macbeth, Macbeth*, you bore me to death.") Just as sharp is Burnich's brand-new guide to *Hamlet*. Here's the Web site to visit if your children are reading that play from the Bard:

http://www.webcom.com/falcon/htable.html

All the plays of William Shakespeare are available for reading (and printing) on the World Wide Web.

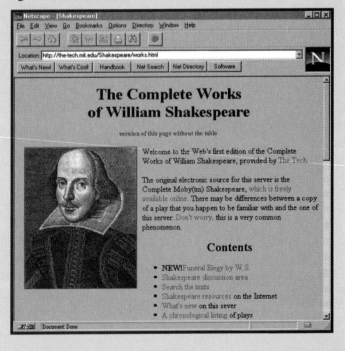

Chapter 12

Speak the Language

English-Language Dictionaries and Foreign-Language Studies

ARE YOUR KIDS LEARNING ANOTHER LANguage or just wrestling with the nuances of their native tongue? Regardless of whether your kids are studying English, German, Japanese, or Estonian, they should be tutored by the family's computer.

The magic of multimedia makes it possible for kids to study a language in much the same way as they do in school: by listening, by speaking, by writing, and by reading. And when it comes to the mother tongue of most Americans, the home PC or Mac offers a wealth of references and resources — including dictionaries that are both general and specific — to help children learn the language, explore its possibilities, and use it correctly.

Because language studies often come home as homework, we dedicate an entire chapter to the topic. We highlight the English- and foreign-language software you need, lead you to some unusual but useful online resources, and even help you fight the homework battle with some tactical advice.

Want to talk the talk? It's easy when your home computer is there to add its voice.

Look It Up in the Dictionary

Trying to learn a language without using a dictionary is like trying to build a house without using a blueprint. A dictionary is an indispensable tool for studying any language, whether it's the mother tongue or a foreign language.

You already have one or more paper dictionaries in the house, but you probably don't have a digital dictionary in your home-learning software library. Although you can do without, we strongly recommend that you add one to your child's rack of CD-ROMs. Such programs function as more than word lists. They open multimedia worlds that entice your child to explore

Animation, photos, and sound make this digital dictionary a top choice for children in grades K through 2.

the magic of language in much the same way a multimedia encyclopedia entices kids to explore different subjects.

In the following sections, we put the *spotlight* (a projected spot of light used to illuminate brilliantly a person, object, or group on a stage) on a pair of electronic dictionaries and an all-around excellent reference work that your kids can use for a myriad of language chores.

Let's go word *spelunking* (the hobby or practice of exploring caves)!

My First Incredible Amazing Dictionary

Ages 4–7

FamilyPC's family testers found My First Incredible Amazing Dictionary so incredible and so amazing that they awarded it the

FamilyPC Recommended rating.

A smart pick for children in grades K through 2, My First Incredible Amazing Dictionary contains 17,000 words, with definitions for 1,000 of them. (For example, it has a definition for *bicycle*, but not for *spoke* or *pedal*, which it displays in a photo called *bicycle words*.) It also includes 1,000 illustrations, 1,000 animations, and 4 hours of audio. Unlike other dictionaries for the very young, My First Incredible Amazing Dictionary narrates not only the words, but also the definitions of those words.

For example, on the screen that describes the word *petal*, your kids find an icon labeled *flower words*. When they click on this icon, a picture of a daisy appears, with *leaf*, *stem*, and *petal* labeled. If they click on any of these labels, the program takes them taken to that entry in the dictionary. My First Incredible Amazing Dictionary also contains a trio of games to help kids learn all about words.

GET SMART: *Every program worthy of the name word processor includes a spell checker and a thesaurus. The former checks the spelling of words in a document, and the latter offers synonyms. However, neither provide definitions or pronunciations of words. For that reason alone, we think a digital dictionary is a good addition to your home-learning library.*

With such a small number of definitions, My First Incredible Amazing Dictionary isn't really suitable as a study aid for young kids who use the computer for writing assignments. But as an exploration of the English language, it's tough to beat.

American Heritage Children's Dictionary
Ages 8–12

Dictionaries on CD-ROM rarely match the convenience of old-fashioned, paper dictionaries. Although this may hold true for the American Heritage Children's Dictionary, this reference work for kids goes a long way toward redefining the value of computer-based dictionaries. Like My First Incredible Amazing Dictionary, this reference work received a *FamilyPC* Recommended label from the magazine's testers.

This CD-ROM succeeds because its goal isn't simply to provide a vehicle for looking up words. Instead, it uses multimedia to

A Free Dictionary

Although less convenient than slipping a CD-ROM in the computer's drive, going online for word definitions has one big advantage: It's free.

The best online dictionary we've found is the Hypertext Webster Interface. To use this dictionary, enter the following address in your Web browser:

http://c.gp.cs.cmu.edu:5103/prog/webster

Type the word you want to look up and press Enter, and the online dictionary displays the definition. What's striking about this dictionary is that the words in the definition are linked to the dictionary via hypertext, so you can access the definitions of *those* words simply by clicking the mouse.

In the Hypertext Webster Interface, the blue shading indicates that a hypertext link exists to that word's definition.

help kids find the fun and fascination in the English language.

For example, enter the word *parrot* in the Word Machine, and the program displays a definition and an illustration of the bird. To hear the word pronounced, you just click on the word. Click on the illustration to hear what a parrot sounds like. And when you click on the Word Wheel, the program lists other exotic birds, and then you can jump to any of these with just another click.

This dictionary pronounces a total of 13,000 words, and it even lets kids click to see syllables, parts of speech, and word forms. It also contains 2,750 illustrations, 800 sound effects and 750 animations. Three word games add to the fun.

Your biggest gripe may be the amount of hard disk space this electronic dictionary requires (about 20MB). But if you have the storage room, the American Heritage Children's Dictionary is a good bet for children in the upper elementary and lower middle-school grades.

Smile

Here's a quick test. When used in an e-mail message, what does the following mean?

:-)

You would know if you had a dictionary of smileys on your Web browser screen. People use *smileys* — small, sideways faces usually built with punctuation marks — in e-mail messages to denote emotions such as sadness:

:-(

Or a smiley might tell you something about the appearance of the person who sent the message. For example, the following smiley tells you that the sender is wearing sunglasses:

8-)

You can find several dictionaries of smileys on the World Wide Web. For starters, check out the Smiley Dictionary by entering the following address in your browser:

http://olympe.polytechnique.fr/~violet/Smileys/

Or head to The Unofficial Smiley Dictionary at the following address:

http://www.eff.org/papers/eegtti/eeg_286.html

Armed with one of these dictionaries (language comes in surprising forms, doesn't it?), you too can type :D (laughter) or :O (yelling).

Microsoft Bookshelf 1996–97
Ages 12 and Up

Microsoft Bookshelf isn't a dictionary. And it's not an encyclopedia. But it *is* one of the best reference values available on CD-ROM.

This collection of nine different digital reference works includes two valuable tools for wordsmiths: The American Heritage Dictionary and The Original Roget's Thesaurus. Microsoft Bookshelf is particularly useful for homework assignments, because you can access its information from within most Windows programs. Just type the topic in the

Search box (for word definitions, you enter the word itself), and the CD pulls information from all its components and displays a list on the screen. You can also create customized searches to look for information in any combination of Bookshelf's books or media types.

In addition to its volumes of text, Bookshelf contains photos, video clips, and animations. The dictionary also has more than 80,000 spoken pronunciations, so you won't embarrass yourself the next time you try to say *onomatopoeia*.

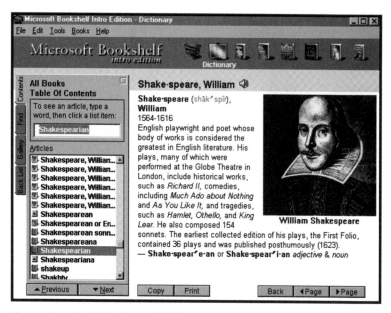

If you subscribe to The Microsoft Network, you can check out the Intro Edition of Bookshelf for no additional charge.

GET SMART: *If you're shopping for an integrated program that runs under Windows 95, take a long look at Microsoft Works & Bookshelf for Windows 95. After installing both programs from this CD-ROM, you can call Bookshelf from the Works toolbar, giving you one-button access to information.*

And the new 1996–97 edition includes The Microsoft Bookshelf Internet Directory 96, a guide to sites on the World Wide Web. You can update this directory monthly by accessing the Bookshelf Web page:

http://www.microsoft.com/bookshelf/updates. htm

If you have an account on The Microsoft Network, you can try out Bookshelf by downloading the Bookshelf Intro Edition engine to your hard disk, then using the online service to look up information. (You don't need the CD-ROM version to do this.)

If you're looking for a top-notch digital dictionary, but you want more than that for your money, we recommend Bookshelf.

Learn a Foreign Language

Foreign languages are making a comeback in school. Many colleges include foreign-language proficiency as an entrance requirement, some school districts have set up language immersion schools, and many parents now realize that the world *is* a small place.

★ TRY THIS! ★

Boogie with Bookshelf

Microsoft Bookshelf is our pick as an all-around reference CD-ROM for young researchers and writers. It offers a first-rate dictionary, the Official Roget's Thesaurus has more synonyms than Greenlanders have words for *snow*, and best of all, you can access all this information from within almost any Windows program.

To prove its versatility, we show you two ways kids can use Bookshelf to complete homework assignments. For more ideas, check out the Ideas for Using Microsoft Bookshelf '95 page by entering this address in your Web browser:

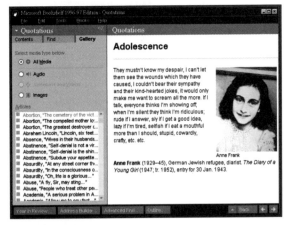

Kids can use many of the quotations in Bookshelf to jump-start journal writing.

http://www.microsoft.com/K-12/Resources/TAGs/
Bk95/bk95idea.htm

When you search using the right keywords, Microsoft Bookshelf's encyclopedia serves up word origins.

The Origins of Words

English is a polyglot language that borrows heavily from languages such as German and Dutch (from its Anglo-Saxon roots), French (due to the Norman conquest of 1066), and Latin (thanks to everything from the legal profession to religion). Kids can use Bookshelf to investigate the origins of words in the English language.

Select the Dictionary from the Books list on the left side of Bookshelf's screen and then choose the Advanced Find command from the Tools menu (or click on the Advanced Find button at the bottom of the screen). Make sure that only the box marked

Continued on page 249

Dictionary is checked and then enter this search phrase:

SPANISH AND "WORD HISTORY"

To search for words that originated in Spanish, click on the Find button. (You can substitute any language for SPANISH.) Did you know that the word *cockroach* comes from the Spanish word *cucaracha*?

Quotes Make Good Starters for Journal Writing

Daily writing assignments often involve a journal. Whether the teacher asks your child to write in a journal during class time or as homework, one of the toughest tasks journal writers face is simply coming up with a new idea.

You can help out by pointing your kid to Microsoft Bookshelf. Choose Bookshelf Daily from the Tools menu, and the program rewards you with a quote of the day. Click on the Next button to see a different quote. You can select the text of each quotation and copy and paste one quote after another into a word-processor document. Print the document and hand it to your child as journal inspiration.

For a more directed list of quotations, select Quotations from the Book list, click on the Find tab, and then enter the name of a famous figure. Bookshelf responds by displaying quotes by or about that person. Alternately, with the Quotations book on the screen, you can click on the Outline button to see a directory of quotations organized by topic.

Studying a foreign language is tough, no matter what the age of the learner. Vocabulary lists, reading and writing assignments, memorization of dialogues, translation chores: All these add up to a time-intensive education. And that means at least some of the language work gets shunted off to home, as homework.

GET SMART: *A multilingual interactive storybook offers one fun way to expose preschoolers to a foreign language. Programs such as those in the Living Books series can display the story in another language (Spanish is the most common) and narrate the tale in that tongue. For more information about interactive storybooks, look to Chapter 3, "The Magic Words."*

The family's multimedia computer is ideally suited to help with this task. With the software we recommend in this section, it can tutor your kids in any of several popular foreign languages (by *foreign*, we mean any language other than English; of course, the term is relative). Using the computer's audio capabilities, such software pronounces foreign-language vocabulary correctly. And like software for math and other subjects that rely on repetitive learning, foreign-language software can drum the basics into your children's brains.

We found a handful of foreign-language programs worth your consideration, and we spotted several intriguing online resources. *Sprechen Sie Deutsch? Parlez-vous français?* As users of the home computer, your kids will answer *ja!* and *oui!*

Go Online!

Dictionaries deal with more than words. Specialized dictionaries list everything from famous historical figures to mathematical terms.

You can find several specialized dictionaries on the World Wide Web. They don't take up any precious hard disk space on your PC or Mac and best of all, they're free. We found our favorites; by using the keyword *dictionary* with any of the Web's search tools, you can, too.

The Biographical Dictionary
http://www.tiac.net/users/parallax/

Containing biographical information on more than 18,000 notable men and women, The Biographical Dictionary is a superb resource for history-class homework research. Each listing includes the person's birth and death years, important achievements, and why he or she is famous. A search mechanism that lets you search by any keyword

The Biographical Dictionary provides a simple, yet solid search tool.

makes this site an excellent tool for historical research. When we used the search keyword *henry viii*, for example, we were rewarded with a long list of that king's wives, children, and important advisors such as Thomas More.

GET SMART: If a homework assignment requires your kids to dig up biographical information on someone who lived during a specific period in history, they can produce a list of people to choose from by using The Biographical Dictionary. To generate a list of people born in the 1800s, for example, use the search keyword _18.

On-line Mathematics Dictionary
http://www.mathpro.com/math/glossary/glossary. html

Do you know the difference between an *abundant number* and a *zeta function*? We didn't either, until we headed to this online dictionary, which lists definitions for those two math terms and everything in between. Especially helpful for parents trying to help their kids decipher math homework, the dictionary contains definitions for basic and advanced mathematical jargon.

The Free On-line Dictionary of Computing
http://wfn-shop.Princeton.EDU/foldoc/

You use a computer, but do you know what a *byte* is? Do you know the purpose of a computer's *cache*? This dictionary of computing terminology comes in handy if your kids know more about computers than you do.

Let's Talk

Ages 8 and Up

In Let's Talk, kids talk in a foreign language and the computer listens. This foreign language sampler includes more than 2,000 words in Spanish, French, Italian, and German. However, Let's Talk is more than a vocabulary builder. Using advanced speech-recognition technology, it prompts kids to talk into a microphone connected to the computer and then rates their pronunciation.

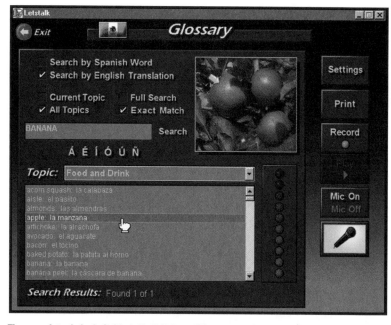

The search tools included in Let's Talk turn this program into a multimedia reference for children studying German, French, Italian, or Spanish.

The foreign-language words and phrases included in Let's Talk are grouped by subject and listed alphabetically. You can also search for words in either English or one of the four foreign languages and then create personalized word lists for more targeted study by your kids.

Although almost anyone can use Let's Talk, the large, colorful photographs accompanying the words make it a particularly effective tutor for elementary-school-aged children. This flash-card-style approach — and the capability of the program to say the words — means you can try Let's Talk with prereaders, too.

As the program speaks the words, kids repeat them into the microphone (unfortunately, the package does not include a mi-

crophone). Let's Talk *listens* and then tells the child how his or her pronunciation compares with that of a native speaker.

The Rosetta Stone PowerPac

Ages 8 and Up

Another excellent foreign-language pick for children is the Rosetta Stone PowerPac. Essentially a language sampler — it introduces English speakers to Dutch, French, German, Russian, and Spanish — the Power-Pac's contents come from the much more expensive ($395 each) but also much more comprehensive Rosetta Stone Level I programs.

Like Let's Talk, the Rosetta Stone Power-Pac uses colorful photographs and speech recognition to teach a foreign language.

★ **TRY THIS!** ★

Read News From Around the World

Older children can use the Internet to hone their foreign-language reading comprehension skills by accessing newspapers and other publications written in that language.

For example, kids studying German can connect to the popular German magazine *Der Spiegel*, by entering this address in their Web browser:

http://nda.net/nda/
spiegel/index.html

Der Spiegel is especially useful for reading practice, because it lets you switch between English and German with a click of the mouse button. Kids can read an article in German and then change to English to check the accuracy of their translation.

Other foreign-language newspapers, magazines, and online news information sources don't offer this back-to-English feature, but they still provide interesting material for reading ac-

tivities. For a large listing of foreign-language publications, head to the News Resources page on the World Wide Web. You access the News Resources Web page by entering the following address in your browser:

http://newo.com/news/

The News Resources Web page lists a multitude of online publications and other news sources from around the globe. Using hypertext links, your kids can easily surf around the world until they find an online newspaper or magazine written in the language they're studying.

You kids can hone their reading skills by using the World Wide Web to call up foreign-language publications such as *Der Spiegel*, a German magazine, which lets you switch between English and German.

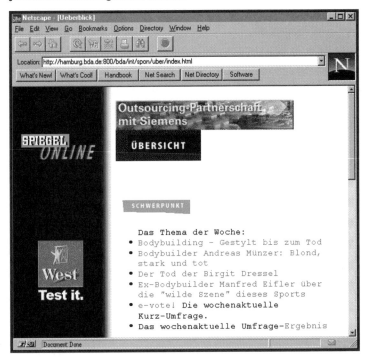

Using an immersion style of teaching, PowerPac displays a series of photos, pronounces a foreign-language word or phrase and then asks you to pick the picture that matches the word or phrase. If you equip your computer with a microphone, your children can say the words or phrases and receive feedback on the quality of their pronunciations.

The Rosetta Stone PowerPac software uses spoken words and pictures to teach a foreign language. What's the correct answer when the computer says ein Mädchen? Click on the picture of the young girl.

If your kids take to one of the languages on Power-Pac, you can move up to a Level I disc. Each Level I program includes 92 lessons (as opposed to only 22 for each language in the PowerPac CD-ROM) and is equivalent to two years of high-school language instruction or a one-year college course.

GET SMART: *If you have a Web browser and a connection to the Internet, you can try the Rosetta Stone language program before you buy. Enter the following address in your browser and then download the demo version of Rosetta Stone (available in both Macintosh and Windows versions):*

http://www.trstone.com/demos/

The demos are quite large (the Windows version is 1.5MB, and each language chapter is approximately 1MB).

Writing in a Foreign Language

Foreign-language homework assignments often resemble those given in English class. Some students — especially those in high school — must read *and* write in the language they're studying.

If you use a full-featured word processor such as Microsoft Word, you may not have to add anything to your computer to write in a foreign language that uses the Roman alphabet. But even these languages — such as German, Swedish, French, Spanish, and Italian — use special characters. In German, for example, you often use an *umlaut* (two small dots above a vowel).

Check your word processor's Help file or its documentation to learn which keys you must press to create such special characters. To place an umlaut over a letter in Mi-

★ TRY THIS! ★

Translate!

Translation is a tedious task. With dictionary in hand, your kids struggle to turn English into Spanish, or French, or German.

In the not-too-distant future, a machine might be able to handle that job. To see this future in action today, point your Web browser to the Globalink home page:

http://www.globalink.com/

Globalink makes various foreign-language-related software programs and has developed a computerized translation technology it calls *Barcelona*. The company created these translation programs primarily for businesspeople who need to translate documents from one language to another, but we decided to take a look, too.

When we visited Globalink's Web site, it offered a free translation service between any two of these languages: English, Spanish, French, Italian, and German. You select the languages for the translation, enter the message (as many as 500 words), and provide your e-mail address. Within 24 hours, they will translate your message and return the translated text via e-mail.

We entered a few sentences from *The FamilyPC Guide to Homework* and asked Globalink to translate the text into German. Here is the text we sent to them:

As parents, our job is to make sure that our kids have the best possible shot at knowing the right

answers to the educational questions, and so give them the best chance of succeeding in school. Of course, that's one of the reasons why we buy a home computer in the first place, and why we keep buying software.

And here's the same passage in German:

Als Eltern ist unsere Arbeit, sicher zu machen, daß unsere Kinder den besten möglichen Schuß haben beim Wissen der richtigen Antworten zu den pädagogischen Fragen, und so gibt ihnen die beste Chance vom Sein Erfolgreich in Schule. Natürlich ist das ein der Gründe, warum wir einen Homecomputer in der ersten Stelle kaufen, und, warum wir das Kaufen von Software behalten.

Pretty cool, huh?

GET SMART: For at-home translations, check out Globalink's Language Assistant, a $50 program that runs on the PC and the Mac. You can order it by calling 800-255-5660 or 703-273-5600.

We're not suggesting that you steer your kids here so they can avoid translation homework (not that we can stop you from doing so). Rather, we want to show you how the family computer can computerize a manual chore. Down the road, children studying foreign languages may have access to such technology, just as kids today often use calculators in advanced math classes.

crosoft Word for Windows, for example, you simultaneously press the Ctrl, Shift, and colon (:) keys *before* typing the letter. In Word for the Macintosh, you press the Option and U keys simultaneously and then the letter key.

Microsoft Word lets you insert special characters of those foreign languages that use the Roman alphabet (such as German).

Languages that do not use the Roman alphabet — for example, Arabic, Chinese, Japanese, Hebrew, and Russian — require special fonts. The best place we've found for obtaining free foreign-language fonts is the Web page of the University of Oregon's Yamada Language Center. The Center offers 112 fonts in 40 different languages; most of these fonts are for the Macintosh (still the computer of choice at many colleges), though a number are available in Windows format, too.

To begin your font search, enter this address in your Web browser:

http://babel.uoregon.edu/yamada/guides.html

After you download a font, you must install it on your computer. Here's how:

● **On the Macintosh:** Drag the font's icon to the System folder (make sure the System folder is closed before you do this). The

Mac asks whether you want to put the font in the Fonts folder. Click on OK.

● **In Windows 3.1:** Double-click on the Main icon in the Program Manager, then double-click on the Control Panels icon. Double-click on Fonts and then click on the Add button. In the file directory dialog box that appears, locate the font file you downloaded. Choose one or more of the fonts in that file and then click on Add. Make sure the Copy Fonts to Windows Directory box is checked and click on OK.

● **In Windows 95:** Open the Fonts folder from within Explorer. (The Fonts folder is inside the Windows folder.) Choose the Install New Font command from the File menu. In the Add Fonts dialog box that appears, locate the folder containing the file you downloaded. Make sure the Copy fonts to Font folder box is checked. Double-click on the icon for the font that you want to add.

Go Online!

The Internet isn't just an American phenomenon. This network stretches across the globe and provides information not only *in* many languages, but *about* many languages, too. That makes the Internet a perfect tool for foreign-language students. The World Wide Web isn't a swift language tutor, but it *does* contain important resources for kids.

Foreign Languages for Travelers

http://www.travlang.com/languages/

This Web page may be aimed at travelers looking to brush up on a language before heading to the airport, but it's also a great spot to send young children when you want to introduce them to any of the 28 languages listed here.

Organized by subject — numbers, shopping, directions, places, and times and dates — the words are both displayed on the screen and pronounced by your computer. (Your Web browser must be properly configured to let you hear the pronunciations; this site includes instructions for doing this.) The Foreign Languages for Travelers page covers languages typically studied in school — such as Spanish, German, and French — as well as other tongues such as Polish, Dutch, Hebrew, and Japanese.

Foreign Language Resources on the Web

http://www.itp.berkeley.edu/~thorne/HumanResources.html

You can search the Web for foreign-language sites or you can

Want to learn a bit of Spanish? Visit the Foreign Languages for Travelers Web page.

head straight to Foreign Language Resources on the Web. This comprehensive collection of hypertext links serves as a launching pad to many of the best and most popular foreign-language pages on the World Wide Web. If your child is studying a language in school, bookmark this place.

BritSpeak

http://pages.prodigy.com/NY/NYC/britspk/main.html

I'm knackered because I've been rabbiting like a lad. Confused? You wouldn't be if you were in Great Britain. This Web page lists scores of British English words and phrases and then matches them with their American English counterparts. Although you can use BritSpeak just for fun, it's also a good starting point for kids researching vocabulary differences within the English language. Still confused? That first line, translates to: *I'm exhausted because I've been chattering like a boy.*

Chapter 13

Creating Presentations

How to Do the Same Old Song and Dance a New Way

PEOPLE DON'T ALWAYS PAY ATTENTION TO the message; sometimes, they focus more on the way you package that message. Kids soon learn this in school, where clear handwriting is rewarded and sharp-looking papers get better grades.

Completed homework assignments — especially reports and projects — are essentially presentations of information. And rest assured, teachers notice how that information is presented.

You can help your children go beyond the typical presentation by showing them what the home computer can do for their reports, papers, projects, and lessons. In this chapter, we highlight several ways you can do that.

Whether your

kids are putting information on paper, displaying it on the computer screen, or building awesome multimedia presentations complete with sound and sights, the home PC or Mac can put a whole new spin on the old song and dance.

Projects Go on Paper

We parents got grades the old-fashioned way: by putting stuff on paper.

Kids can still dazzle teachers and classmates without resorting to high-tech, multimedia presentations. Rather than provide a light and sound show, children can present their school reports the low-tech way, on paper. But by using the computer, they can give those presentations the extra *oomph* that's needed to make them stand out from the rest of the crowd.

They can do this by packaging the report creatively with the help of desktop publishing software. Professionals use such programs to design newsletters, magazines, books, and pamphlets. Kids can do much the same thing by using home-appropriate desktop publishing programs — which cost a lot less and are much easier to use than the programs the pros use.

In the following sections, we outline several ways to assemble reports and papers, give you plenty of tips and hints to pass along to your kids, and recommend the best software we've found for the job.

It's Not Fancy, It's Just Sharp

All Ages

Your computer already has the simplest tool for punching up a report: your word processor.

GET SMART: *Any kids in the house who don't type? If your family is looking for a typing tutor, we recommend Mavis Beacon Teaches Typing to Kids (Mindscape, 800-234-3088, for Windows or Mac, $40). Most schools teach this skill at some point, but you can give your children a head start as early as age five or six.*

Sure, handwritten reports and papers can look charming, but they present a big problem. Need to make a change, even an extra word or two? If so, your child has to rewrite the entire paper. From scratch. (We can hear the whining from here!) With a word pro-

All word processors — even the less powerful ones within integrated packages — offer one-click footnotes. In ClarisWorks on the Mac, for example, you just pick Insert Footnote from the Format menu.

cessor, however, changes are a snap.

Unless you're acting as typist, your kids need to know their way around the keyboard and your word-processing program. That said, here are some tips for keeping the kids on track:

- If the teacher requires a specific format for the paper, make sure your kids follow the teacher's guidelines. For example, does the paper or report have to be double-spaced? If so, make sure the document is set up that way.

- When possible, keep it simple. Use a single-column layout and choose basic, not fancy, fonts. On a Windows-equipped PC, for example, we recommend 12-point Times New Roman as the font choice for the main text; on the Mac, we like Times. Both are classic, easy-to-read fonts — important qualities for long stretches of text. (Elementary-school-aged kids may want to try 14-point type rather than 12-point; the larger size is similar to what they see in their schoolbooks.) Headlines — such as the title of the paper or report — should be in a contrasting font. On your PC, try 24- or 36-point Arial in boldface; Helvetica works well on the Mac.

- Make sure your kids use at least one-inch margins on the sides of the page (1 1/4-inch margins are even better) and one-inch margins at the top and bottom. The margins should be wide enough that you can hold the paper at its edges without covering up any of the text.

- Demonstrate the power of the word processor's automatic footnote feature to older children. With a word processor, they can easily add footnotes without worrying about how much fits on one page. The program automatically makes the footnotes fit.

Great-Looking Documents, Easy as Pie
Ages 10 and Up

Although a plain old word processor is a super tool for many kids, a more specialized program is sometimes a better bet for putting thoughts on paper. If the elementary-school-aged children in your house want to use the family computer for producing slick-looking documents, we recommend The Learning Company's Student Writing Center for the PC or the Mac, and the Student Writing and Research Center for Windows.

Why should you buy another program that does essentially the same thing as one that you already have? Because these packages provide preformatted document de-

Word Processor Picks

For schoolwork as well as writing chores around the house, kids have a wealth of word processor choices. But which is best for your children? We think three titles are especially effective:

- For grades 2–5: Amazing Writing Machine offers a bright interface and cartoon-style graphics, and it's one solid writing program.

- For grades 6–8: Microsoft Works' word processor includes the writing tools this age range needs (such as footnotes), but isn't so feature-packed that kids will get lost.

- For grades 9–12: Microsoft Word is the preferred word processor for high-school-aged kids (and those almost in high school). It includes an outliner, has tools that mark revisions, and can easily accommodate tables for numerical information.

signs, which means your kids can concentrate on the message, and not the way they package it.

These programs offer two distinct document formats that are both appropriate for elementary-school homework assignments: a single-column report and a multiple-column newsletter. And they include a wealth of clip art — pictures your kids can select and drop into a document. (The Student Writing and Research Center also includes such advanced word-processing extras as a bibliography maker, footnotes, and an integrated encyclopedia.)

Although these packages do a lot of handholding as they guide your children through the document-creation process, you can still pass along some helpful tips:

Word processors made especially for kids let young writers pick from several predefined document types so they can get right to work on reports, newsletters, or personal journals.

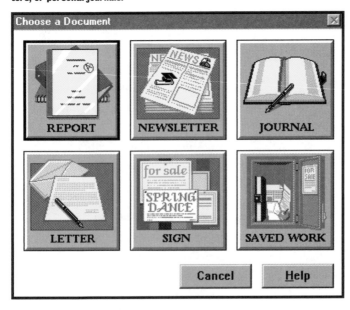

- The report template creates single-column documents; use this format for such projects as book reports and short research papers.

- Use the journal template for free-form creative writing.

- The Student Writing Center can import graphics in two popular Windows formats: PCX and BMP. You can download many images in the PCX format from online services or the Internet and use them to punch up a report or a newsletter.

Go Professional
Ages 10 and Up

If your family computer is already equipped with an integrated package such as Microsoft Works or ClarisWorks (and it should be; see Chapter 2, "The Bare Necessities"), older children have the tools in hand for creating spectacular documents. These packages, which each feature a word processor, a spreadsheet program, a graphics or charting module, and other programs, can turn out a variety of document styles.

The key to creating successful documents with an integrated program comes from two traits of these packages. First, integrated programs make it relatively easy to combine words with other ele-

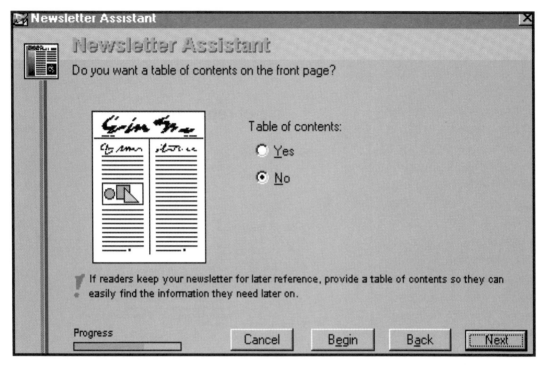

Both ClarisWorks and Microsoft Works include helpful assistants (Microsoft Works calls them Wizards) that automatically create a ready-to-use newsletter design for you and your children.

ments, such as artwork, drawings, charts, and numerical tables. Second, the most recent versions of Works and ClarisWorks include a variety of templates that do the design work for your children. After selecting the template that best meets their needs, your kids simply fill in the blanks.

How about creating a pair of documents to get them going? We use ClarisWorks for Windows 95 in the following projects, but you use a similar process in Microsoft Works. You might want to create these templates for your children the first time and then save them using recognizable names. Later, the kids can open the files themselves and start to work.

Document 1: Letting the Computer Do the Work

In ClarisWorks, create a new document by pressing Ctrl-N and then click on the Use Assistant or Stationary box. Pick the Newsletter Assistant and answer the questions it asks. The program then creates the newsletter template. Type the text for the report or import it from another word-processing file, by choosing the Insert command from the File menu.

Document 2: A One-Page Report That Catches the Eye

Unbalanced documents can attract attention. To create a two-column report template that lets kids enter main points in the first column and the rest of the text in the second column, create a new word-processing document by pressing Ctrl-N. When the blank page appears on the screen, choose Section from the Format menu and enter 2 in the Number of Columns box. Click on Variable Width Columns (to create columns of un-equal widths) and, in the Settings boxes, enter 2 inches for column 1, and 4.17 inches for column 2.

You can add a title for the report by creating a graphics frame (click on the tool icon that looks like

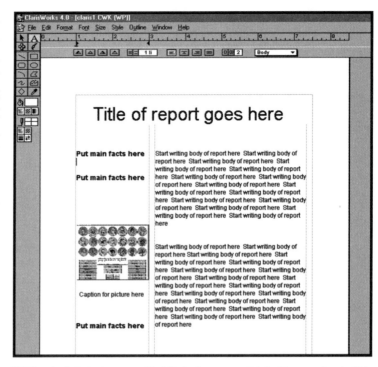

Middle-school students can use ClarisWorks to prepare slick-looking reports using this single-page template.

a paintbrush and drag a box into place across the entire page). You're now ready to enter text in either column. (To start typing text in the right column, keep pressing Return until the cursor appears in that column.) If your homework workers want to spice up this template with a piece of clip art or a table, create additional graphics frames or a spreadsheet-style frame ready for numbers.

Projects Go Digital

Getting up in front of an audience is tough, even for adults. So, when our children come home from school moaning about an up-coming oral report, it's easy to sympathize.

It's also easy to help out. Although we used to do the job with note cards and a prop or two — methods that work as well today as they did 30 years ago — our computer-equipped kids can do even better. After all, presenting a school report isn't much different from delivering a business report. At work, you might use *presentation software*, which makes slick-looking slides and over-head transparencies. Kids can do the same thing with the same sorts of tools.

And even if they don't present their work at school, kids can learn just by assembling the presentation. (If you coach them in the right way, they might even have fun.) To assemble a presentation, they must do research, organize their thoughts, create an outline of notes, and blend words with pictures, charts, or numbers.

Real-world presenters make their points using powerful programs such as Microsoft Powerpoint or Lotus Freelance Graphics. If you have such software — perhaps because you use it — you can demonstrate it to older children. In fact, kids can usually master such software, because it typically includes ready-made slide templates with predefined images and backgrounds, and fill-in-the-blanks spaces for text and charts.

But we're not recommending that you spend your hard-earned money on a presentation package just for the kids. In the following sections, we show you a pair of kid-perfect programs that include digital slide show makers.

Pint-Sized Presenters Can Wow 'em, Too

Ages 8 and Up

Although younger kids may not take to the idea of creating a slide show for schoolwork (one of the stumbling blocks is actually showing the slides on a computer at school; see the sidebar "Tips for At-School Presentations," later in this chapter), they can still learn while building a presentation about something that interests them. Of course, if they print out the picture-packed presentation — assuming you have a color ink-jet printer

— the show can go to school.

We think Kid Pix Studio is the perfect program for young presenters. You can easily manipulate digitized pictures, sound, and text and then exhibit the information in the form of a self-running slide show, complete with transitions and other special effects.

To get started, help your child collect the data for the presentation. For example, if your daughter is fascinated by dogs, you and she can conduct a personal survey by taking pictures of friends' canines. Bring along a camera and a notebook you can use as a logbook for important information, including each dog's name, breed, sex, age, time and date seen, location, owner's name and address, and distinguishing features.

After you and your child collect the dog data, the next step is to digitize the photographs so that you can import them into Kid Pix Studio. If you didn't use a digital camera (which plugs directly into the computer) and you don't have a scanner at home, you can usually have the photo prints

Getting Pics into PCs (and Macs)

Some print shops or photo stores transfer photographs onto floppy disks (in BMP format for Windows, or PICT for the Mac) for about $10 or less per picture. You can also send the film to photo developers such as Konica (800-669-1070) or Seattle Filmworks (800-445-3348); these firms put the images on floppy disks for $10 to $21 per roll. Another method to consider is to take the undeveloped film to a photo shop that offers Photo CD service. Such shops put as many as 100 photos on a single CD-ROM for around $70.

scanned at a quick-print shop.

Now, launch Kid Pix Studio and open each image as a separate file. Be sure to set up your pages based on the orientation of the image (in other words, *portrait* for vertical shots, and *landscape* for horizontal pictures). Enter the details of each dog in large type and bright, contrasting colors. The best place for this text is at the corners or to the side of the dog's image. Use the Save As command to save each page with a name, such as Dog 1; this helps you assemble the show in the right order.

When several pages are complete, open the SlideShow feature and place the pages in the proper order, starting with a title page — how about "Dogs I Know?" — by clicking on the icon representing each page. In Kid Pix Studio, add sound effects by clicking on the sound icon. Your child can pick from recorded sounds (such as a dog's bark) or, if you're adventurous and have a microphone-equipped computer, record her own narration or comments. Be sure to keep the

Tips for At-School Presentations

In most cases, it will be difficult, if not impossible, to actually show the presentation on a computer at school. Even if the classroom has a computer and the right software (not likely), unless you can talk the teacher into crowding the class around the monitor, you need a link between the computer and a television or a big-screen display (even less likely). For this reason, we recommend that your child either prints out the presentation as a handout, with copies for each classmate, or prints out the presentation on overhead transparencies.

If you have a color ink-jet printer, your child can create color transparencies, which are much more effective for presenting a message than boring black on white. Most schools have an overhead projector. You can find transparencies for your home laser or ink-jet printer at most office supply stores.

When the presentation is the backbone of an oral report, your child can't simply distribute the handouts or show transparencies on the screen. Help your child rehearse his speech, just as you would if he was using note cards and a prop or two. You should also time the presentation to ensure that it fits within the length requirement set by the teacher.

Max
Soft-coated Wheaton Terrier
8 month old

Favorite Thing: Kissing Photographers

Encourage your kids to use bright colors and large type for the text in their Kid Pix Studio presentation. The slides will be easier to read, especially for an audience watching the presentation from halfway across a classroom.

narration brief, because sound files consume large quantities of hard disk space. (Skip the sound effects if your child plans to print out the pages and take them to school for an old-fashioned, pass-around report.)

Kid Pix has 16 different slide transitions — including fades, wipes, and dissolves — which you can place between each page if the presentation will be shown on the computer. At the bottom of each panel in the presentation, click on the transition button, choose an effect, and then click on Select. To make sure the audience gets a chance to read and see everything, set the slide bar below each window so that each slide stays on the screen for at least 8 to 10 seconds.

Each page in a ClarisWorks document is a separate slide in the digital presentation and can hold pictures and text.

Show Time!

Ages 10 and Up

Older students who want to produce a dazzling slide show presentation can turn to ClarisWorks for help. Not only is this integrated program an able assistant for many other homework chores, it also includes a slide show feature that turns the computer into a presenter with considerable flair.

For the most part, slide show creation in ClarisWorks is a manual process. Unless you use the single Assistant that steps you through the process, you have to do all the work on your own. For this reason, creating slide shows with ClarisWorks is a task best suited for older children — those in upper elementary, middle school, and high school grades.

As in any report or project, the first job is doing the research. Convince your child of the benefits of using lots of images in the presentation; the capability to include pictures with text really distinguishes digital presentations from the old stand-up-and-talk report. (If the report is all text, assembling a digital presentation is overkill.

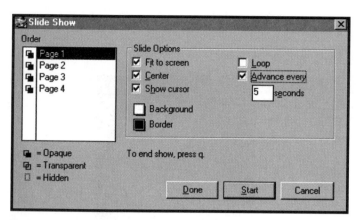

Slide Show

Order
- Page 1
- Page 2
- Page 3
- Page 4

Slide Options
- ☑ Fit to screen
- ☑ Center
- ☑ Show cursor
- ☐ Background
- ■ Border
- ☐ Loop
- ☑ Advance every
- 5 seconds

= Opaque
= Transparent
= Hidden

To end show, press q.

[Done] [Start] [Cancel]

The Slide Show dialog box lets kids change the organization of the slide show by dragging the pages at the left into the proper order.

In such cases, kids are much better off focusing their creative energies on producing a snappy-looking document; see the section "Projects Go On Paper," earlier in this chapter.)

Among the best places for gathering images are online services, the Internet, or — if the computer lacks a modem — an electronic encyclopedia. (For more information on doing research with the home computer, see Chapter 7.) For example, if you're assembling a report on space for a science project, you might search for some interesting images at the following Internet address:

http://www.jpl.nasa.gov/archive/images.html

This is the image archive for NASA's Jet Propulsion Laboratory, where a library of space pictures is available for downloading.

Launch ClarisWorks — the Mac and the Windows versions both include the necessary tools — and create a new Draw document, by selecting New from the File menu. Next, choose Document from the Format menu and enter the number of pages — or slides — for this presentation. (Don't worry about entering the right number; you can add more pages at any time.) To see the individual pages on the screen, pick Page View from the Window menu.

To add one or more images to each page, choose the Insert command from the File menu. Create a text box by clicking on the text tool and then type the description for each picture. To give the text a more dramatic appearance, use a bright, bold color. Continue the process until you have all the pages — or slides — on disk. Finally, save the file.

To run the slide show, pick Slide Show from the Window menu. In the dialog box that appears, you can organize the slides, set special effects, and specify the length of time that each slide appears on the screen. ClarisWorks' special effects aren't as flexible or dynamic as those in Kid Pix Studio, but they work well for straightforward presentations.

One advantage of using ClarisWorks is that many schools also use this program. A slide show file created in the Windows version of ClarisWorks can even be opened and run on a Mac (and vice versa). If your child's classroom has a computer with ClarisWorks, he can save the file on a floppy disk, and run the show at school.

Chapter 14

Homework
Software

The Complete List

T HE COMPUTER IS A TERRIFIC TEACHER AND a superb homework helper. That is, when it's running the right software.

To help you find the right software, this chapter lists all the programs we highlight throughout *The FamilyPC Guide to Homework*. But the software collection used in this book isn't exhaustive. That's why we also list other winners of the *FamilyPC* Recommended seal of approval. For more thorough descriptions of these programs — as well as software recommendations in categories outside the focus of this book, such as games — look for *The FamilyPC Software Buyer's Guide*. This companion book to *The FamilyPC Guide to Homework* describes more than 200 programs and is an excellent resource for families trying to sift through

the overwhelming number of available CD-ROMs.

As an additional aid to picking the best software, this chapter identifies the *FamilyPC* Recommended programs (look for a star next to the program's name) and lists the scores (in parenthesis) those programs received during real-world testing. (To earn the *FamilyPC* Recommended seal, a program must rank at 85 or higher out of a possible score of 100.)

Chapter 1
The Family Computer

★ **KidDesk Family Edition (85)**
Edmark, 800-691-2985 or 206-556-8484; Mac, Windows, and Windows 95 CD-ROM, about $40

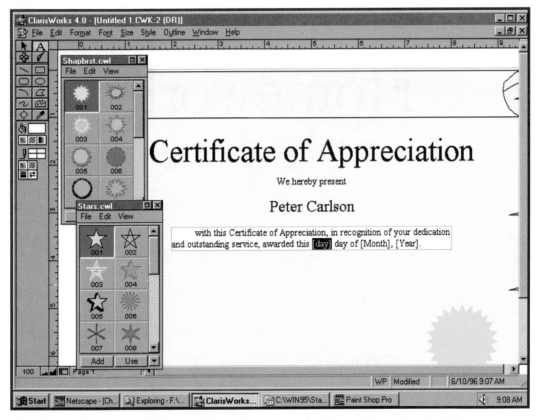

"ClarisWorks is the single most important software on our machine," said Barry Goldbarg from San Diego.

Chapter 2
The Bare Necessities

★ **America Online (85)**

America Online, 800-827-6364; Macintosh and Windows, $9.95 per month for the first five hours of connect time (includes access to all services), and $2.95 for each additional hour

Bailey's Book House

Edmark, 800-691-2985 or 206-556-8400; Mac and Windows disk or CD-ROM, about $35

★ **ClarisWorks (86)**

Claris, 800-544-8554 or 408-727-8227; Mac disk, about $130, and Windows 95 disk, about $70

★ **EasyPhoto Reader (88)**

Storm Software, 800-275-5734; Mac and Windows, about $250

★ **Hewlett-Packard DeskJet 600C or DeskWriter 600C (87)**

Hewlett-Packard, 800-752-0900; Macintosh (DeskWriter) and PC (DeskJet), about $299

★**Kidboard (88)**
Kidboard, 800-926-3066; Macintosh and Windows; $99 (Mac), $69 (Windows)

★**Kid Pix Studio (90)**
Brøderbund, 800-521-6263 or 415-382-4700; Mac and Windows CD-ROM, about $40

★**Microsoft Encarta 96 (85)**
Microsoft, 800-426-9400 or 206-882-8080; Mac and Windows CD-ROM, about $55

★**Microsoft Works for Windows 95 (86)**
Microsoft, 800-426-9400 or 206-882-8080; Windows 95 CD-ROM and disk, about $80

★**Millie's Math House (85)**
Edmark, 800-691-2985 or 206-556-8400; Mac and Windows disk or CD-ROM, about $35

★**Netscape Navigator Personal Edition 2.0 (88)**
Netscape, 415-528-3777; Mac and Windows disk, about $50

PC Pals Mouse 'N House
Sima, 800-345-7462 or 708-966-0300; Windows, about $35

★**Sammy's Science House (89)**
Edmark, 800-691-2985 or 206-556-8484; Mac and Windows disk or CD-ROM, about $39

★**Wacom ArtPad II (86)**
Wacom, 800-922-6613 or 360-750-8882;

Mac and Windows, $174.99 ($189.99 bundled with Dabbler)

Chapter 3
The Magic Words
Mentioned in *The FamilyPC Guide to Homework*

★**The Amazing Writing Machine: CD-ROM Edition (86)**
Brøderbund, 800-521-6263 or 415-382-4700; Mac and Windows CD-ROM, about $45

★**Chicka Chicka Boom Boom (85)**
Simon & Schuster Interactive, 800-910-0099 or 212-698-7000; Windows CD-ROM, about $35

★**ClarisWorks (86)**
Claris, 800-544-8554 or 408-727-8227; Mac disk, about $130, and Windows 95 disk, about $70

★**Dr. Seuss's ABC (90)**
Living Books, 800-397-4240 or 415-382-7818; Mac and Windows CD-ROM, about $40

KidWorks Deluxe
Davidson & Associates, 800-545-7677 or 310-793-0600; Mac and Windows CD-ROM, about $45

★**Microsoft Works for Windows 95 (86)**
Microsoft, 800-426-9400 or 206-882-8080; Windows 95 CD-ROM and disk, about $80

★**StoryBook Weaver Deluxe (86)**
MECC, 800-685-6322, ext. 529, or 612-569-1529; Mac and Windows CD-ROM, around $45

Student Writing and Research Center
The Learning Company, 800-852-2255 or 510-792-2101; Windows CD-ROM, about $99

★**Winnie the Pooh and the Honey Tree (90)**
Disney Interactive, 800-900-9234 or 818-841-3326; Windows CD-ROM, about $30

Other *FamilyPC* Recommended Reading and Writing Software

★**Alien Tales (86)**
Kids take part in an extraterrestrial game show in which aliens claim to have written some of Earth's finest children's literature. Your child sets the record straight by reading passages from great books, answering questions, and solving puzzles.

Brøderbund, 800-521-6263 or 415-382-4700; Mac and Windows CD-ROM, about $40; ages 9–13

★**Arthur's Teacher Trouble (91)**
Arthur's Teacher Trouble — an interactive storybook based on a book by Marc Brown — recounts the story of Arthur the aardvark, who discovers that he has "The Rat" — the infamous Mr. Ratburn — as his third-grade teacher.

Living Books, 800-776-4724 or 415-382-7818; Mac and Windows CD-ROM, about $40; ages 4–10

★**Casper Brainy Book (88)**
Adapted from the movie *Casper*, Casper Brainy Book contains an interactive storybook plus reading games for prereaders and early readers.

Knowledge Adventure, 800-542-4240 or 818-246-4400; Mac, Windows, and Windows 95 CD-ROM, about $35; ages 3–8

★**Disney's Animated StoryBook: The Lion King (85)**
The Lion King contains 21 beautifully illustrated pages that tell the tale of Simba the lion cub, who loses his father — and almost his will to live — before triumphantly returning to rescue his kingdom from the destructive paws of Scar, his evil uncle.

Disney Interactive, 800-688-1520 or 818-841-3326; Mac and Windows CD-ROM, about $30; ages 3–9

★**Franklin's Reading World (87)**
In Franklin's Reading World, words and sentences abound as kids learn about phonics, word recognition, reading, and spelling.

Sanctuary Woods, 800-943-3664 or 415-286-6000; Mac and Windows disk, about $30, CD-ROM, about $39; ages 4–7

★**Great Word Adventure (86)**
Featuring the voice of comedian Howie Mandel, the Great Word Adventure takes your child on a wacky journey into the world of language skills inside Lil' Howie's Fun House.

7th Level, 800-884-8863 or 214-437-4858; Mac and Windows CD-ROM, about $40; ages 6–9

The bell rang. The first day of school was over. Kids ran out of every classroom-every one but Room 13. Here, the students filed out slowly, in alphabetical order. "See you tomorrow," said their teacher, Mr. Ratburn.

"There are all kinds of neat things to click on in Arthur's Teacher Trouble!" —Jessica Manson, age eight, of Austin, Texas.

★Kiyeko and the Lost Night (86)

In Kiyeko and the Lost Night, your kids enter the magical world of the Amazon rain forest, where they meet a young boy named Kiyeko, who is trying to discover who stole the night. This interactive storybook, based on Vladimir Hulpach's *The Snakes Who Stole the Night*, contains 8,000 hand-drawn frames and 45 minutes of original music and sound effects.

Ubi Soft Entertainment, 800-824-7638 or 415-464-4440; Mac and Windows CD-ROM, about $30; ages 4–10

★The Multimedia Workshop (85)

The Multimedia Workshop lets kids creatively combine video, sound, graphics, and text and gives them a taste of what it's like to be a professional producer of video presentations and slide shows.

Davidson & Associates, 800-545-7677 or 310-793-0600; Mac and Windows CD-ROM, about $30; ages 8 and up

★Read, Write and Type (89)

With the dexterous assistance of Lefty LaDee and Right Way McKay — two animated, talking hands — kids get a head start with reading, phonics, and typing skills.

The Learning Company, 800-852-2255 or 510-792-2101; Mac and Windows CD-ROM, about $60; ages 6–8

★Reader Rabbit's Reading Development Library Level 1 (86)

Reader Rabbit's Reading Development Library Level 1 contains two interactive storybooks that build reading comprehension skills for beginning first-grade readers.

The Learning Company, 800-852-2255 or 510-792-2101; Mac and Windows CD-ROM, about $45; ages 5–7

★Reading Blaster Jr. (85)

Reading Blaster Jr. is an interactive, intergalactic adventure that teaches kids ages four to seven to read by using phonics.

Davidson & Associates, 800-545-7677 or 310-793-0600; Windows CD-ROM, about $35; ages 4–7

★Sesame Street: Let's Make a Word (89)

Let's Make a Word is an interactive game in which kids discover words, spelling, vocabulary, phonics, and more.

Creative Wonders, 800-245-4525 or 415-571-7171; Mac and Windows CD-ROM, about $39; ages 3–6

Chapter 4
Numbers Are Cool
Mentioned in *The FamilyPC Guide to Homework*

★Adi's Comprehensive Learning System 2nd & 3rd Mathematics (89)

Sierra On-Line, 800-757-7707 or 206-649-9800; Windows CD, about $44

Alge-Blaster 3

Davidson & Associates, 800-545-7677 or 310-793-0600; Mac and Windows disk and CD-ROM, about $45

★ClarisWorks (86)

Claris, 800-544-8554 or 408-727-8227; Mac disk, about $130, and Windows 95 disk, about $70

Cruncher

Davidson & Associates, 800-545-7677 or 310-793-0600; Mac and Windows disk and CD-ROM, about $45

DinoPark Tycoon

MECC, 800-685-6322 or 612-569-1529; Mac and DOS disk, about $30

Gazillionaire

Spectrum Holobyte, 800-695-4263 or 510-522-3584; Windows CD-ROM, approximately $13

★James Discovers Math (91)

Brøderbund, 800-521-6263 or 415-382-4700; Mac and Windows CD-ROM, about $39

★JumpStart First Grade (87)

Knowledge Adventure, 800-542-4240 or 818-246-4400; Mac and Windows CD-ROM, about $35

★**Math Rabbit (89)**
The Learning Company, 800-852-2255 or 510-792-2101; Mac and Windows disk, about $45, or CD-ROM, about $50

★**Math Workshop (87)**
Brøderbund, 800-521-6263 or 415-382-4700; Mac and Windows CD-ROM, about $40

★**Microsoft Works for Windows 95 (86)**
Microsoft, 800-426-9400 or 206-882-8080; Windows 95 CD-ROM and disk, about $80

★**Millie's Math House (85)**
Edmark, 800-691-2985 or 206-556-8400; Mac and Windows disk or CD-ROM, about $35

★**SimCity 2000 Special Edition (89)**
Maxis, 800-526-2947 or 510-933-5630; Mac, DOS, and Windows disk, about $45, or CD-ROM, about $60

Other *FamilyPC* Recommended Math Software
★**How Many Bugs in a Box? (86)**

"I love using Nick Jr. Play Math. I have not gotten bored, because there are so many areas to play in." Gabrielle Siskind, age five, of Owings Mills, Maryland.

Based on David A. Carter's best-selling pop-up book of the same name, How Many Bugs in a Box? is an interactive journey with ports of call in counting and sorting, reading, matching, memory, and hand-eye coordination.

Simon & Schuster Interactive, 800-910-0099 or 212-698-7000; Mac and Windows CD-ROM, about $35; ages 3–6

★ JumpStart Preschool (92)

JumpStart Preschool presents a colorful, fun preschool curriculum that helps two- to five-year olds leap toward an early understanding of numbers, shapes, letters, and colors.

Knowledge Adventure, 800-542-4240 or 818-246-4400; Mac and Windows CD-ROM, about $35; ages 2–5

★ Logical Journey of the Zoombinis (88)

Hidden inside this delightful animated odyssey is instruction in graphing, logic, set theory, data analysis, and algebraic thinking.

Brøderbund, 800-521-6263 or 415-382-4400; Mac and Windows CD-ROM, about $40; ages 8–12

★ Money Town (86)

In Money Town, kids help Greenstreet's characters earn money to reopen the town park and in the process learn the basics of dollars and cents.

Davidson, 800-457-8357 or 310-793-0600; Windows CD-ROM, about $35; ages 5–8

★ Nick Jr. Play Math (90)

For young fans of TV's Nickelodeon network, Nick Jr. Play Math offers a colorful, animated computer alternative for learning basic math skills.

Viacom NewMedia, 800-469-2539 or 212-258-6000; Mac and Windows CD-ROM, about $25; ages 3–6

★ Peter Rabbit's Math Garden (85)

The instructive power of nature's ways blooms in Peter Rabbit's Math Garden. This entertaining program employs Beatrix Potter's classic characters to teach your child basic number concepts through four fun activities.

Mindscape, 800-234-3088 or 415-897-9900; Mac and Windows CD-ROM, about $35; ages 4–8

★ Snootz Math Trek (85)

In Snootz Math Trek, an intergalactic math adventure for kids ages six to 10, Snootians crash their spaceship into Earth. Your child can help them fix their ship — and find all the items on their Big List — by solving math and logic problems.

Theatrix, 800-955-8749 or 510-658-2800; Mac and Windows CD-ROM, about $34; ages 6–10

★ Zaark and the Night Team (85)

In this two-CD set, Zaark and the Night Team help your children discover the patterns and symbols all around them.

Maxis, 800-336-2947 or 510-933-5630; Windows CD-ROM, approximately $35; ages 6–9

Chapter 5
People and Places
Mentioned in *The FamilyPC Guide to Homework*

Africa Trails
MECC, 800-685-6322, ext. 529, or 612-569-1529; Mac and Windows CD-ROM, about $50

Cartopedia
DK Multimedia, 212-213-4800 or 800-356-6575; Mac and Windows CD-ROM, about $49

★**Kid Pix Studio (90)**
Brøderbund, 800-521-6263 or 415-382-4700; Mac and Windows CD-ROM, about $40

Microsoft Encarta 96 World Atlas
Microsoft, 800-426-9400 or 206-882-8080; Windows 95 CD-ROM, about $55

Material World
Starpress Multimedia, 800-782-7944 or 714-833-3838; Mac and Windows CD-ROM, about $30

★**PC Globe Maps 'N' Facts (86)**
Brøderbund, 800-521-6263 or 415-382-4700; Mac and Windows CD-ROM, about $30

★**Passage to Vietnam (90)**
Against All Odds Productions, 908-370-3801; Mac or Windows CD-ROM, about $40, book and CD-ROM, about $75

★**3D Atlas (86)**
ABC/EA Home Software, 800-245-4525 or 415-571-7171; Mac or Windows CD-ROM, about $80 (Mac) or $65 (Windows)

★**Where in the U.S.A. is Carmen Sandiego? (91)**
Brøderbund, 800-521-6263 or 415-382-4400; Mac and Windows CD-ROM, about $50

Other *FamilyPC* Recommended Geography Software
★**Carmen Sandiego Junior Detective Edition (89)**
In the junior edition of the popular Carmen Sandiego series, kids solve puzzles and follow a trail of clues to track down the ever-elusive Carmen Sandiego.
Brøderbund, 800-521-6263 or 415-382-4700; Mac and Windows CD-ROM, about $40; ages 5–8

★**GeoSafari Multimedia (85)**
GeoSafari is a fun, informative multimedia trek that quizzes kids eight and up about geography, history, and science.
Educational Insights Interactive, 800-381-0381 or 615-381-9066; Mac and Windows CD-ROM, approximately $49; ages 8 and up

★**Ozzie's Travels: Destination Japan (85)**
In Ozzie's Travels: Destination Japan, kids embark with Ozzie S. Otter on a voyage of cultural discovery through 55 games, puzzles, and activities.
Digital Impact, 800-775-4232 or 918-

"I thought Morgan's Adventures in Ancient Greece was fun overall," said Kristin Happe, age 10, of Arlington, Virginia. "It really will help me since I'm going to be studying Greece in school."

742-2022; Mac and Windows CD-ROM, about $30; ages 5–10

★ Rand McNally TripMaker (87)

With Rand McNally TripMaker, you and your children can use the family computer to plan the perfect car trip, right down to the exact route. TripMaker, which is bundled with (and cross-referenced to) Rand McNally's 1996 Road Atlas, is the best among at least five trip-planning programs on the market.

Rand McNally New Media, 800-671-5006 or 708-329-8100; Windows CD-ROM, about $40

★ Morgan's Adventures in Ancient Greece (92)

Morgan's Adventures in Ancient Greece is a cartoon romp that follows — though not always faithfully — the story of the Iliad. Your kids will be entertained, but they'll also learn about ancient Greece.

Harper Kids Interactive, 415-616-6856; Mac and Windows CD-ROM, about $35; ages 7–14

Chapter 6

The Past Is a Blast

Mentioned in *The FamilyPC Guide to Homework*

Conquest of the New World
Interplay, 800-468-3775 or 714-553-6678; DOS CD-ROM, about $50

★**Family Tree Maker Deluxe Edition II (90)**
Brøderbund Software, 800-521-6263 or 415-382-4700; Windows CD-ROM, about $60

500 Nations
Microsoft, 800-426-9400 or 206-882-8080; Windows CD-ROM, about $40

Gettysburg Multimedia Battle Simulation
Swfte International, 800-237-9383 or 302-234-1740; Windows CD-ROM, about $70

How Would You Survive?
Grolier Electronic Publishing, 800-285-4534 or 203-797-3530; Mac and Windows CD-ROM, about $50

Microsoft Ancient Lands
Microsoft, 800-426-9400 or 206-882-8080; Windows CD-ROM, about $35

★**Microsoft Encarta 96 (85)**
Microsoft, 800-426-9400 or 206-882-8080; Macintosh and Windows CD-ROM, approximately $55

Microsoft Encarta 96 World Atlas
Microsoft, 800-426-9400 or 206-882-8080; Windows 95 CD-ROM, about $55

Oregon Trail II
MECC, 800-685-6322 or 612-569-1529; Macintosh and Windows CD-ROM, approximately $55

Sid Meier's Civilization
Microprose, 800-695-4263 or 510-522-3584; Macintosh, DOS, and Windows disk, approximately $27

Beyond the Wall highlights real soldiers who served in Vietnam, and tells their stories with their own words, family photos, and letters home.

Other *FamilyPC* Recommended History Software

★**Beyond the Wall (90)**

Magnet Interactive has come close to re-creating the power of the Wall on its new CD-ROM. Beyond the Wall is a comprehensive look at the Vietnam Memorial, including how it was built and the effect it has on its visitors.

Magnet Interactive Studios, 202-625-1111 or 800-966-0011; Mac and Windows CD-ROM, about $45

★**Doonesbury Flashbacks: 25 Years of Serious Fun (91)**

The Doonesbury clan has made the move to a CD-ROM that documents the history of the comic strip and the history of our times.

Mindscape, 800-234-3088 or 415-897-9900; Windows CD-ROM, about $40

★**Our Times Multimedia Encyclopedia of the 20th Century (85)**

The Our Times Multimedia Encyclopedia of the 20th Century covers a rich, international mix of politics, art, film, sports, personalities, statistics, and milestones of all sorts. It strikes a balance between the earth-shattering global events and everyday minutiae that give history a sense of reality. For example, in 1930, as scientists at MIT built the first computer, a *Vogue* article noted that a woman in tasteful makeup can still be a good wife and mother.

Vicarious, 800-465-654, ext. 900, or 415-610-8300; Mac and Windows CD-ROM, about $70

Chapter 7

Wading into the Information Pool

Mentioned in *The FamilyPC Guide to Homework*

★**America Online (85)**

America Online, 800-827-6364; Mac and Windows, $9.95 per month for first five hours (includes access to all services), $2.95 each additional hour

★**Microsoft Encarta 96 (85)**

Microsoft, 800-426-9400 or 206-882-8080; Mac and Windows CD-ROM, about $55

Other *FamilyPC* Recommended Reference Software

★**My First Encyclopedia (85)**

My First Encyclopedia gives kids a big boost in their first climb up the tree of knowledge. It contains 575 entries that cover such categories as space, geography, arts and music, sports, food, animals, Earth, and nature.

Knowledge Adventure, 800-542-4240 or 818-246-4400; Windows CD-ROM, about $35; ages 3–6

Chapter 8

Science Is Fact, Not Fiction

Mentioned in *The FamilyPC Guide to Homework*

★**A.D.A.M.: The Inside Story (86)**

A.D.A.M. Software, Inc., 800-408-2326 or 619-549-0222; Windows and Mac CD-ROM, about $40

"My First Encyclopedia is a really great learning program for kids," said Emily Delgado, a teacher from Chino, California. "It teaches them that researching information can be fun and informative."

★The Incredible Machine 2 (95)
Sierra On-Line, 800-757-7707 or 206-649-9800; Mac and Windows CD-ROM, about $40

★The Magic School Bus Explores the Solar System
Microsoft, 800-426-9400 or 206-882-8080; Windows CD-ROM, about $50

★Microsoft Dinosaurs (87)
Microsoft, 800-426-9400 or 206-882-8080; Mac and Windows CD-ROM, about $59

★RedShift 2 (89)
Maris Multimedia, distributed by Maxis, 800-526-2947 or 510-933-5630; Mac and Windows CD-ROM, about $55

★Science Sleuths, Volume 1 and Volume 2 (85)
Videodiscovery, 800-548-3472 or 206-285-5400; Mac and Windows CD-ROM, about $35 each

★3-D Body Adventure (86)
Knowledge Adventure, 800-542-4240 or

818-542-4400; Windows and Mac CD-ROM, about $35

Volcano: Life on the Edge
Corbis Publishing, 800-246-2065 or 206-641-3997; Mac and Windows CD-ROM, about $50

★**What's the Secret? and What's the Secret? 2 (85)**
3M Learning, 800-219-9022 or 612-736-7072; Mac and Windows CD-ROM, about $33 each

★**Widget Workshop (85)**
Maxis, 800-526-2947 or 510-254-9700; Mac and Windows disk, about $34

Other *FamilyPC* Recommended Science Software

★**Adi's Comprehensive Learning System: Science 4th & 5th (85)**
This two-CD set covers Earth science, life science, and physical science.
    Sierra On-Line, 800-757-7707 or 206-649-9800; Windows CD, about $44; ages 10–12

"I thought Fun with Electronics was going to be boring, but I had so much fun! I did every single project. This is my favorite software so far." Tashina Maxon, age 13, Spring Valley, California.

★Adventures with Edison (85)

Adventures with Edison is a triple serving of colorful, animated fun in which kids seven to 14 learn about science, logic, and music through three activities.

Corel, 800-455-3169 or 613-728-3733; Windows CD-ROM, about $20; ages 7–14

★Cybercrafts: Hands-On-Learning Fun with Electronics (90)

Fun with Electronics combines a mini workbench, 100 electrical components, and a CD-ROM, to teach kids how to build 25 electronic projects, including a burglar alarm, a siren, and a traffic light.

Philips Media Home and Family Entertainment, 800-883-3767 or 310-444-6100; Mac and Windows CD-ROM, about $44; ages 8 and up

★The Way Things Work (85)

From electric kettles and kites to telephones and tower cranes, The Way Things Work takes your child inside objects to see what makes them tick.

DK Multimedia, 800-356-6575 or 212-213-4800; Mac and Windows CD-ROM, about $39; ages 8 and up

Chapter 9
Our Planet

Mentioned in *The FamilyPC Guide to Homework*

The Animals 2

Mindscape, 800-234-3088 or 415-883-3000; Mac and Windows CD-ROM, approximately $50

Dangerous Creatures

Microsoft, 800-426-9400 or 206-882-8080; Mac and Windows CD-ROM, about $45

Microsoft Oceans

Microsoft, 800-426-9400 or 206-882-8080; Windows CD-ROM, about $35

★Microsoft Publisher CD Deluxe for Windows 95 (85)

Microsoft, 800-426-9400 or 206-882-8080; Windows 95 CD-ROM, about $80

★Ozzie's World (87)

Digital Impact, 800-775-4232; Mac and Windows CD-ROM, about $40

★Wide World of Animals

Creative Wonders, 800-543-9778 or 415-573-8500; Mac, Windows, and Windows 95 CD-ROM, about $40

Other *FamilyPC* Recommended Environmental Software

★Discovering Endangered Wildlife (88)

Discovering Endangered Wildlife takes kids on an educational tour of the Earth's creatures that are in the greatest danger of extinction.

Lyriq International, 800-433-4464 or 203-250-2070; Windows CD-ROM, about $29; ages 8 and up

★Explorapedia: World of Nature (86)

Full of facts and figures presented with color, animations, youthful narration, and lots of fun, Explorapedia groups information in logical ways, and includes dozens of games

"If any of our curriculum deals with the environment, I would definitely use Discovering Endangered Wildlife as a supplement," said Jan Brown, a teacher in East Greenwich, Rhode Island. "Most kids love animals, and the slides are great."

and 26 projects to do away from the computer.

Microsoft, 800-426-9400 or 206-882-8080; Windows CD-ROM, about $34; ages 6–10

★How Animals Move (89)

For kids who want to move beyond the basic animal encyclopedia to delve into a different side of animal life, How Animals Move offers an in-depth look at how animals get around, including jumping, crawling, running, flying, and burrowing.

Discovery Channel Multimedia, 800-678-3343 or 317-579-0400; Mac and Windows CD-ROM, about $50; ages 10 and up

★The Multimedia Bug Book (87)

In this interactive field guide, kids can observe more than 50 insects up close and learn tips on capturing and identifying their creepy-crawly neighbors.

Swfte International, 800-759-2562 or 305-567-9990; Mac and Windows CD-ROM, about $49; ages 5–10

★One Small Square: Backyard (86)

In One Small Square: Backyard, kids explore the world of nature as seen in a three-dimensional rendition of a small square of earth.

Virgin Sound and Vision, 800-814-3530 or 310-246-4666; Mac and Windows CD-ROM, about $35; ages 8 and up

★SimIsle: Missions in the Rainforest (86)

The tropical rain forest is the setting for SimIsle: Missions in the Rainforest, another Sim title from Maxis. In this simulation program, you choose an island from an archipelago located near the equator. You are the island's governor, and its resources are at your disposal.

Maxis, 800-526-2947 or 510-933-5630; Windows and Mac CD-ROM, about $40; ages 12 and up

★Zoo Explorer/Ocean Explorer (86)

This two-CD set takes kids on fun and colorful explorations among creatures of land and sea.

Compton's NewMedia, 800-862-2206 or 619-929-2500; Mac and Windows CD-ROM, about $32; ages 3–8

Chapter 10
Artistic License

Mentioned in *The FamilyPC Guide to Homework*

★Adobe Art Explorer (86)
Adobe, 800-888-6293 or 415-961-4400; Mac CD-ROM, about $29

★Crayola Art Studio 2 (85)
Micrografx, 800-676-3110 or 214-234-1769; Windows and Mac CD-ROM, about $40

★Dabbler 2 (86)
Fractal Design, 800-297-2665 or 408-688-5300; Mac and Windows CD-ROM, about $70

★Kid Pix Studio (90)
Brøderbund, 800-521-6263 or 415-382-4700; Mac and Windows CD-ROM, about $40

Le Louvre
BMG Interactive, 800-221-8180 or 212-930-4000; Mac and Windows CD-ROM, about $50

★Masterpiece Mansion (89)
Philips Media, 800-883-3767 or 310-444-6500; Mac and Windows CD-ROM, about $40

Other *FamilyPC* Recommended Art Software
★Adobe PhotoDeluxe (92)
PhotoDeluxe contains much of the power of Photoshop, the market leader for professional image editing, but Adobe has eliminated all the unwieldy and complicated functions (and the $800 price tag) that only professionals can handle.

Adobe, 800-888-6293 or 415-961-4400; Mac CD-ROM; about $90

★Corel Gallery 2 (86)
Corel Gallery 2, the latest version of the im-

"Excellent graphics and neat stamps — Flying Colors makes a picture seem alive and real!" Sarina Yospin, age nine, of Newton, Massachusetts.

pressive Corel Gallery (the previous version contained 10,000 high-quality images, for $50), has something for every burgeoning multimedia artist. The new version has 15,000 clip-art images, 500 photos, 500 fonts, and a few sounds and animated video clips.

Corel, 800-772-6735 or 613-728-3733; Mac or Windows CD-ROM, about $100

★Flying Colors (87)

Flying Colors doesn't feature activities or projects, such as coloring books, like those found in other paint programs. Instead, it provides kids with a stunning selection of colors, tools, and images to spark their imaginations.

Davidson & Associates, 800-545-7677 or 310-793-0600; Mac and Windows disk or CD-ROM, about $35; ages 8 and up

★Great Artists (87)

The CD-ROM focuses on 40 of Europe's greatest painters, including Monet, Van Gogh, da Vinci, and Rembrandt. It explores in great detail one painting from each artist, allowing you to study each painting within the context of history, art techniques, and themes.

Cambrix Publishing Inc., 800-992-8781 or 818-993-4274; Windows CD-ROM, about $60; ages 10 and up

★A Passion for Art: Renoir, Cézanne, Matisse, and Dr. Barnes (89)

Art lovers will be thrilled to explore the private collection of Dr. Albert C. Barnes, available in its entirety on CD-ROM.

Corbis Publishing, 800-246-2065 or 206-641-3997; Mac and Windows CD-ROM, about $45

★Print Shop Ensemble II (85)

Twelve years after it first brought publishing into the home, The Print Shop — in its latest incarnation as Ensemble II — continues to impress families with its versatility and its broad selection of graphics.

Brøderbund, 800-521-6263 or 415-382-4400; Mac and Windows CD-ROM, about $80

★Sesame Street: Art Workshop (85)

Sesame Street: Art Workshop is designed to draw out the creative side of your preschooler.

Creative Wonders, 800-543-9778 or 415-513-7555; Mac and Windows CD-ROM, about $35; ages 3–6

★With Open Eyes (85)

Using With Open Eyes, kids can view photographs of more than 200 works of art from the Art Institute of Chicago.

The Voyager Company, 800-446-2001 or 212-431-5199; Mac and Windows CD-ROM, about $39; ages 3 and up

Chapter 11

In Song and On Stage

Mentioned in *The FamilyPC Guide to Homework*

★Hollywood (85)

Theatrix Interactive, 800-955-8749 or 510-658-2800; Mac and Windows CD-ROM, about $40

★Kid Pix Studio (90)

Brøderbund, 800-521-6263 or 415-382-4700; Mac and Windows CD-ROM, about $40

KidRiffs

IBM Multimedia Studio, 800-898-8842 or 615-793-5090; Windows CD-ROM, about $50

★Lamb Chop Loves Music (85)

Philips Media, 800-340-7888 or 310-444-6500; Mac and Windows CD-ROM, about $40

★Macbeth (90)

The Voyager Company, 800-446-2001 or 212-431-5199; Mac and Windows CD-ROM, about $50

Making Music

The Voyager Company, 800-446-2001 or 212-431-5199; Mac and Windows CD-ROM, about $40

Microsoft Composer Collection
Microsoft, 800-426-9400 or 206-882-8080;
Windows CD-ROM, about $70

★**Microsoft 3D Movie Maker (86)**
Microsoft, 800-426-9400 or 206-882-8080;
Windows 95 CD-ROM, about $45

★**Microsoft Works for Windows 95 (86)**
Microsoft, 800-426-9400 or 206-882-8080;
Windows 95 CD-ROM and disk, about $80

Music Mentor 2.0
Midisoft, 800-776-6434 or 206-391-3610;
Windows disk or CD-ROM, about $100

Opening Night
MECC, 800-685-6322, ext. 529, or 612-569-
1529; Mac and Windows CD-ROM, about
$48

★**Print Shop Ensemble II (85)**
Brøderbund, 800-521-6263 or 415-382-
4400; Mac and Windows CD-ROM; about
$80

★**Romeo and Juliet (89)**
Attica Cybernetics, 800-992-8781 or 818-
993-4274; Windows CD-ROM, about $50

Other *FamilyPC* Recommended Music and Drama Software

★**eMedia Guitar Method (87)**
If your teen is an air-guitar addict and wants
to learn the real thing, get this multimedia
instructional CD-ROM.
    eMedia, 20-329-5657; Windows and Mac
CD-ROM, about $60; ages 10 and up

★**Fisher-Price Sing-alongs: Barnyard Rhythm & Moos (86)**
This colorful CD features a host of classic
kid songs and fun animation for the toe-tap-
ping preschooler to explore.
    Davidson & Associates, 800-545-7677 or
310-793-0600; Mac and Windows CD-
ROM, about $30; ages 3–7

★**Of Mice and Men (85)**
John Steinbeck's classic tale of alienation
among migrant farm workers in depres-
sion-era California is a natural for multimedia adaptation. Byron Preiss and Pen-
guin Electronic do justice to the author's
work in this first title in a projected Steinbeck CD-ROM library.
    Byron Preiss Multimedia and Penguin
Electronic, 800-253-6476 or 212-989-6252
ext. 149; Mac and Windows CD-ROM,
about $50

★**Play Blues Guitar with Keith Wyatt (88)**
If the blues are in your bones but not your
fingers, dust off your guitar and load up
Play Blues Guitar with Keith Wyatt. If you
have some previous guitar experience, you
will benefit quickly from video demos, animated fretboards, and music that loops for
continuous practice.
    Play Music, Inc., distributed by Hal
Leonard, 800-887-7529 or 818-766-2958;
Windows CD-ROM, about $60

★**Plugged-In: Classic Rock Guitar (86)**
Rock and roll is here to stay, so grab your
guitar, tune to the digital tuner, and choose

In eMedia Guitar Method, you learn how to strum chords and advance quickly into various finger-picking techniques.

one of eight classic rock songs, to learn rock techniques such as the shuffle, arpeggios, harmonics, scratching, hammer-ons, and slides.

Ubi Soft, 800-824-7638 or 415-464-4440; Windows and Mac CD-ROM, about $60

★**Robert Winter's Crazy for Ragtime (89)**
In Crazy for Ragtime, Robert Winter — the UCLA professor who brought classical music to CD-ROM in his esteemed Composer series for Voyager — lends his scholarly expertise and a great sense of fun to this unforgettable episode in American music.

Calliope Media/Distributed by Maxis 800-336-2947 or 310-829-1100; Mac and Windows CD-ROM, about $50

Chapter 12

Speak the Language

Mentioned in *The FamilyPC Guide to Homework*
★**American Heritage Children's Dictionary (85)**
Houghton Mifflin Interactive, 800-829-7962 or 617-351-5000; Windows CD-ROM, about $40

Let's Talk
Syracuse Language Systems, 800-688-1937;
Windows CD-ROM, about $45

⭐**My First Incredible Amazing
Dictionary (87)**
DK Multimedia, 800-356-6575 or 212-213-4800; Mac and Windows CD-ROM, about $29

⭐**Microsoft Bookshelf 1996–97 (90)**
Microsoft, 800-426-9400 or 206-882-8080;
Mac and Windows CD-ROM, about $55

The Rosetta Stone PowerPac
Fairfield Language Technologies, 800-788-0822 or 540-432-6166; Windows or Mac CD-ROM, about $100

Chapter 13

Creating Presentations

Mentioned in *The FamilyPC Guide to Homework*
⭐**ClarisWorks (86)**
Claris, 800-544-8554 or 408-727-8227; Mac disk, about $130, and Windows 95 disk, about $70

⭐**Kid Pix Studio (90)**
Brøderbund, 800-521-6263 or 415-382-4700; Mac and Windows CD-ROM, about $40

⭐**Microsoft Works for Windows 95 (86)**
Microsoft, 800-426-9400 or 206-882-8080;
Windows 95 CD-ROM and disk, about $80.

Other *FamilyPC* Recommended Presentation Software
⭐**Microsoft Publisher CD Deluxe for Windows 95 (85)**
Microsoft Publisher gives you the best of both worlds: a home publishing program that can handle anything from club bulletins to paper airplanes, and a desktop publishing program with which you can produce pages that would please any design professional.
    Microsoft, 800-426-9400 or 206-882-8080; Windows 95 CD-ROM, approximately $80

⭐**The Multimedia Workshop (85)**
The Multimedia Workshop lets kids creatively combine video, sound, graphics, and text and gives them a taste of what it's like to be a professional producer of video presentations and slide shows.
    Davidson & Associates, 800-545-7677 or 310-793-0600; Mac and Windows CD-ROM, about $30; ages 8 and up

Chapter 15

Online Hot Spots
Recommended Web Sites

Y OUR FAMILY COMPUTER IS A FIRST-RATE homework helper. It tutors kids in foreign languages, transforms itself into an artistic canvas, and provides the tools your children need for producing reports and projects. But one of its most important responsibilities is to bring the outside world — the world of information — into your home.

Throughout *The FamilyPC Guide to Homework*, we highlight more than 100 online resources — most of them found on the Internet's World Wide Web — that we think demonstrate the awesome information opportunities available to today's children. For your convenience, this chapter lists all the Web addresses we mention in this book. To view any of these resources, simply enter its address in your Web browser.

Remember, however, that the Internet

and the Web are always changing. Although we checked and double-checked the addresses we list in this chapter, Web pages *do* move — and in some cases, even disappear — overnight. If you enter an address and it takes you nowhere fast, use one of the Web's search tools to find the new address for the Web site you're seeking. You can search by using the name we list or the subject area that best describes the site. (For details on how to use these search tools, see Chapter 7, "Wading into the Information Pool.")

We also highlight our favorite Web homework helpers — the sites that are especially useful for kids working on homework assignments — by marking them with this symbol: ★

Ready to send your children on an information exploration? Just open your Web browser and start clicking!

Chapter 3
The Magic Words

The BookWire
http://www.bookwire.com/links/readingroom
/echildbooks.html

For fairy tales and other classic children's literature your children can read at the computer or print and read later, visit the BookWire.

★The Book Nook
http://i-site.on.ca/Isite/Education/Bk_report/
BookNook/default.html#Nook

The young bibliophiles in your family can share their book reports by e-mailing a text file or by filling out a book report form while they're online.

At the Book Nook, kids can add their own book report to the library by filling out a form.

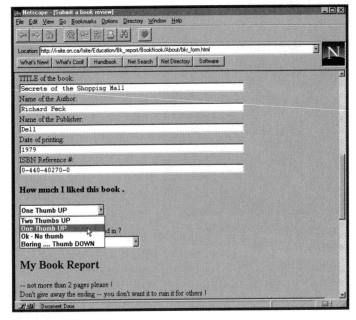

Purdue University's On-Line Writing Project (OWL)
http://owl.english.purdue.edu/

Purdue's project is packed with writing tips, including "Writing Research Papers: A Step-by-Step Approach."

The Story Resources on the Web
http://www.swarthmore.edu:80/~sjohnson/stories/

Story Resources offers links and more links to other storytelling-related Web pages, including children's stories, stories by children, and tales from various cultures.

★University of Calgary's Book Lists
http://www.ucalgary.ca/~dkbrown/awards.html
http://www.ucalgary.ca/~dkbrown/lists.html

The University of Calgary's Book Lists are the places to be if you're looking for lists of recommended children's books (including Newbery Award winners) and reading lists from organizations such as the American Library Association.

Chapter 4
Numbers Are Cool

★Ask Dr. Math
http://forum.swarthmore.
edu/dr.math/

Ask math masters any question you want via e-mail, or search through Dr. Math's archives of questions others have asked.

Helping Your Child Learn Math
gopher://gopher.ed.gov/00/
publications/full_text/
parents/math.dos

Filled with tips you can pass along to your kids to bolster their math confidence, this document by the U.S. Department of Education also includes lots of good at-home activities for exploring math.

Online Calculator
http://www.math.scarolina.
edu/cgi-bin/sumcgi/
calculator.pl

Enter an expression in this online calculator, and the answer appears in the box at the bottom of the screen.

★ Steve's Dump: Math Sites on the Internet
http://forum.swarthmore.
edu/~steve/steve/mathlevels.
html

The best place to go when your kids want help with math, Steve's Dump categorizes math links by school level.

21st Century Problem Solving
http://www2.hawaii.edu/
suremath/home.shtml

This site offers up dozens of example word problems in algebra, chemistry, and physics; shows how to solve those problems (and

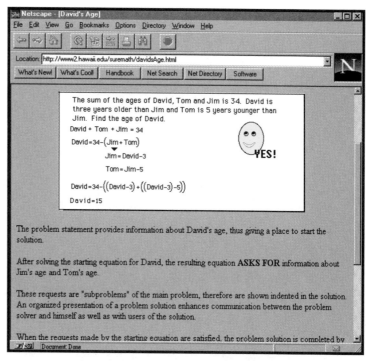

The sum of the ages of David, Tom and Jim is 34. David is three years older than Jim and Tom is 5 years younger than Jim. Find the age of David.

$$David + Tom + Jim = 34$$
$$David = 34 - (Jim + Tom)$$
$$Jim = David - 3$$
$$Tom = Jim - 5$$
$$David = 34 - ((David - 3) + ((David - 3) - 5))$$
$$David = 15$$

YES!

The problem statement provides information about David's age, thus giving a place to start the solution.

After solving the starting equation for David, the resulting equation **ASKS FOR** information about Jim's age and Tom's age.

These requests are "subproblems" of the main problem, therefore are shown indented in the solution. An organized presentation of a problem solution enhances communication between the problem solver and himself as well as with users of the solution.

When the requests made by the starting equation are satisfied, the problem solution is completed by

Word problems get a workout on the 21st Century Problem Solving Web site.

word problems in general); and provides an encyclopedia of solved word problems for additional study.

Chapter 5
People and Places

★ The CIA World Factbook 1995
http://www.odci.gov/cia/publications/95fact/
index.html

Our tax dollars are spent wisely on this Web page, which provides information on all the world's countries, including tons of facts about geography, people, and resources.

Color Landform Atlas of the United States
http://fermi.jhuapl.edu/states/states.html

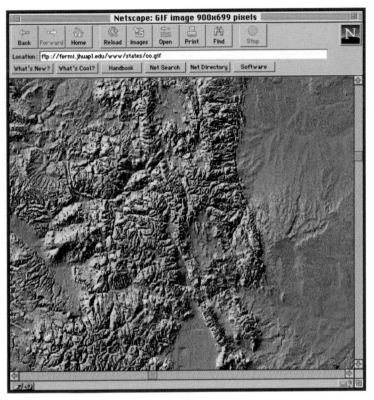

Netscape: GIF image 900x699 pixels

Back Forward Home   Reload Images Open Print Find   Stop

Location: ftp://fermi.jhuapl.edu/www/states/co.gif

What's New? What's Cool? Handbook Net Search Net Directory Software

Recognize this place? It's part of the state of Colorado, as seen from space.

Look for keyboard pals from outside North America here, or on the sibling Rigby Keypal List at the following address:

http://www.reedbooks.com.au/rigby/global/keypal.html

Historical Atlas of Europe and the Middle East
http://www.ma.org/maps/map.html
If your kids need top-notch historical maps for periods up to and including the Renaissance, bookmark this site.

Investigations
http://www.microsoft.com/ewa/investigate.htm
Microsoft's Investigations Web site has three activities suitable for school reports and projects. All three rely on the Microsoft Encarta 96 World Atlas.

★ The Mail Office at Kids' Space
http://plaza.interport.net/kids_space/mail/mail.html
If your kids are looking for keyboard pals, they should check out this Web page. It has lots of *want-a-pal* listings from children in the U.S.

Xerox PARC Map Viewer
http://pubweb.parc.xerox.com/map

This excellent U.S. map resource includes relief and county maps for all 50 states.

The Electric Postcard
http://postcards.www.media.mit.edu/Postcards/
Pick a postcard (you can choose from lots of famous paintings), type your message, and off it goes. The Electric Postcard is a great place for kids who want to send a keyboard pal something snappier than a plain-text e-mail message.

Heinemann Keypal List
http://www.reedbooks.com.au/heinemann/global/keypali.html

The Map Viewer lets you create a color map of any location on the planet.

Chapter 6
The Past Is a Blast

★ The Ancient World Web
http://atlantic.evsc.virginia.edu/julia/AncientWorld.html

With hundreds of sites listed by subject or geographical location, this mega index lets kids easily locate Internet resources offering everything from ancient Roman recipes to a virtual tour of the Acropolis.

Britannica Lives
http://www.eb.com:84/cgi-bin/bio.pl

A free service from the electronic version of Encyclopedia Britannica, this site can be used by kids to create a calendar that lists the birthdates of famous people.

★ The Civil War Home Page
http://funnelweb.utcc. utk.edu/~hoemann/cwarhp.html

The Civil War Home Page offers links to hundreds of Civil War-related Web sites, ranging from pages that cover specific battles and unit rosters to those that offer personal accounts and picture files containing photos from the Library of Congress.

Diary of a Prospector
http://uts.cc.utexas.edu/~scring/index.html

For a firsthand account of a trip from New York to California during the Gold Rush of 1849, read the mem-oirs of miner/adventurer Eugene Ring (1827–1912).

★ The Gettysburg Address
http://lcweb.loc.gov/exhibits/G.Address/ga.html

Head to the Library of Congress' Web site to see digitized images of the actual speech.

The Legacy of the Horse
http://www.horseworld.com/imh/kyhpl1a.html

If your child wants to tackle the Try This! project, "Do The Time-Line Tango," in Chapter 6, send her to this virtual exhibit sponsored by the International Museum of the Horse. She'll find information about how the horse was domesticated, where stirrups originated, and what a day at the track (at Rome's Circus Maximus) was like.

Electronic newspapers such as the *New York Times* Web site usually offer a search tool, so you can dig through old stories as well as current news.

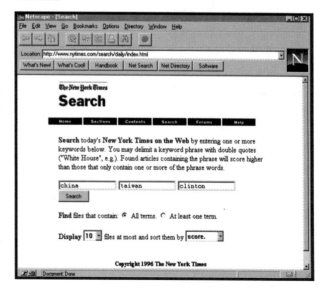

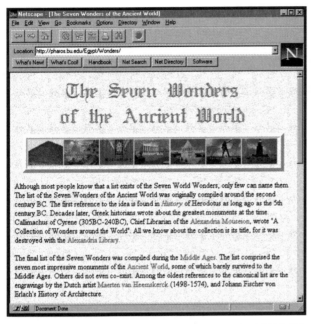

Netscape - [The Seven Wonders of the Ancient World]
File Edit View Go Bookmarks Options Directory Window Help

Location: http://pharos.bu.edu/Egypt/Wonders/

What's New! What's Cool! Handbook Net Search Net Directory Software

The Seven Wonders of the Ancient World

Although most people know that a list exists of the Seven World Wonders, only few can name them. The list of the Seven Wonders of the Ancient World was originally compiled around the second century BC. The first reference to the idea is found in *History* of Herodotus as long ago as the 5th century BC. Decades later, Greek historians wrote about the greatest monuments at the time. Callimachus of Cyrene (305BC-240BC), Chief Librarian of the Alexandria Mouseion, wrote "A Collection of Wonders around the World". All we know about the collection is its title, for it was destroyed with the Alexandria Library.

The final list of the Seven Wonders was compiled during the Middle Ages. The list comprised the seven most impressive monuments of the Ancient World, some of which barely survived to the Middle Ages. Others did not even co-exist. Among the oldest references to the canonical list are the engravings by the Dutch artist Maerten van Heemskerck (1498-1574), and Johann Fischer von Erlach's History of Architecture.

Document: Done

Quick. Can you name the Seven Wonders of the Ancient World? This Web page describes all seven in detail.

The Letters of Captain Richard W. Burt
http://www.infinet.com/~lstevens/burt/
Get a perspective on life in the field by reading the letters of Captain Richard W. Burt, a veteran of the Civil War.

Name Search
http://www.census.gov/ftp/ pub/ genealogy/www/namesearch.html
More fun than educational, the Name Search Web site lets you enter your family's last name (or your first name) and then see how it ranks in popularity.

★ The New York Times
http://www.nytimes.com/
Steer your middle-school and high-school-aged children here if they're looking for na-

tional and international current-events news, two areas in which this online newspaper shines.

★ The Oregon Trail
http://www.isu.edu/~trinmich/ Oregontrail.html
By visiting the Oregon Trail Web page, your kids can follow the real route, read fantastic pioneering facts, and view a list of supporting materials, including a free study guide originally created for teachers.

The Seven Wonders of the Ancient World
http://pharos.bu.edu/Egypt/Wonders/
A cultural touchstone even today, the Seven Wonders of the Ancient World are described in great detail on this Web site. Illustrations show artists' representations of the Seven Wonders, a map pinpoints their locations, and descriptions and a brief history of each are provided.

The 76th Ohio Volunteer Infantry
http://www.infinet.com/~lstevens/civwar/
March along the battle trail with the 76th Ohio Volunteer Infantry as it fights in 44 skirmishes and loses 351 soldiers.

★ USA Today
http://www.usatoday.com/
Almost as colorful on the Web as it is on paper, *USA Today* is a super online paper pick for children ages eight and up who want to keep up with current events.

★ **The Valley of the Shadow: Living in the Civil War in Pennsylvania and Virginia**
http://jefferson.village.virginia.edu/vshadow/vshadow.html

For a you-were-there view on the Civil War, your kids should dig into this huge Web resource, which uses thousands of digitized pages of period newspapers, census returns, and army rosters to illustrate what two towns went through during the conflict.

Yahoo!'s Genealogy Index
http://www.yahoo.com/Arts/Humanities/History/Genealogy/

Spend time at the Valley of the Shadow Web site, and you'll think you were really in the Civil War.

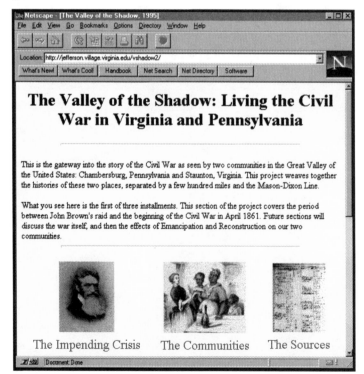

Yahoo!'s index is an excellent launching pad into the Web's genealogical sites.

Chapter 7
Wading into the Information Pool

★ **Electric Library**
http://www.elibrary.com/

This remarkable and easy-to-use compilation of resource material from daily newspapers, radio and television transcripts, books, encyclopedias, maps, and atlases costs $9.95 a month.

Infoseek
http://www.infoseek.com/

Infoseek sports some solid Web site categorizations, but its search engine is slow.

Lycos
http://www.lycos.com/

Lycos features a fast, flexible Web search tool, and includes connections to the just-as-useful Point review page.

OpenText
http://www.opentext.com/omw/f-omw.html

While search sites such as Yahoo categorize the information you can find on the Web, the OpenText search engine examines all the words within Web documents and pages during its searches.

Teacher's Guide to Encarta 96
http://www.microsoft.com/k-12/resources/
tags/encarta96/default.htm

An excellent resource for parents and kids who use Microsoft's Encarta electronic encyclopedia, the Teacher's Guide to Encarta 96 includes 40 learning lessons in subjects ranging from creative writing to architecture.

★Yahoo!
http://www.yahoo.com

One of the premier where-is-it? directories to the Web, Yahoo! also offers excellent search tools. This is a great starting point when you're doing research via the Web.

★Yahooligans!
http://www.yahooligans.com

A version of Yahoo designed for kids ages eight to 14, Yahooligans' search tools aren't as thorough as Yahoo's, but the sites it highlights are *all* kid-perfect.

Chapter 8
Science Is Fact, Not Fiction

★Ask-A-Geologist
http://walrus.wr.usgs.gov:80/
docs/ask-a-ge.html

By visiting the Ask-A-Geologist Web site, anyone can quiz real scientists from the United States Geological Survey about geology. If your kids

wonder whether your part of the country ever had a quake, or you're curious about why Texas is flush with oil while West Virginia has coal deposits, you can ask the experts.

Beakman's Electric Motor
http://fly.hiwaay.net:80/~palmer/motor.html

At the Beakman's Electric Motor Web site, an engineer who put together one of the projects for the television show "Beakman's World" has posted simple instructions and several illustrations to help you and your kids make this gizmo: an electric motor made from, of all things, the cardboard tube inside a roll of toilet paper.

Yahooligans, a searchable index for children ages eight to 14, uses colorful graphics and lists kid-appropriate Web pages, but its search tool isn't as powerful as Yahoo's.

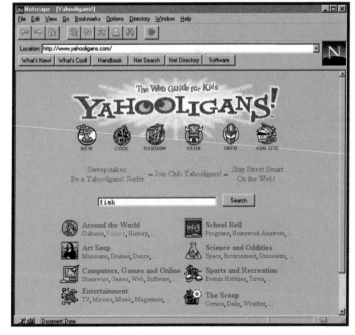

Bill Nye, the Science Guy
http://nyelabs.kcts.org/nyeverse/shows/
shows.html

"Bill Nye, the Science Guy," another PBS science show for kids, uses its Web page to post an episode-by-episode guide, with one home how-it-works experiment per episode. These projects are perfect for preschoolers and kids in the early elementary-school grades. The projects might not take first prize at a science fair, but they can be completed with stuff you have around the house.

★Click the Bones You Wanna See
http://www.cs.brown.edu/people/art035/Bin/
skeleton.html

Send your children to Click the Bones You Wanna See, a click-and-hear Web page, where they can point to any bone in the skeleton and hear the bone's name pronounced.

★Dinos to DNA
http://www.bvis.uic.edu/museum/
Dna_To_Dinosaurs.html

An interactive walk through a premier exhibit at the Field Museum of Natural History in Chicago, Dinos to DNA is one of the best dino sites on the Web.

Dinosaur Hall
http://ucmp1.berkeley.edu/exhibittext/dinosaur.html

Your young paleontologists can cruise through a virtual version of the University of California Museum of Paleontology, where they can read about dinosaur diversity and myths, view skeletons, and dig up information about everything from how

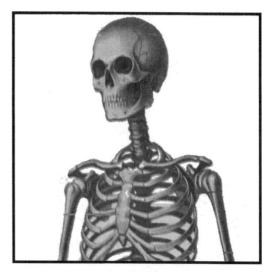

This skeleton from the Click the Bones You Wanna See site may look like a Halloween joke, but it's really a super teaching tool.

fast dinosaurs moved to why most scientists now believe birds are descendants of these great beasts.

Earth Science HyperStudio Stacks
http://volcano.und.nodak.edu/downloads/stack.html

If you have a Macintosh, head to the Earth Science HyperStudio Stacks, where you and your kids can download a slew of excellent earth-science adventures.

Earthquake Information
http://www.civeng.carleton.ca/cgi-bin/quakes

The Web page of the National Earthquake Information Service (NEIS) lists information about the latest quakes, including their location, their magnitude, and the date they occurred. This is a great resource for kids working on earthquake-related reports and projects.

Exploring Earth's Volcanoes
http://volcano.und.nodak.edu/vwdocs/volc_images/volc_images.html
Pick a region of the world and you can peek at several images taken by orbiting astronauts, giving you and your kids a view rarely seen in textbooks and paper encyclopedias.

Hands-On Science
http://www.exploratorium.edu/publications/Hands-On_Science/Hands-On_Science.html
San Francisco's Exploratorium, famous for its kid-appropriate, hands-on science exhibits, also publishes *The Exploratorium Science Snackbook*, a collection of 107 experiments and demonstrations that are essentially scaled-down interactive exhibits. Before you spend $30 for the book, check out the eight sample projects at this Web site.

★ The Heart: A Virtual Exploration
http://sln.fi.edu/biosci/heart.html
Part of the Franklin Institute Science Museum, this journey through the human heart lets kids watch QuickTime movies of the heart, listen to heartbeats of various speeds, look at X-rays, and see animations of blood pumping and the heart working.

Helping Your Child Learn Science
http://www.ed.gov/pubs/parents/Science/index.html
An online collection of 16 at-home science projects, the Helping Your Child Learn Science Web site describes simple experiments kids and parents can do together.

★ NASA Educational Sites
http://quest.arc.nasa.gov/nasa-resources.html
For a full list of all the NASA-sponsored education-oriented Web sites, check out the NASA Educational Sites listing. From here, you can launch to virtually every part of NASA.

The Newton Science Try Its Web Page
http://ericir.syr.edu/Projects/Newton/
Look to this Web site for a half-dozen kitchen science projects suitable for preschoolers and young elementary-school-aged kids.

NASA's Online Interactive Project area sure doesn't look bureaucratic; it's waiting to take kids on fascinating interactive journeys with real scientists.

★Online Interactive Projects
http://quest.arc.nasa.gov/interactive.html
Although the "Sharing NASA" projects are meant to bring together schoolchildren in collaborative explorations, kids at home can use them, too. Each multimedia project lasts one to three months, letting kids share in the thrill of real-life space missions.

★The Royal Tyrrell Museum of Paleontology
http://www.tyrrell.com/
The Tyrrell's Web site is easily understandable to younger viewers but still packed with enough stuff about dinosaurs to keep mom and dad at the screen.

By going to the Tyrrell Museum's Web page, you can walk through this Canadian museum without stretching your legs.

Science at Home
http://education.lanl.gov/RESOURCES/Science_at_Home/SAH.rocket.html
The *Science at Home* hands-on activity science book for grades 4–8 isn't on the Web any longer, but one cool sample experiment remains. Head to this page for step-by-step instructions for making a seltzer-tablet rocket and to learn a bit about how propulsion works.

Science Fair Research Directory
http://spacelink.msfc.nasa.gov/html/scifairt.html
Kids gathering information for science-fair projects can find lots of links to science-related Web sites at the Science Fair Research Directory, which lists scores of references in subjects ranging from biology to zoology.

U.S. Geological Survey Earthquake Maps
http://quake.wr.usgs.gov/QUAKES/CURRENT/
Check out recent earthquake locations in California and Hawaii by heading to the U.S. Geological Survey Earthquake Maps Web site. You can find tremor maps for Los Angeles, San Francisco, the Mojave, Monterey, the island of Hawaii, and others.

★University of Bradford
http://www.eia.brad.ac.uk/eia.html
Head to the University of Bradford site if you want to control a real robotic telescope. After you register, you can ask the telescope to look anywhere in the northern sky.

★VolcanoWorld
http://volcano.und.nodak.edu/vw.html
Manned by professional volcanologists and educators, VolcanoWorld is an everything-you-want-to-know kind of place. It offers lesson plans, tons of photographs, and a library full of facts.

★Welcome to the Planets
http://stardust.jpl.nasa.gov/planets/
Welcome to the Planets is a superb guided tour of the Solar System, complete with full-color pictures of the planets (taken from space probes) and vital statistics about each.

You Can with Beakman & Jax
http://www.nbn.com/youcan/
Based on the popular TV show "Beakman's World" (and the *Beakman & Jax* books), this site presents several how-things-work projects and other science information.

Chapter 9
Our Planet

The Bear Den
http://www2.portage.net/~dmiddlet/bears/
The Bear Den offers facts and more facts about the bears of the world, with lots of pictures and an amazing amount of background information.

E-E Link
http://www.nceet.snre.umich.edu/index.html
With a huge amount of educational material and links to other eco-sites on the Internet, E-E Link is a good starting point for kids doing environmental research.

★The Electronic Zoo
http://netvet.wustl.edu/e-zoo.htm
When your kids want homework help about animals, tell them to try The Electronic Zoo.

Hypercard Stack of Great Whales
http://unite.ukans.edu/UNITEResource/
783750390-447DED81.rsrc
From this Web site, Mac owners can download a superb Hypercard stack of illustrations and other information about the world's whales.

In Memoriam: RMS Titanic
http://www.xnet.com/~cmd/titanic/
On this Web page, your children can explore one of history's worst nautical disasters.

★The Jason Project
http://seawifs.gsfc.nasa.gov/JASON/
HTML/JASON.html

Bearish on bears? Then head to The Bear Den, which includes information on all the world's bears.

Schools participate in the Jason Project's electronic oceanographic field trips, but kids at home can follow along, too.

Keiko the Killer Whale
http://www.presys.com/ohwy/k/keiko.htm
The star of the movie *Free Willy* also stars on this Web page.

★Miami Museum of Science
http://www.miamisci.org/hurricane/weatherstation.html
Kids who want to build a weather station should check out the detailed how-to instructions here.

The National Weather Service — Interactive Weather Information Network
http://iwin.nws.noaa.gov/iwin/graphicsversion/main.html
Visit the Interactive Weather Information Network to check out the local weather conditions for anywhere in the U.S.

Ocean Planet
http://seawifs.gsfc.nasa.gov/ocean_planet.html
Based on an actual Smithsonian exhibit in Washington, D.C., Ocean Planet is a fun Web stop for anyone in the family.

★RMS Titanic: 83 Years Later
http://www.lib.virginia.edu/cataloging/vnp/titpref.html
Newspapers of the period documented the sinking of the Titanic, and this site lets kids

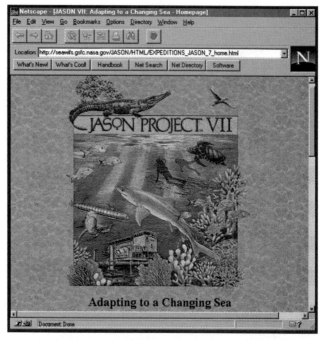

The Jason Project is one of the best sites on the Web for kids interested in oceans.

read the same news as the people who lived during those times.

The Storm Chaser Home Page
http://taiga.geog.niu.edu/chaser/chaser.html
Filled with too-close-for-comfort images of twisters snapped by brave photographers, the Storm Chaser Home Page can be used as an informational source about severe weather.

★TerraQuest
http://www.terraquest.com/
TerrQuest takes kids on virtual scientific expeditions to exotic (and environmentally important) parts of the world, such as Antarctica and the Galapagos Islands.

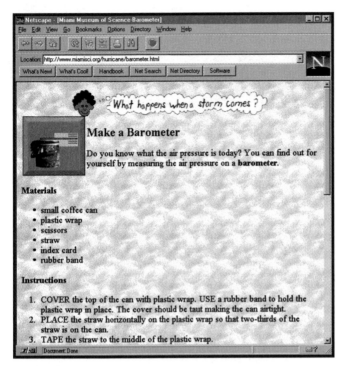

A barometer measures air pressure and is a good tool for predicting storms. The Miami Museum of Science Web site shows how to make one by using common household materials.

Titanic Home Page

http://iccu6.ipswich.gil.com.au/~dalgarry/

Set sail for the Titanic Home Page Web site, where your kids can take a virtual tour of the ship, hosted by its builder, Thomas Andrew (who perished when the liner went down).

Virtual Safari

http://www.period.com/safari/safari.shtml

By visiting the Virtual Safari Web site, kids get to go on digital trips into the field and learn about several different species of animals through maps, fun and fascinating facts, and pictures.

WhaleNet

http://whale.simmons.edu/

Your children can read accounts of whale migration tracking efforts on WhaleNet.

★ WeatherNet

http://cirrus.sprl.umich.edu/
wxnet/software.html

Visit WeatherNet to download weather-related shareware.

ZooNet Image Archives

http://www.mindspring.com/
~zoonet/gallery.html

Does your child need pictures of animals to use in a report? Then turn to ZooNet.

Chapter 10

Artistic License

Aunt Annie's Craft Page

http://www.coax.net/annie/

Aunt Annie describes how to use common household materials to make projects such as homemade stamps, homemade paper, and cool appliqués.

Barry's Clip Art Server

http://www4.clever.net/graphics/clip_art/clipart.
html

This Web site has hundreds of black-and-white images that make good coloring book material.

Carlos's Coloring Book Home

http://www.ravenna.com/coloring/

At this online coloring book, young kids can paint a half-dozen pages. The process is slow — even slower than coloring with an art program — but it's a neat trick.

The Georges Seurat Home Page
http://www.pride.net/~dbirnbau/seurat/index.html
Check out some original paintings by Seurat by pointing your Web browser here.

★National Museum of American Art
http://www.nmaa.si.edu:80
Your home computer can take you and your kids to the National Museum of American Art, part of the Smithsonian Institute, where you can view more than 1,000 works of art and take any of several self-guided tours.

The Refrigerator
http://www.seeusa.com/refrigerator.html
Your child's artistic masterpiece can be seen by anyone with access to the World Wide Web, when you transmit it to this Web page.

★Sistine Chapel
http://www.christusrex.org/www1/sistine/0-Tour.html
Just one of several pages that highlight art at the Vatican, this spectacular site lets you view the awe-inspiring artwork of Michelangelo without getting a crick in your neck.

★WebMuseum: Famous Paintings Exhibition
http://sunsite.unc.edu/wm/paint/
This massive collection of the world's most recognizable art on canvas includes hundreds of images of paintings as well as short biographies of scores of painters, which your kids can use for elementary research.

Chapter 11
In Song and On Stage
ClassicalNet
http://www.classical.net/music/
For a one-stop information shop catering to

One of Michelangelo's gifts to the ages, the Sistine Chapel, is accessible online. The close-ups are awesome.

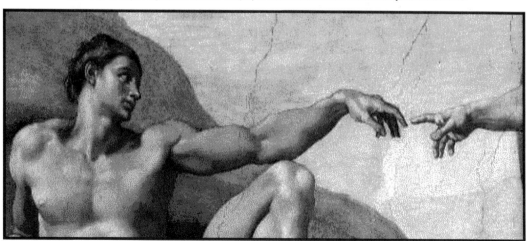

anyone interested in classical music, you can't beat ClassicalNet. It includes extensive informational files, links to other classical music Web pages, and where-to-buy advice for anyone searching for the best audio CDs on the subject.

★ The Complete Works of William Shakespeare
http://the-tech.mit.edu/Shakespeare/works.html

This super site — maintained by the Massachusetts Institute of Technology (MIT) — not only contains all of Shakespeare's plays but also lets you search through all the text of all the plays.

Jack's Harp Page
http://www.volcano.net/~jackmearl/index.html

Does your child want to learn how to play the harmonica? Jack Earl will send your child 10 free lessons via e-mail.

Macbeth
http://www.webcom.com/falcon/Macbeth.html

Among the many nifty resources on the Web site maintained by Roger Burnich, a high school teacher in Stamford, Connecticut, you can find this eminently readable, scene-by-scene summary of *Macbeth*.

Mozart Among Us
http://www.io.com/~glenford/Mozart_Among_Us_TOP.html

If your kids are casting their research net for the next Mozart, point them to this site, which highlights notable composers of this century.

Playbill On-Line's colorful interface sends kids to several areas of dramatic interest, including some nifty quizzes and transcripts of online interviews with real theater people.

★ Mozart's Musikalisches Wurfelspiel
http://mendel.berkeley.edu/~jchuang/Music/Mozart/mozart.cgi

With this electronic version of a dice game created by Mozart, you can compose a minuet in moments by letting the computer pick random numbers.

Playbill On-Line
http://wheat.symgrp.com/playbill/html/home.html

Playbill On-Line's colorful interface is attractive to kids and offers plenty of information for middle- and high-school-aged children looking for research resources for theater-related homework.

Rock and Roll Hall of Fame
http://www.rockhall.com/

Send your kids to the virtual version of the

Rock and Roll Hall of Fame, where they can view the list of the "500 Songs That Shaped Rock and Roll," read short biographies of many of the bands and performers, and even download and listen to snippets of many of the songs.

★ **Theatre Central**
http://www.theatre-central.com/

The acknowledged one-stop drama shop on the World Wide Web, Theatre Central, may be more useful to professional actors and dramatists, but kids who are involved in acting and producing plays in middle or high school can use these links, too. Because Theatre Central is so popular, however, this site is often inaccessible. If you have trouble accessing Theatre Central try it at night or on weekends.

TV Bytes: The WWW TV Themes Home Page
http://themes.parkhere.com/themes/tvthemes.html

This site is pure fun, but it could serve as an excellent resource for kids writing reports and papers on popular culture. You can download scores of TV theme songs from shows past and present.

Chapter 12

Speak the Language

★ **The Biographical Dictionary**
http://www.tiac.net/users/parallax/

The Biographical Dictionary offers a snappy search tool and biographical information on more than 18,000 notable men and women, making this site a good resource for history homework.

Rather than go to Cleveland, you can tour the Rock and Roll Hall of Fame from the comfort of your chair, read biographies of famous performers and bands, and even listen to some of their music.

BritSpeak
http://pages.prodigy.com/ NY/NYC/britspk/main.html

This Web page lists British English words and phrases and then matches them with their American English counterparts. It's a good starting point for kids researching vocabulary differences within the English language.

Der Spiegel
http://nda.net/nda/ spiegel/ index.html

Kids studying German can head here to read a German-language magazine. Best of all, they can switch between German and English with a click of the mouse button, to check the accuracy of their translations.

Foreign Language Resources on the Web
http://www.itp.berkeley.edu/~thorne/HumanResources.html
This site offers one of the Web's most comprehensive collections of hypertext links to foreign-language resources.

★Foreign Languages for Travelers
http://www.travlang.com/languages/
Introduce your kids to 28 languages. They can hear the pronunciations of common words and phrases.

The Free On-line Dictionary of Computing
http://wfn-shop.Princeton.EDU/foldoc/
This dictionary of computing terminology comes in handy for parents whose kids know more about the machines than they do.

★Globalink
http://www.globalink.com/
This page offers a free translation service between any two of these languages: English, Spanish, French, Italian, and German. Enter a message, and Globalink returns the translated text via e-mail.

★Hypertext Webster Interface
http://c.gp.cs.cmu.edu:5103/prog/webster
The best English-language dictionary on the Web uses hypertext links to take you to the definition of almost any word.

Ideas for Using Microsoft Bookshelf '95
http://www.microsoft.com/K-12/Resources/TAGs/Bk95/bk95idea.htm
Although these activity ideas are made for teachers, you can modify them for at-home use with Microsoft Bookshelf, the versatile, multibook reference CD-ROM.

News Resources
http://newo.com/news/
This site provides a collection of links to online publications and other news sources from around the globe.

On-line Mathematics Dictionary
http://www.mathpro.com/math/glossary/glossary.html
This math-specific online dictionary defines scores of math terms and is especially useful for kids in advanced math classes in middle and high school.

The Smiley Dictionary
http://olympe.polytechnique.fr/~violet/Smileys/
The Smiley Dictionary offers definitions of *smileys*, those graphical faces made from punctuation marks that some people use to show emotion in e-mail messages.

The Unofficial Smiley Dictionary
http://www.eff.org/papers/eegtti/eeg_286.html
See The Smiley Dictionary.

★Yamada Language Center
http://babel.uoregon.edu/yamada/guides.html
Looking for foreign-language fonts for your Mac or PC? The Center's font archive offers 112 fonts in 40 different languages.

Index

FREE ISSUE

Introducing **FamilyPC** — the new computer magazine for parents and kids! It's more colorful, more educational, more fun than you ever dreamed a computer magazine could be! That's because it's published jointly by Disney (the world's top expert on fun) and Ziff-Davis (the world's top publisher of computer magazines)!

Whether you have a DOS/Windows computer or a Macintosh, you'll find **FamilyPC** is packed with ideas on how to get the most value, use and fun out of your family computer. Every issue brings you:

Reviews: The best hardware, software, online services, games & gear
Activities: Dozens of creative art, music, science, craft & learning projects
Learning: Effective ways to teach kids the computer skills they need
Help: Troubleshooting tips and practical advice
PLUS: A mini-magazine created by kids, for kids!

FamilyPC – it's just exactly what you need to make the most of your family's computer!

To receive your FREE trial issue of **FamilyPC**, call **1-800-888-9688**. If you like **FamilyPC**, you'll receive 11 more issues (for a total of 12) for just $12.95 – you save 63% off the $35.40 annual cover price! Otherwise, simply write "cancel" on the bill, return it and owe nothing. The first issue is yours to keep or give to a friend.

Canadian and foreign orders, include U.S. funds and add $10 for GST/postage.
FamilyPC's annual cover price is $35.40. ©1996 FamilyPC

CBK1AA